W. E. B. Du Bois

Photograph by Carl Van Vechten

William Edward Burghardt DuBois

W. E. B. DuBois

NEGRO LEADER
IN A TIME OF CRISIS

by

Francis L. Broderick

STANFORD UNIVERSITY PRESS
Stanford, California
1959

STANFORD UNIVERSITY PRESS
STANFORD, CALIFORNIA

© 1959 by the Board of Trustees of the
Leland Stanford Junior University

Printed in the United States of America

Library of Congress Catalog Card Number: 59–7422

PUBLISHED WITH THE ASSISTANCE OF THE FORD FOUNDATION

To Mother and Dad

ACKNOWLEDGMENTS

A study of the public career of a complex figure like William Edward Burghardt DuBois, who has put so much on the record and who has been a controversial figure for over half a century, invites controversy at almost every chapter. It is not the job of the historian to avoid controversy. It is his job to reconstruct the past as accurately as his limitations permit, even when his judgments contradict existing judgments. This is what I have done. My intention has been neither to exalt nor to demean Dr. DuBois; it has been to understand him in the context of his time.

My work has put me in debt to many people. At the head of the list is Dr. DuBois himself. Not only did he ease my way into sources of information, such as the Harvard archives, which otherwise would have been unavailable; he also gave me unlimited access to his own voluminous papers. Since he has kept full and well-organized files since his adolescence, this opened up a sizable body of material without which it would have been almost impossible to look into the first half of his life. Unfortunately my research had been carried only to 1910 when, at the time of his indictment by a federal grand jury in 1951, he closed his papers to outsiders. My chapters for the period following 1910 had to rely on other material, published and unpublished. I am grateful for his permission to use the material already collected. While I worked in Dr. DuBois's office, first at the National Association for the Advancement of Colored People and then at the Council on African Affairs, I had the continuing cooperation of his secretary, Lillian Murphy, and, in the early months of my work, of his research assistant, Hugh H. Smythe. Dr. Smythe did much to orient me in Negro history and made available to me a number of DuBois's speeches in 1948.

Many others have helped along the way. I have a continuing obligation to Oscar Handlin, who guided the work from the beginning and gave the final version a close critical reading, both for style and for content. His own published work suggests what a valuable aid this has been. Walter P. Metzger read through the manuscript carefully; almost every page is better because of his suggestions. Richard F. Niebling and Janet Wicks Gillespie went over the text with me chapter by chapter, and Henry W. Bragdon gave me some valuable tips on organization. Eric F. Goldman advised me in the early stages. Herbert Aptheker did much to ease my orientation in the DuBois papers and generously made available to me the work he had done in the DuBois papers on the Niagara Movement. Leslie H. Fishel, Jr., pointed out many bits of material on DuBois in the Negro press. I profited a great deal from conversations with C. Flint Kellogg, who worked in the DuBois papers at the same time as I, and even more from a three-day exchange of views and notes with Elliott M. Rudwick, who was studying DuBois from a different point of view. Arna Bontemps helped me track down a reference on DuBois and gave me a revealing comment on DuBois's influence on the "Negro Renaissance." The late Walter White allowed me to look at the files of the National Association for the Advancement of Colored People and to study the minutes of its board of directors. Until the late stages of my work, I knew August Meier only through his writings. Personal acquaintance has confirmed what is apparent in his published work—that is, a subtle grasp of Negro history of the past hundred years.

Library and librarians carried toleration far. I am grateful for the courtesies of the Widener and Houghton Libraries at Harvard, the Davis Library at Phillips Exeter Academy, the manuscript division of the Library of Congress, the Sterling Memorial Library at Yale, the New York Public Library and its branch, the Schomburg Collection, the Union Theological Seminary Library, the Boston Public Library, the State University of Iowa Library, the Howard University Library, and the Congregational Library in Boston. I owe a special debt to Jean Blackwell at the Schomburg Collection and to Margaret P. Tate at the Davis Library.

My wife, Barbara Baldridge Broderick, has put up with much in the name of DuBois. Her patience has been admirable, but her judgment and skepticism have been worth even more. I can see why scholars want wives, but I do not understand how they can get them.

Though everybody knows it, I suppose I must say explicitly that none of these people bears responsibility for anything which appears below.

Parts of the material in this book have appeared, in different form, in the *Progressive,* the *Journal of Negro Education, Phylon,* and (without my permission) in the *Negro History Bulletin.*

A word on the footnotes. I am reluctant to weigh down the book with them, yet anxious to satisfy the curiosity of the reader about the precise time and place of something Dr. DuBois has said. The result is a compromise which, like most compromises, will satisfy nobody. I have given the source for quotations close to the length of a sentence, but not for single words or phrases picked up because of their characteristic flavor. In borderline cases, I have followed my own whim. When I discuss Dr. DuBois's books at some length, it has not seemed necessary to add dozens of useless citations for each page from which a quotation was drawn.

F. L. B.

Exeter, New Hampshire
November 1, 1958

PREFACE

American Negroes greeted liberation from slavery as the "day of jubilee," not realizing that emancipation only freed them for a long struggle, the end of which is still not in sight. That struggle has now been carried on beyond three generations, and for each of these there arose a leader whose career symbolized an epoch.

For thirty years, from 1865 to 1895, Frederick Douglass spoke for Negro America. A crusading abolitionist, he carried the tradition of democratic idealism into the period when the goal of freedom was not the abrogation of slavery but the enjoyment of political, civil, and social equality. A loyal Republican office-holder, Douglass continued to demand full rights for Negroes even after they were set adrift by the party of Lincoln, and when the South began to impose ever narrower limitations on Negro equality. Until his death in 1895, he spoke brave words. But by 1895 they were hollow words.

As if by prearrangement, Booker T. Washington came to national prominence the year Douglass died. The principal of a Negro industrial school in Alabama, Washington viewed the Negro's plight from its lowest economic level, not from the plane of justice. The period of his leadership coincided with the great retreat into disfranchising constitutions and Jim Crow legislation in the South. Though he never repudiated a single long-range goal of Douglass's program for Negro progress, Washington was prepared to move cautiously through a dark night, speaking soft words to white men and careful words to colored men. For twenty years Washington appealed to a national mood of moderation on Negro rights: economic progress, especially through industrial education, and postponement of civil, political, and, above all, social equality.

At Washington's death in 1915, the Negro—and perhaps the nation as a whole—was ready for the uncompromising demands of W. E. B. DuBois. Some would say that the leadership passed years before; but that would be hard to concede. Long restive under Washington's acquiescence in second-class citizenship, DuBois ordered the Negro to be a man and demanded that white America recognize him as such. Slowly at first and then in increasing numbers, the race responded, so that even when DuBois faltered after thirty years of shouting, enough of the race had heard him to carry on without him. A generation looking for Negro equality by 1963, the hundredth anniversary of the Emancipation Proclamation, is using his great ideas.

CONTENTS

W. E. B. DuBois

I

THE SEARCH FOR A CAREER

After his birth in Great Barrington, Massachusetts, in 1868, Will DuBois took twenty-six years to settle on a career. A black man in a white culture, he learned that the barrier of color created two worlds: a dominant white society and a separate Negro community. Alert and sensitive, he became a part of both worlds. In the process, nothing impressed him so much as the intensity of the hostility between them, yet he came to see in each the roots of reconciliation: among white men, a commitment to Christianity, democracy, and truth; among Negroes, a wealth of undirected talent avid for leadership. Here was the task for a young man's lifetime: to set his talents as the mediator between two cultures. With that goal in view, young Will DuBois, bright pupil and high-school orator, moved on to his career as Dr. W. E. Burghardt DuBois, historian, sociologist, teacher, and missionary to both races.

Doing the Groundwork

A mulatto of French Huguenot, Dutch, and Negro ancestry, Will DuBois—the name is pronounced Du-Boyce—was born into Great Barrington's small Negro community, perhaps fifty strong in a town of five thousand.[1] It was a confined, provincial group. It kept in touch with the colored families in the nearby town of Lee, but as a rule its world did not stretch beyond the Berkshires. When the National Convention of Colored Men met in Louisville, Kentucky, in 1883—a meeting which attracted Frederick Douglass, the best-known spokesman for the race, and other leaders from twenty-four states—Great Barrington Negroes took no interest except to disapprove of this sort of concerted action. These same older, established families also looked down their noses at "contraband" Negroes immigrating from the South and breaking in on their comfortably settled society.

The Burghardts, Will's mother's family, had been in the community since Revolutionary days; Will's maternal great-grandfather, born a slave, had been manumitted after fighting briefly for the colonial forces. Ever since, the family had had small farms in nearby Egremont Plains. Will's father's family lived farther east. His paternal grandfather, Alexander DuBois, had been a steward on a ship on the West Indies run, and Will's father, Alfred, had been born in Santo Domingo. When the family settled down in New Haven, Connecticut, Alfred fled from his stern parent and found his way west to Great Barrington to ply his trade as a barber. There he married Mary Burghardt. When Will was still quite young, his father wandered away and did not return, and the young lad and his mother moved to grandfather Burghardt's farm.

When Will reached school age, his mother left her father's farm and came to town, determined to give her son every possible educational opportunity. In town he could attend the public school regularly. If she could get him a good education, then success, she was sure, was just a matter of sacrifice and hard work. Ambitious for her son, she gave him her sense of purpose, and in turn enjoyed his little successes as her own. Her brother, also a barber, shared their cramped tenement and helped with their expenses. She pieced out their income by occasional domestic service; some unobtrusive charity added a little more; and, as Will grew older, he helped a bit with boyish chores: splitting kindling, mowing lawns, firing a stove in a millinery shop.

For young Will it was a happy life. In an unpublished short story written some years later, DuBois, under a thin disguise, recalled his boyhood as almost idyllic: a "demure" town with its winding Housatonic River searching out the way from the Great Hoosac Range to the Taconic Hills; skating by moonlight on Mansfield Pond, coasting down Castle Hill (where the railroad added the spice of real danger), and playing Indians during the summer. There was a brook running through the little yard in front of his house. There were the sweet eyes and filmy dresses of his landlady's niece.

The white community found room for him in its social life, for in this Northern region the color line was faint. Years later,

he could recall "almost no experience of segregation or color discrimination."² His schoolmates, mostly white, welcomed him
readily in their activities and in their homes, and when occasional
quarrels grew into pitched battles, they followed boyish logic
rather than the color line. Like the richer white children, whom
Will "annexed" as his "natural companions," young Will felt
the native's patronizing scorn for the overdressed children of summer colonists. Social divisions were defined more clearly by class
than by color. When the influx of an Irish and South German
working class into the town's manufacturing plant added an alien
element to the homogeneous community of Americans of English and Dutch descent, the Burghardts, resident in the neighborhood for several generations, associated themselves with the established families rather than with the newcomers. For his part,
young Will "cordially despised" the mill workers as a "ragged,
ignorant, drunken proletariat, grist for the dirty woolen mills
and the poor-house."³ From his companions, as well as from his
mother, he learned the capitalist ethic of late nineteenth-century
America: "Wealth was the result of work and saving and the rich
rightly inherited the earth. The poor, on the whole, were to be
blamed. They were lazy or unfortunate, and if unfortunate their
fortunes could easily be mended by thrift and sacrifice."⁴

DuBois's own experience in school confirmed this philosophy:
without financial resources, he achieved success on his ability
alone. He took the standard "classical" college preparatory course:
four years of Latin and three of Greek; arithmetic, algebra, and
geometry in three of the four years; one year of English; a year of
ancient and American history; and scattered bits of geography,
physiology, and hygiene. In addition, like every other student,
he presented compositions, declamations, and recitations, and performed occasional exercises in reading, spelling, and music. Competing with the children of the town's leading families, he matched
his talent against theirs and usually won. DuBois recalls that
while they struggled to perform well for visitors, he answered
glibly, tauntingly. His high-school principal, Frank A. Hosmer,
encouraged him to plan for college and even helped to provide
the necessary textbooks. Will rewarded Hosmer's confidence by
completing the high-school course with high honors, along with

various extracurricular distinctions such as the presidency of the high-school lyceum. (Many years after DuBois's school days at Great Barrington, DuBois wondered what would have happened if Hosmer had been "born with no faith in 'darkies.' ")[5]

Several decades later, as DuBois recalled these experiences with wonder, he realized that if the high school had had fraternities, honor societies, and dances, there might have been more color discrimination. As it was, however, the color line only faintly crossed his educational experience. When students differed, it was merely a difference in levels and types of talent: Art Gresham could draw caricatures for the *High School Howler*; DuBois could express his meaning better in words; Mike McCarthy, a perfect marble player, was dumb in Latin. Will was inferior in ball games but could lead the pack in exploring, story-telling, and planning intricate games. He happened to have a lively intellect—he accepted the fact and reveled in it. At the home of Maria Baldwin, a teacher at the high school, he would make himself the center of argument: this was, as he says himself, his "hottest, narrowest, self-centered, confident period, with only faint beginnings of doubts," when he knew most things "definitely" and argued with a "scathing, unsympathetic finality that scared some into silence."[6] The important fact was that neither the argument nor the silence arose from color. Indeed Miss Baldwin, herself a Negro instructor of hundreds of white children, effectively symbolized Great Barrington's apparent indifference to race.

In the Negro community DuBois came to hold a special place. As a member of one of the oldest families, as the only Negro in his high-school class of twelve, as one of the two or three students who would go on to college, and as the local correspondent for a Negro newspaper, he took on seriousness and self-importance all out of proportion to his sixteen years. Already DuBois was fascinated by the record of his own intellectual development. At the age of fifteen, he was gathering and annotating his collected papers. In the same year, he had started to use his newspaper column in the New York *Globe* as a running critical commentary on the internal activities of the Negro community. The *Globe* (later the New York *Freeman*) was a pioneer newspaper published by T. Thomas Fortune to serve as a chronicle for Negroes of the northeast. It gave much space to national news, but it kept its local touch through short columns of items supplied by dozens of local correspondents. Few reporters were as young as Will, yet there was probably no one in the neighborhood of Great Barrington better equipped by education and interest. The reporter quickly became a social critic. The services at the African Methodist Episcopal Church he found "interesting," though not as fully attended as they might have been. He recorded the general regret among "our people" that they had no local businessmen. On another occasion, "those intending to replenish their libraries" were advised "to consult the *Globe* correspondent before so doing." He encouraged the suggestion of forming a literary society in the colored community as the "best thing" for people there. He condemned "another wrangle" in the Negro church at Lee as a "shocking scene." During the Christmas season of 1884, the Sons of Freedom, of which DuBois was secretary-treasurer, decided to take up the history of the United States at its next meeting and "pursue it as far as possible." Two weeks later he reported that it had been pursued with profit. The citizens of the town formed a law-and-order society to curb the sale of liquor; DuBois said it would be a "good plan" for some colored men to join. Alarmed by the numbers of Negroes absent from town meeting, he warned his readers sternly that they took too little interest in politics to protect their rights. He even proposed a caucus to line up a solid bloc of Negro votes. Little escaped his interest. Week by week, he awarded gold stars to the local Negro community, or turned himself into the village scold.[7]

Toward the end of his high-school course, he escaped the sheltered valley, and as he visited the larger Negro concentrations in Connecticut and Rhode Island, he felt overwhelmed by the full grandeur of the race. At New Bedford he met his grandfather, old Alexander DuBois, a formidable figure—short, thick-set, taciturn; curt but civil with his grandson; awesome with the dignity of eighty years. At Rocky Point, Rhode Island, where Will witnessed an unusually large congregation of Negroes "of every hue and bearing," he was "transported with amazement and dreams." Noting nothing of poverty and degradation, he saw only "extraordinary beauty of skin-color and utter equality of mien."[8]

Characteristically, in his reports on these trips he balanced satisfaction and regret: he found evidences of industry and wealth but not enough literary societies, which "of all things ought not to be neglected."[9]

During that time DuBois sensed little slights which he associated with his color. Among the older girls with whom he had played for years, coolness developed when strangers or summer boaders came to town. One summer visitor cut Will by refusing his "visiting card" in a juvenile (and therefore very serious) burlesque of a custom of their elders. In school he came to sense an aloofness rooted in something other than resentment of his superior academic ability. In politics the color line was more perceptible. On the one hand, the *Globe* recorded that Negroes took part in town meetings as a matter of course and marched in political parades without being "tucked in the rear nor parcelled off by themselves."[10] But, on the other hand, when the Republican town committee selected a white Democrat for night watchman over a Negro Republican, DuBois could not doubt that racial bias had dictated the appointment. When the town determined to push Will's career along, he was characteristically shunted off to Fisk, a Negro college in Tennessee training young Negroes to lead their own people, rather than prepared directly for Harvard, the goal of his ambitions, or for Amherst or Williams, closer at hand. His Negro friends resented his being sent off to school in the South (among "his own people," as his white supporters put it), for the South had an "unholy name" in DuBois's community, and his family and his colored friends regarded the citizens of Great Barrington, not the Southern Negroes, as "his people." Yet, as DuBois himself noted later, Great Barrington could not expect that a colored person of his talents would find an adequate role in the local social system.

Despite these occasional hints that New England was not altogether color blind, DuBois left Great Barrington in the summer of 1885 with little first-hand awareness of discrimination. The town had accepted him as a person, admitting him to its select society and sharing with him its disdain for the newcomers who worked in the mills and worshipped in the Catholic church. It had trained him. It had encouraged him to higher education, and had even contributed to his college expenses.

Young Will set out for Tennessee in the fall of 1885. Seventeen years old, slight in build, he had a handsome bronze skin, dark hair, sharp features. He moved and spoke rapidly—a young man in a hurry. His mother died just before he left, too soon to see his exciting career develop, but not too soon to see him well launched upon it. A simple and untutored woman, she had left young Will her pride in a family free since Revolutionary times, her ambition for his success, and her determination to make every sacrifice necessary for that success. To his credit, DuBois remembered this legacy with deep gratitude each time he reflected on his early years. The mature DuBois linked her name with William James in describing the formative influences crucial for his development.

During his three years at Fisk—the quality of his work at Great Barrington admitted him to sophomore standing upon entrance— he found himself in a very different world. Later he would recall the experience:

> I was tossed boldly into the "Negro Problem." From a section and circumstances where the status of me and my folk could be rationalized as the result of poverty and limited training, and settled essentially by schooling and hard effort, I suddenly came to a region where the world was split into white and black halves, and where the darker half was held back by race prejudice and legal bonds, as well as by deep ignorance and dire poverty.[11]

Yet what resources appeared to meet the problem! When Will was set down at Fisk among two hundred students from all parts of the South, a new world opened up to him—not a little lost group, but "a world in size and a civilization in potentiality." At Great Barrington high school, he had been almost alone. But at Fisk, thirty-five Negroes were registered in the college department. Here, he thought, was the advance guard of the Negro civilizing army; here the yearning for truth which would bring the Negro race abreast of modern civilization; here the variety of hue in both sexes which showed the immense physical richness of the Negro mass; here the difference in background, a catalog of Negro experience in nineteenth-century America. To Will, who had never been south of New Haven, fellow students from Georgia, Alabama, Mississippi, Louisiana, and Texas, for the most part five to ten years older than he, "could paint from their own experience a wide and vivid picture of the post-war South and of its black millions. There were men . . . who knew every phase of insult and repression."[12] DuBois's two summer sessions of teaching in Wilson County introduced him to the Southern rural Negro, whose poverty made every day spent in school during the summer months a financial drain, but who nonetheless sought out education for himself and for his children.

As DuBois saw them all, his spirit took possession of them, and his ambition told him to lead them. In a "public rhetorical" he told his Fisk classmates, "ye destined leaders of a noble people": "I am a Negro; and I glory in the name! I am proud of the black blood that flows in my veins. From all the recollections dear to my boyhood have I come here, not to pose as a critic but to join hands with this, my people." He spoke with passion of the "mission of the black orator of the 20th century" to raise his people by the power of truth.[13] Almost sixty years later, DuBois could still remember the fervor of those days: "The excellent and earnest teaching, the small college classes; the absence of distractions, either in athletics or society, enabled me to re-arrange and re-build my program for freedom and progress among Negroes. I replaced my hitherto egocentric world by a world centering and whirling about my race in America. . . . Through the leadership of men like me and my fellows, we were going to have these enslaved Israelites out of the still enduring bondage in short order."[14]

Along with similar colleges, such as Atlanta and Howard, Fisk had been founded after the Civil War to help train Negro youth as a leaven of intelligence for the race as a whole. Supported largely by Northern white philanthropic organizations or by denominational groups, and at one time aided financially by the Freedmen's Bureau, these colleges drew students from all parts of the South. Fisk itself, founded and supported by the American Missionary Society, spoke of its purpose in its catalog for 1884–

1885: "Fisk University aims to be a great center of the best Christian Educational forces for the training of the colored youth of the South, that they may be disciplined and inspired as leaders in the vitally important work that needs to be done for their race in this country and on the continent of Africa." The college hoped "to thoroughly establish among the colored youth the conviction of the absolute necessity of patient, long-continued, exact and comprehensive work in preparation for high positions and large responsibilities."[15]

Within the walls of the University, accepting and accepted by the all-white teaching staff, DuBois had three enriching years. In his first year, he studied the *Iliad*, the *Odyssey*, and the Greek Testament; conic sections and the calculus; rhetoric; French grammar and literature; and botany. In junior year, he read Livy and Tacitus along with Demosthenes' *Oration on the Crown* and Sophocles' *Antigone*, studied German grammar and translations, and found time for physiology, hygiene, and astronomy. Finally in his senior year, he and six classmates studied "mental sciences," using John Bascom's *Science of Mind* and James McCosh's *Laws of Discursive Thought*. Ethics, political economy, English literature, and a laboratory course in chemistry rounded out a heavy schedule. The university explicitly rejected industrial education as part of its formal curriculum, but, as the catalog put it, "manual labor is dignified and made honorable."[16]

Almost forty years later, on the occasion of a commencement address at Fisk, and perhaps under the influence of the occasion, DuBois recalled those three years of "splendid inspiration" and "nearly perfect happiness" with teachers whom he respected, amid surroundings which inspired him. The ten years after Fisk he chronicled as "a sort of prolongation of my Fisk college days. I was at Harvard but not of it. I was a student of Berlin but still the son of Fisk."[17] At Fisk Adam Spence taught him Greek, and Frederick A. Chase the natural sciences. DuBois came to think of these two, along with William James and Albert Bushnell Hart at Harvard, as the persons outside his own family who had influenced him most. With a missionary commitment to the uplift of the Negro race, this devoted band, headed by President Erastus Cravath, spurred DuBois on by judging his skills and knowledge without attention to his color. When, at the end of three years at Fisk, DuBois looked North to Harvard, they endorsed his application with praise beyond the usual platitudes of letters of recommendation. Though Fiske did not have a regular marking and ranking system, President Cravath spoke of DuBois's high rank, noted his "unusually quick, active mind," and could hardly fail to mention that Will was ambitious. Other teachers referred to his manliness, faithfulness to duty, earnestness in study, and excellent scholarship. Chase in the physical sciences gave a more revealing picture by recording that in addition to his regular assignments, Will had done outside work in anatomy, and, though he never overworked and had a remarkable capacity for sleep, he achieved "first grade" in scholarship. Chase admitted that DuBois might give the impression of being somewhat conceited, but added that this trait would not prevent faithful work.[18] In DuBois's mind, this encouragement from his Fisk teachers did something to compensate for the discriminatory pattern of Southern life.

They had much to redeem. Away from Fisk, DuBois was not a promising student, but simply a Negro; and thus the "race question" at last became an intimate experience pressing in on him daily. The move toward legal segregation and Negro disfranchisement had not yet gained ground in the South, but informally enforced etiquette and extralegal coercion made personal affronts routine. In a generous mood, DuBois could explain the South's attitude in terms of ignorance or misunderstanding: in an unpublished short story written in these years, he tells of a young Negro teacher who recognizes, after a conversation with two white men in a village store, that the white South's intentions are good and that its prejudice would yield to education. But how long could patience and generosity mask the hostile white world which, this hot-tempered Negro boy was sure, rejected black men as "aliens, strangers, outcasts from the House of Jacob—niggers."[19] In his own person, he saw the kind of teacher and the sort of education which Tennessee was giving to the Negro—a college student who for two months in the summer worked for $28 or $30 in an antique shack in Wilson County to bring culture to Negroes who had had only one other school session since the Civil War.

In his junior or senior year, DuBois put together a full statement of the Negro's grievances. In "An Open Letter to the Southern People,"* written about 1887, DuBois assailed the arbitrary
line between the white man and the Negro in the South; they were,
respectively, patrician and plebeian, capitalist and laborer, Democrat and Republican. He pointed to an anomaly: while justifying
disfranchisement by Negro ignorance, the white South refused
equal educational opportunities. Trial by peers, a free ballot,
free entrance into the various callings of life—all had been denied
to the Negro. The white South placed the Negro at the level of
a dog or a horse. He warned that Negroes, forced into the galley,
the hovel, and the Jim Crow car, responded with hatred, which
retarded the progress of both races. Yet there was hope: if the
"best of you" in the white South would lay aside race prejudice
and make common cause with educated Negro leaders, together
they could give direction to the masses. This appeal was directed
at Southern white conservatives who, as C. Vann Woodward says,
held to "an aristocratic philosophy of paternalism and *noblesse
oblige*" and who felt more comfortable with mannerly colored
men than with what a Charleston paper called "unmannerly and
ruffianly white men."²⁰ DuBois rejected their paternalism, for he
felt that he, and educated Negroes like him, shared this *noblesse*;
yet he was anxious to work with them, for he hoped that the black
and white men of taste and education could join hands to lead the
ignorant of both races. Needless to say, this appeal went unheeded—the walls rarely come tumbling down in response to
manifestoes by college students.

About the same time that DuBois was urging enlightened white
men to join hands with educated Negroes, he made a dramatic
appeal to Negroes as well. Speaking at an intercollegiate convention of Negro students, the fiery young orator told them to throw
off their "political serfdom" in the Republican party and to vote
on issues, specifically issues important to the Negro, like federal
aid to education, civil rights, and lynching. If Negroes voted
thoughtfully, he said, "gratitude for services rendered would be
due not to the party but to the principles upon which it stands.

---

* The letter, now in the DuBois papers, was probably never published.

When it leaves those principles, it leaves it[s] right to your suf-
frages. Too often have men forgotten the substance *principle* and
gone after the shadow *party*. . . . Neglecting the sacred duties of
citizenship more sacred in a Republic than elsewhere, they have
given up the manipulation of parties into the hands of political
bosses and ward machines who represent no principles but those
of dishonesty and avarice; then taking a ballot labelled with the
name of their patron saint they march to the ballot box." Republicans, he said, had abandoned the principles of Lincoln; therefore, they had no right to Negro votes. DuBois longed for a Negro
Parnell dangling a bloc of votes between the two great parties; but
if not a Parnell, at least an independent vote responsive to political wooing.

Neither party, he said, liked Negroes, but both wanted votes,
and Negroes should be willing to bargain with Democrats,* especially since the recent administration under Grover Cleveland
had, much to the Negro's surprise, treated him like a man. Times
had changed: the South of slavery was dead. DuBois denied that
the outrages of caste prejudice could be laid at the door of the
Democratic party: "They arise from the blind race prejudice
which, however reprehensible, is nevertheless natural when a
horde of ignorant slaves are suddenly made the equals of their
one-time masters." Then he added, very significantly in view of
his later development: "We ourselves make the color line broader
when in defiance of our principles and best interests we vote in
opposition to the people of this section *because* they're *white* and
we're *black*. Our interests are not antagonistic, they are one and
the same, and to blind you[r]selves to any party in spite of these
bonds of mutual interest . . . [is] to keep alive the smoldering
coals of Race antagonism."[21]

* The idea for this switch to the Democrats probably came to DuBois
through the influence of T. Thomas Fortune, editor of the *Globe* and the
Freeman (the papers to which DuBois contributed Great Barrington news)
and author of *The Negro in Politics* (New York, 1885), where the idea of
"*Race first; then party*" (p. 38) is developed at length. DuBois has never
acknowledged this influence, for he and Fortune feuded in later years. But
the parallels between Fortune's ideas and DuBois's, their close relationship
through the newspaper, and Fortune's substantial prestige in the Negro community as a pioneer newspaper editor lend support to this assumption.

Though it had no political significance—DuBois himself, aged nineteen or twenty, could not even vote—this notion had some plausibility, for in the late 1880's the Democratic party, both in the South and under the national administration of Cleveland, was making efforts to woo the Negro vote away from its sentimental Republican moorings. (Frederick Douglass said he would as soon divide the Negro vote "between light and darkness, truth and error, Heaven and Hell" as divide it between Republicans and Democrats.)[22] Not raised in slavery and therefore less responsive to the appeal of the party of Lincoln, DuBois wanted Negroes to respond calculatingly. He looked for a level of independent judgment and political maturity that colored men had not yet attained. Therefore, the first step in Negro emancipation was a program to train Negroes to overcome their prejudices. He was proud that the "heart of Africa" was broader than its mind; but now the mind must gain equal breadth.

It would be a long struggle. DuBois saw himself leading it.

Harvard and Berlin

The years at Fisk left DuBois with a sense of the "absolute division of the universe into black and white."[23] In this state of mind he approached Harvard. The admissions office wanted to know his "special reason for wishing to enter Harvard College." His blunt reply, which someone at Fisk intercepted and revised before it went out in the mail, was: "I have very little money and think I can get more aid there than elsewhere."[24] He never developed any affection for the university. Glorying in his isolation and eschewing Harvard life except as a "laboratory of iron and steel" where he could extend his knowledge, he came to think of Harvard as a library and a faculty, nothing more. He found himself a corner room at 20 Flagg Street, a ten-minute walk from the Yard and a block or so from the Charles River. He boarded at the common refectory in Memorial Hall his first year, but finding it too expensive he took modest meals in his room, or in town, or at an inexpensive eating club. For four years he commuted from his room to his classes and to the library without ever feeling himself a part of the university's social community.

DuBois's academic plans were fluid. Fisk had given inspiration
but not direction. DuBois had already rejected President Cravath's suggestion of the ministry as a career. Trained in a Congregational Sunday school, he had during his first year at Fisk
proudly joined the Fisk congregation and asked for the prayers
of his Great Barrington Sunday school to "help guide me in the
path of Christian duty." He approved of a recent revival which
had won forty converts.[25] But during the next three years, organized religion ceased to be meaningful: he believed too little
in Christian dogma to become a minister. In his autobiography
DuBois attributed this attitude to the heresy trials, especially those
controversies over "higher criticism" of the Bible which eventually led to the suspension of Charles A. Briggs from the Presbyterian Church, and to the insistence of the local church at Fisk
that dancing was a sin. Furthermore, the compulsory "book of
'Christian Evidences' "* struck him as a "cheap piece of special
pleading."[26] Rejecting Christianity as dogma, he also became
distrustful of Christian ethics, for he could find scant ethical commitment on the race issue in Christian churches. At the first symptoms of higher longings among Negroes, DuBois said the year after
he left Fisk: "There is no devil in Hell that would countenance
more flagrant infringements upon Human Liberty, to crush the
rising genius of a People, than the average deacon of the Methodist Church South."[27]

What career, if not the ministry? It took DuBois several years
to decide. His diary for the Harvard years shows him tussling with
the problem. On occasion he saw himself the tragic hero—"What
care I though death be nigh?" he asked; sometimes as an epic poet;
again as a philosopher, author of "A Philosophy by Me"; or as an
orator sending light into civilization. Whatever the role, the underlying motive remained constant: to develop himself as a Negro
leader who would use his talents to improve the condition of the
race as a whole. In a course paper for William James, DuBois
wrote that the fundamental question of the universe, past and
future, was Duty.[28] In preparation for duty, "Work is but play

---

* The reference is probably to William Paley, *A View of the Evidences of
Christianity* (London, 1794), a text written in the spirit of rationalism to
prove the truth of Christian doctrines. It was widely used in the nineteenth
century.

with an end in view." Such an attitude invested every action with high seriousness. On a trip to New York, he wrote, one must see Brooklyn Bridge, Central Park, the Statue of Liberty, the Battery, and Broadway, for these were "the *only* things to really repay such a visit."[29]

In later years DuBois reconstructed his education as a straight-line preparation for the life's work which in shadowy form he had planned from his youth. Actually the decision came relatively late as the terminal point of desultory intellectual meandering.[30] His preliminary inquiry to the secretary of the university spoke of study leading to a Ph.D. in political science, with political economy as a special field. Six months later, in his application for scholarship aid, he proposed to give "especial attention to the sciences and Philosophy" as preparation for a postgraduate course, probably in philosophy. At Harvard, where he repeated the junior and senior years of college, his first-year courses favored the sciences. In addition to a prescribed course in English composition, a half course in "earlier English Ethics," and an economics course, he concentrated on scientific subjects: qualitative analysis based chiefly on laboratory work, a beginner's laboratory course in geology, and a more advanced geology course given by Nathaniel Shaler. Though he scored A's in all his science courses, the following year the exact sciences disappeared from his schedule without explanation. Perhaps chemistry and geology seemed too remote from Negro problems and deprived DuBois of an adequate outlet for what he regarded as his talent for creative writing.

In the second year, the bulk of his work was in philosophy—George Santayana's French and German philosophy, William James's logic and psychology, and F. G. Peabody's ethics of social reform. To these he added the senior composition course; a half course in elocution; an economic survey of railroads and bimetalism; and Albert Bushnell Hart's Constitutional and Political History of the United States from 1783 to 1861.

This philosophical schedule was more appealing. There was inspired teaching by Santayana and James. Furthermore, DuBois's admission into the realm of speculative ideas allowed him to see himself as a Negro at the frontiers of knowledge, working under the developing philosophy of pragmatism and participating in the most advanced developments of modern thought. DuBois

thoroughly enjoyed jousting with ideas. His account book and
diary for this period is full of random sentences reflecting his current notions about basic questions. "The very conception of the
Caused carries with it the conception of the Uncaused." "The Infinite—that specious invention for making something out of nothing." "I hold it Truth: that every argument rests on an unprov-
able postulate which contains *implicit* the whole conclusion."
"Science is Mathematics. Mathematics is Identity. Science is
Identity."

Yet philosophy did not hold DuBois either, and in graduate
school he shifted to political economy and history. The reason for
this second change is only slightly clearer than for the first. Years
later DuBois recalled that James, like Chase at Fisk, had urged
him away from philosophy: "It is hard to earn a living with
philosophy."[31] Perhaps DuBois's recollection of James's advice was
milder than the original. James, famous for his gentleness in dealing with his students, may have preferred this way of saying that
DuBois's talents were ill suited for the logical and speculative
disciplines. Perhaps the two B's which DuBois received in senior
year from James and Santayana compared to the A plus from Hart
in constitutional and political history of the United States indicated that the latter was a field better oriented to his talents. Perhaps the inductive study of social problems such as charity, divorce,
labor, prisons, and temperance under Peabody impressed DuBois
as more germane to Negro problems than French philosophy or
James's logic. Maybe the explanation is simpler: he may have regarded the natural sciences and philosophy as basic equipment;
having surveyed them, he was ready to turn to the more specialized
social sciences which had figured prominently in his early plans.
In any case, by the spring of 1890, when DuBois applied for a
graduate fellowship, he had decided to pursue the Ph.D in social
science "with a view to the ultimate application of its principles
to the social and economic rise of the Negro people." Having can-
vassed the catalog thoroughly, DuBois bombarded the graduate
school with applications for every type of aid even remotely connected with his project and finally received the $450 Rogers schol-
arship for the study of ethics in relation to jurisprudence or sociology.

For the next two years DuBois dug into political and constitutional history. The historians of the generation of Hart and Herbert Baxter Adams sought to understand the present through a study of the development of institutions; Hart's course, which DuBois had already taken, was devoted almost exclusively to this type of history, and little else was included in Harvard's history offerings. Hart had helped to introduce the German universities' research seminar into Harvard's history department a few years before DuBois entered the graduate school. DuBois joined Hart's "seminary" and, following the methodology of his mentor, combed the statutes of the United States, colonial and state laws, the *Congressional Record*, executive documents, and "contemporary sources" for material on the African slave trade. It was slow, painstaking research: by March 1891, he reported to the faculty that he had located 146 pertinent statutes on the period from 1638 to 1788. At the same time he was carrying a full course load: in his first year, another course in history, one in English composition, one in political economy, and one in Roman law; in his second year, four half-year courses in history and one in political economy. Once in a while he took time out to compete for a prize in a field related to his work. But as a rule his research had first claim; indeed it consumed so much of his time that his course work suffered. Eventually his hours in the library stacks gave him the material for his doctoral dissertation and his first book.

In general, DuBois's record at Harvard justified the confidence of his friends at Fisk, though it did little to increase his modesty. His five A's and one C (in English composition) in junior year, four A's and three B's in senior year, and honorable mention in philosophy at graduation constituted a creditable showing, and his A-plus in History 13 led Hart to scribble a note of recommendation of DuBois as a good candidate for a graduate fellowship. In two years of graduate school residence he was awarded five A's and five B's, and though the completion of his degree took somewhat longer than he intended, his thesis, *The Suppression of the African Slave-Trade to the United States of America, 1638-1870*, was published in 1896 as the first volume in the *Harvard Historical Studies.**

* For discussion of this work, see below, pp. 35–36.

Will found other successes outside the classroom. When he gave an address, "Jefferson Davis as a Representative of Civilization," to the commencement audience at Harvard at the end of his senior year, the *Nation* recorded his distinct personal triumph. "DuBois not only far excelled Morgan [Clement Morgan, the other orator, also a Negro] in mere delivery, but handled his difficult and hazardous subject with absolute good taste, great moderation, and almost contemptuous fairness." In contrast to the type represented by Davis—the white "Teutonic" ideal of "stalwart manhood and heroic character" badly smeared with "moral obtuseness and refined brutality"—DuBois set up "the patient, trustful, submissive African as a type of citizen the world would some day honor," the *Nation* continued. "For the moment the audience showed itself ready to honor this type as displayed in the orator."[32] Here was the way to a hearing in the white world: a Negro abreast of modern civilization and devoted to truth could make people listen. Heartened, DuBois returned the following year to argue that the Negro problem could be solved if the spirit of Harvard, "that spirit of intellectual breadth and liberty that seeks Truth for Truth's sake," prevailed over misunderstood economic principles in the South.[33] That winter, a joint meeting of Harvard's history and political-economy seminars heard a preliminary summary of DuBois's research on the slave trade, and when DuBois repeated this report at one of the early meetings of the American Historical Association, Herbert Baxter Adams praised it as a "scholarly and spirited paper."[34]

Successful as a student, DuBois felt that he had to share his education; as he later expressed it himself, he "tried to take culture out into the colored community of Boston."[35] He promoted local plays: he took a part in a production entitled "Sampson and Delilah, or the Dude, the Duck and the Devil," a burlesque of the Negro hair-tonic business. Six months later, on Thanksgiving night, he was at it again, this time with the *Birds* of Aristophanes at the Charles Street Church.

One long address—"Does Education Pay?"—written in 1891 when DuBois was a first-year graduate student, carried the burden of his message, and incidentally revealed a good deal about the speaker, whose lack of tact later became a Negro legend. Speaking to the National Colored League of Boston,* DuBois reported his alarm that "a people who have contributed nothing to modern civilization, who are largely on the lowest stages of barbarism in these closing days of the 19th century," were unfitting themselves for modern life by neglecting education, even high-school education.† At the moment of basic economic and political change, he said, Negroes were throwing away the road to truth, beauty, and virtue by ignoring the wisdom of man's past experience. By doing this, he warned, they disqualified themselves for a part in the future of mankind and, indeed, destroyed their only legitimate reason for existence.

He especially defended college life as a time of leisure to study under a faculty gathered to guide work. He dismissed the usual criticisms of higher education—that it was irreligious, snobbish, and expensive. The charge that college made a man irreligious he mocked as "mere fol-de-rol": if religion were not true, men should not believe it; if it was true, college would confirm it. "A religion that won't stand the application of reason and common sense," he said, "is not fit for an intelligent dog." Nor was the charge of snobbery a fair criticism, he went on, for no thoroughly educated man ever turned his nose up at a fellow human being, though "on the other hand, as long as one man is lazy, and another industrious, you will, you *must* have social classes." On the matter of cost, DuBois cited his own expenses to prove that any boy "with grit and average ability" could get through without a penny.‡

DuBois complained that Boston Negroes ("you people," he

---

* The occasion and date of this speech are marked on the manuscript in the DuBois papers. But DuBois failed to show up for a scheduled speech about that time, and this may have been the occasion.

† DuBois's prose in this period is worth sampling: "With a coldly critical world looking on, when every passion, every precedent is calling for the strained nerve & master hand, when this battle of life never offered dearer booty, when the blanched face of the coward should never mock our lines, when the blood of our fathers is shrieking from the soil, to cheer a battle as much nobler than other battles as the moral and intellectual is nobler than the dust—This day, I have seen—I have seen an army throwing away its arms."

‡ Income: summer work, $125; scholarship, $200; tutoring, $50; monitorships, $10; prizes, $45—total, $430.
Expenses: tuition, $150; books, $25; room, $22; board, $114; fuel, light, $11; clothes, $60; washing, $18; sundries, $30—total, $430.

called them) were neglecting existing facilities for a rich cultural life. He found Negro ideas of recreation stunted: amusements lacked literary achievement; churches in condemning respectable dances, card parties, and decent fun of any kind as immoral drove Negro youth into less reputable establishments. There were other complaints: churches contributed nothing to practical social work or to manly character; sermons never contained thoughtful discourses of any kind; and revivals concealed deviltry instead of saving souls. To meet a real need, DuBois outlined a complete program for Negro Boston's social life: libraries, lectures, Chautauqua circles, literary societies, and churches that stood for "education and morality." According to his estimate, the Boston community spent $5,000 a year on amusements. If that were true, he said, the money should be concentrated in an amusement center which would provide cultural uplift and still have a surplus to support some students at Harvard.

The Negro world, he continued, lacked the leadership worthy of the race. Ethiopia, he asserted, "is calling for the strong man, the master-felt man, the honest man, and the man who can forget himself." And in return she has received a "reign of the coward" —scamps among the politicians, rascals among the leaders, "a time-server for our Moses and a temporizer who is afraid to call a lie a lie."* Even the great mass of the Negro people, though honest and generous, he said, seemed afraid to take a stand for "truth, honor, and grit," though they saw the rottenness. The whole race must become dutiful and moral: "No Negro can afford to stoop to an Anglo-Saxon standard of morality."

This type of speech did little to ingratiate DuBois with the Boston community. On his arrival at Harvard, the established Negro urban communities had opened their social life to him. His English themes record various evenings with girls—one at which the girls took advantage of the privileges of leap year, another at which two young ladies "apparently did not notice me." One girl teased this self-conscious intellectual until he decided in despair: "She

---

* In a poem mourning Douglass's death in 1895, DuBois softened this judgment: the death of "our mightiest" is as a "watchfire / Waving and bending in crimson glory" which "Suddenly flashes to the mountain and leaves / A grim and horrid blackness in the world."

is a thorough trifler in philosophy—a still better explanation perhaps . . . a woman." His fantasy carried him even further: a
short story written in this period describes the adventures of four
young blades who courted two sets of girls the same evening and
had to steal a trolley to make proper connections.

But the longer he stayed, the less welcome he became. During
DuBois's undergraduate years, the Boston correspondent for the
New York *Age* had praised his scholastic accomplishments and
noted that, popular and genial, DuBois had made many friends in
and out of school. As he entered graduate school, the praise leveled
off to perfunctory notice, and then dipped into criticism. His
failure to appear for a scheduled speech was reported. His dramatic efforts were unappreciated and resented. When he went to
Europe, criticism followed him. His letters to the *Age* about his
European adventures led the Cleveland *Gazette* to comment:
"Much of W. E. B. DuBois's letters from Europe published in the
New York *Age* make one very tired. 'I, I, I, I, Me, me, me, Black
bread and butter,' *Scat!*"[36]

DuBois's own memory of these years conjures up nothing but
a parade of successes. Actually, there were distinct disappoint-
ments. Toward the end of his first term of graduate school, his
English 12 instructor summarized DuBois's work sharply: "Un-
thinking seems to me the word for your style. With a good deal
of emotional power, you blaze away pretty much anyhow. Occasionally, a sentence or a paragraph, and sometimes even a whole
composition, will be fine. Oftener there will be a nebulous, almost
sulphorous indistinctness of outline. As for reserve of power, it is
rarely to be found. More than most men, you need . . . an appreciation of good literature."[37] The graduate school, at the end of
his second year, apparently felt some reservation about his progress,
for his application for a fellowship for the third year, preferably
to be taken abroad, was not approved, and the defensive tone of
DuBois's application suggests that he was under criticism for in-
attention to course work and for his slow progress toward his doctoral examinations.

In general, however, DuBois could regard his academic career
at Harvard with satisfaction. His sampling of courses in the first
two years gave breadth to his education; his specialization in gradu-

ate school gave depth in a single subject. He had heard applause from scholarly and popular audiences.

Not so much can be said, however, for his life in the white community surrounding the classrooms. He never felt himself a part of his class or of the college, and he deeply resented the color line, which proved to be more obvious around Cambridge than it had been at Great Barrington.

There were occasional breaks in the pattern. A program for a class dinner at the Parker House during Will's undergraduate years is preserved in his papers. He at least bought a ticket to Class Day exercises in the Yard during his senior year. Robert Morss Lovett, a contemporary at Harvard, recalls long hikes with him (one to Quincy to see "drumlins and dunes") and says he never thought of DuBois as a Negro until DuBois achieved some honor as a prize orator.[38] But these were the exceptions. When DuBois met a fellow undergraduate on the trolley into Boston, an inquiry about the "race's statistics at Harvard" served to remind him again of his color—as he was regularly reminded, he observed, by 90 per cent of the visitors to the college. He generally lived apart from college life. Even marginal organizations such as the Graduates Club, with mingled social and intellectual interests, were closed to him.* He trained himself, as most Negroes who circulated among white men had to train themselves, to ignore stares as he sat down to a meal. He stayed with his books and was satisfied with his reputation as a "grind." He pitied the absence of purpose among his white contemporaries and mocked the pageant of Harvard: seeing an anachronistic portrait of Jared Sparks, the nineteenth-century historian, in a toga, DuBois looked for Socrates in wig and top boots, or Minerva in a corset.

Early in his career at Harvard, DuBois drew a distinction between the treatment of the Negro in the North and in the South. In the South, he said, the Negro sustained positive outrage as liberty was throttled by prejudice and fear. In the North, he went on, conditions stung the pride of the ambitious and educated—i.e.,

---

* Thomas E. Will, a classmate, later told DuBois that he, Will, had declined membership in the Graduates Club because DuBois was "said to have been blackballed because of your color." Will to DuBois, January 1, 1906, DuBois papers.

himself—but Negroes had grown up in the hope that obstacles would finally disappear. Now, however, after noble hearts like Garrison, Sumner, and Phillips had helped raise the Negro from slavery, the Negro "arisen, educated and willing, fired by memory of the past," found no door open save that to the dining room and the kitchen.[39]

The church seemed especially at fault. To help defray the expenses of his education, DuBois gave "readings" to church groups for an admission charge of twenty-five cents, shared by the church and the orator. In the scrapbook for his first year at Harvard, he chronicled a recent trip to see the rector of "– – – church." On the way everyone stared, for it was the God-given right of American ladies, he said, to eye a social inferior from head to foot without losing their self-respect. The domestic at the rectory was astonished to see a Negro calling, but the lady of the house was cordial. She made a show of how nice she could be to colored people, mentioned casually the vast debt owed to the Anglo-Saxon race because of the great interest "her" people had in "your" people and the pile of clothing sent to Tuskegee the previous winter. In turn, DuBois gave her an account of the "extraordinary" fact that he was at Harvard, and "a verbal census of all other such past and future anomalies." Then the rector rejected the reading project; rejected politely, but rejected. So DuBois returned to Flagg Street: "Mind not, little heart," he wrote in his diary, "if the world were you I could love it. And so we have spent a sample day. We are disappointed. And yet I have spent the happiest hours of my life when I have come home in the twilight with a life plan in my bosom smashed—and alone—sturdy man, forsooth: laid my head on my table, and wept."[40] Evidence of a recurring hostility to the white Christian church appears time after time. He writhed at what he called the Anglo-Saxon's "high Episcopal Nicene creed" which justified the white man in putting his heel on the neck of the man down. He commented on the text: "Ethiopia shall in these days stretch forth her hands to God." That may be, DuBois wrote, but "the spectacle [of] the venerable colored dame in this rather unbalanced position in regard to the Anglo-Saxon god has become somewhat nauseating to the average young Negro of today."[41] Only the "self-forgetful Quakers," he said, still remembered God.[42]

By the end of his Harvard years, the range of DuBois's hostility to American white society had broadened considerably. Despite some exceptions such as Lovett (even this exception is recorded by Lovett and not by DuBois), rejection by the white world evoked in DuBois a mounting bitterness against it. In response to exclusion, he countered with an exclusiveness which frequently reduced him to a group of one. The four years in Cambridge had given DuBois his fill of social slights, of coolness from Harvard organizations, of patronizing wives, and of fellow students who saw him as a Negro rather than as a classmate.

The Harvard faculty departed dramatically from this pattern of discrimination. Shaler, who taught DuBois in several courses, was sensitive to, if not particularly informed about, the Negro problem. Barrett Wendell flattered DuBois by reading a part of one of his themes to a crowded class. Hart not only guided his work, but helped him secure successive Harvard scholarships and probably arranged for his appearance before the American Historical Association. A "smoker" of history professors, instructors, and graduate students included DuBois as a member. William James, to whom DuBois refers as "my favorite teacher and my closest friend" and "guide to clear thinking," welcomed him to his home "repeatedly" and encouraged his work.[43] James commended DuBois's long course paper, "The Renaissance of Ethics: a critical comparison of scholastic and modern ethics," as very original, full of independent thought, vigorously expressed—an "exceptionally promising production."[44] George Santayana read Kant privately with DuBois. From Ephraim Emerton and Frank W. Taussig, President Charles W. Eliot, Josiah Royce, and Charles Eliot Norton came invitations to call on specified evenings.

In short, at the top level of intellect and scholarship, DuBois found that he was being accepted, if not as a peer, at least as a prospective peer. If his color entered into the appraisal of his work, he did not know it; as far as he could see, the faculty at Harvard was free from racial prejudice. Looking back, DuBois could say: "God was good to let me sit awhile at their feet and see the fair vision of a commonwealth of culture open to all creeds and races and colors."[45]

Meanwhile he had etched a clear picture of life behind the Veil.

With a wonder tinted with sentimentality, he dwelt lovingly on the varied beauty of Negroes and on their patience, generosity, and submissiveness. As discrimination limited the extent of his identification with white culture, he took up this minority group passionately and defended it against its white critics. This group, he thought, could contribute much to American life.

On the other hand, it could receive much more: a vision of the panorama of modern Western culture. In an age requiring reason and education, Negroes languished in prejudiced ignorance. The fault, DuBois thought, lay not with the Negro people themselves —their hearts and souls were sound; the fault lay with incompetent leadership unprepared to bridge the gap between the "lowest stages of barbarism" and modern civilization. In DuBois's view, the first task for the Negro was to develop his cultural resources, to catch up with his white neighbors.

An unnoticed trap lay under this image of life behind the Veil. DuBois assumed that the Negro's cultural advance would qualify him for a full part in modern civilization and presumably for integration in white society. Yet, ironically enough, cultural advance might actually confirm separation. An increase in Negro businessmen might broaden the Negro's range of achievement, presumably a cultural advance, but it would also set Negroes apart, because Negro merchants would for the most part serve customers of their own race. A larger turnout at a town meeting might symbolize Negro participation in American life; yet if Negroes met in caucus as a preliminary to bloc-voting, as DuBois suggested, they were separating themselves from the rest of the town. The notion of the Negroes as balance of power overlooked the possibility that such a political device might not compel white justice, but might invite the alternative of removing the Negro from politics entirely.

DuBois's own experience in Great Barrington illustrated the dilemma. The same academic success which gave impetus to his career disqualified him from a role in the town's social system. His mother might deny discrimination on account of color—"it was all a matter of ability and hard work"[46]—but Will's ability and hard work led to a scholarship at a Negro college, not at Amherst or Williams. The very process of catching up with modern civilization created obstacles to integration by exciting opposition among white men unable to conceive of the Negro at any but the most servile level. The cure was, to be sure, not worse than the condition, nor could the condition be met except by applying the cure. Yet this paradox of Negro progress did exist, and DuBois at this stage of his career was unaware of it.

Two years at the University of Berlin gave DuBois a chance to think objectively about the Negro's status and his own relation to it. In 1892, after two years of graduate study at Harvard, DuBois went abroad on a grant—half gift, half loan—from the Slater Fund, a philanthropic foundation headed by former President Rutherford B. Hayes. DuBois's travels in England, France, Italy, and Germany, his visits to Vienna, Cracow, and Budapest, and his studies at Berlin released him from his consuming preoccupation with color. "From the physical provincialism of America and the psychical provincialism of my rather narrow race problem into which I was born and which seemed to me the essence of life," he recalls, "I was transplanted and startled into a realization of the real centers of modern civilization and into at least momentary escape from my own social problems and also into an introduction to new cultural patterns."[47] He went to the theater every week and to the symphony now and again. He learned to regard an art gallery as a house for a single picture, all the others serving simply as a frame for it. As he sailed down the Rhine, a German family took him under its wing, and a young Fräulein may even have fallen in love with him. Except where Americans had penetrated in some numbers, DuBois found little in Europe to parallel the racial discrimination inescapable even in the North. In the student beer halls he was as welcome as any other foreigner. When his exotic color was a cause for comment at all, it never created a barrier; if anything, it added to his welcome. During his vacations he traveled to the limit of his budget. He was fascinated by the rise of anti-Semitism in Germany: it "has much in common with our own race question," DuBois said, "and is therefore of considerable interest to me."* In Prague he was surprised to find the surge of nationalism

* DuBois to Daniel Coit Gilman, undated, *ca.* April 1893, DuBois papers. DuBois appears to have absorbed some anti-Semitism himself. In his "Diary of my Steerage Trip across the Atlantic" (summer 1895) he says that he had

which led people to avoid the study of German. He made a long analysis of German socialism, which later apparently served as a lecture. At the University of Berlin, Heinrich von Treitschke lectured on the superiority of the Anglo-Saxon race and snarled at the backwardness of colored peoples, but he greeted DuBois cordially on a casual meeting before vacation time. Those glorious months abroad made DuBois realize that "white folk were human."[48]

At the university DuBois observed that Harvard's red tape seemed paralyzing only because Americans had never seen the "deeper crimson" of Berlin's variety. To the newcomer Berlin's academic halls glistened with that "ethereal sheen which, to the fresh American, envelopes everything European," but by Christmas time the sheen wore off, and the young scholar settled down to his ambitious program in the social sciences.[49]

His work for the fall term of his first year, for example, included a course in politics under Treitschke; a study of the beginnings of the modern state; Rudolph von Gneist's Prussian state reform; theoretical political economy and "industrialism and society" under Adolph Wagner; and Gustav Schmoller's Prussian constitutional history. In addition, he was admitted to Schmoller's seminar and, as at Harvard, spent the bulk of his time preparing a research paper, "The Plantation and Peasant Proprietorship Systems of Agriculture in the Southern United States."

The interlude at Berlin served several purposes. For one thing, Schmoller's cordiality reinforced DuBois's conviction that intellectuals were above color prejudice. For another, Schmoller, with one of the brightest reputations in German economic thought, drew DuBois away from history into a type of political economy which could easily be converted into sociology, and, at a more general level, encouraged him to a career devoted to scholarship. Again DuBois could look back at a chapter with satisfaction. Though his plan to take a degree at Berlin never materialized, he brought

---

seen the aristocracy of the Jewish race and the "low mean cheating pöbel," but he had seldom seen "the ordinary good hearted good intentioned man." He found two congenial Jews on the trip, but he shunned the rest—"There is in them all that slyness that lack of straight-forward openheartedness which goes straight against me."

back to America flattering testimonials from Schmoller and Wagner along with Schmoller's tentative commitment to publish DuBois's Berlin research paper in his "yearbook."

On his twenty-fifth birthday DuBois paused to take stock. Looking back over his education and forward to his career, he dedicated himself as the Moses of his people. After a "sacrifice to the Zeitgeist" of Mercy, God, and Work, and a curious ceremony with candles, Greek wine, oil, song, and prayer, he dedicated his library to his mother and then went on to compose a long note in his diary, speculating on his own place in the modern world:

> I am glad I am living, I rejoice as a strong man to run a race, and I am strong—is it egotism is it assurance—or is it the silent call of the world spirit that makes me feel that I am royal and that beneath my sceptre a world of kings shall bow. The hot dark blood of that black forefather born king of men—is beating at my heart, and I know that I am either a genius or a fool . . . . this I do know: be the Truth what it may I will seek it on the pure assumption that it is worth seeking—and Heaven nor Hell, God nor Devil shall turn me from my purpose till I die. I will in this second quarter century of my life, enter the dark forest of the unknown world for which I have so many years served my apprenticeship—the chart and compass the world furnishes me I have little faith in—yet, I have none better —I will seek till I find—and die. There is grandeur in the very hopelessness of such a life—life? and is life all? If I strive, shall I live to strive again? I do not know and in spite of the wild sehnsucht for Eternity that makes my heart sick now and then —I [grit?] my teeth and say I do not care. Carpe Diem! What if life but life, after all? Its end is its greatest and fullest self— this end is the Good. The Beautiful its attribute—its soul, and Truth is its being. Not three commensurate things are these, they three dimensions of the cube—mayhap God is the founder, but for that very reason incomprehensible. The greatest and fullest life is by definition beautiful, beautiful—beautiful as a dark, passionate woman, beautiful as a golden hearted school girl, beautiful as a grey haired hero. That is the dimension of *breadth*. Then comes Truth—what is, cold and indisputable: That is *height*. Now I will, so help my Soul, multiply breadth by height, Beauty by Truth and then Goodness, strength, shall bind them together into a solid whole. Wherefore? I know not

now. Perhaps Infinite other dimensions do. This is a wretched disguise and yet it represents my attitude toward the world. I am striving to make my life all that life may be—and I am limiting that strife only in so far as that strife is incompatible with others of my brothers and sisters making their lives similar. The crucial question now is where this limit comes . . . . God knows I am sorely puzzled. I am firmly convinced that my own best development is not one and the same with best development of the world and here I am willing to sacrifice. The sacrifice is working for the multiplication of (Truth × Beauty) and now here comes the question how. The general proposition of working for the world's good becomes too soon sickly sentimentality. I therefore take the work that the Unknown lays in my hands & work for the rise of the Negro people, taking for granted that their best development means the best development of the world.

This night before my life's altar I reiterate, what my heart has . . .

Here the manuscript breaks off, but it is resumed shortly thereafter:

These are my plans: to make a name in science, to make a name in literature and thus to raise my race. Or perhaps to raise a visible empire in Africa thro' England, France, or Germany.

I wonder what will be the outcome? Who knows?[50]

This remarkable diary entry, inchoate, histrionic, but, above all, moving, reveals much of DuBois's sense of himself as a person destined to redirect the history of his time. This personal assertiveness, however, was modified by a sense of duty: he would subordinate his personal ambition to the central purpose of elevating the Negro people. If occasionally duty coincided with personal ambition, that merely demonstrated the extent to which he had intertwined the two. When he asked the Slater Fund trustees to subsidize a second year abroad, he explained that the experience was absolutely necessary to the completion of his education. He went on to say: "I realize, gentlemen, the great weight of responsibility that rests upon the younger generation of Negroes, and I feel that, handicapped as I must inevitably be to some extent in the race of life, I cannot afford to start with preparation a whit shorter or cheaper than that deemed necessary to the best usefulness of my white fellow student."[51] DuBois was ready to pay for the luxury of his duty, for he offered to renew his fellowship on the same basis as the original award, half grant and half loan, or as a full loan. Actually, the Slater trustees renewed his grant on the same terms, but even so, by the time he started teaching (on a salary of $800 a year), his education had saddled him with a debt of $1,125. In short, he mortgaged his future to prepare himself adequately for the task of serving his race.

A Sense of Mission

The world of DuBois's youth pointed the way to his career. If white men were guilty of race prejudice arising from ignorance, if black men were retarded, remote from the culture of the time, then DuBois must teach both and reconcile them. He knew with conviction that he had the talent and the technique; his missionary sense of duty would permit him to do no less. He decided upon a life's work of teaching and research; as a college teacher he would dispel Negro ignorance by training other missionaries who could carry the gospel back to their communities; at the same time, his research would convert white America to a just appraisal of the Negro. His career would serve a third purpose as well: it would fill a genuine personal need. Among white intellectuals he had always found acceptance. As their peer he would continue to find it. In the Negro world he would be a liberator. Here was a career, a mission, which could consume many lifetimes.

This decision was never, to be sure, consciously plotted out. Yet DuBois had been working toward a scholar's career for several years: from science through philosophy to history and economics.

With DuBois's background in scientific courses, he found great appeal in James's pragmatism, for he assumed that pragmatism gave assurance that ethics, once freed of "scholastic dogma," could be based on empirical observation and on reason. In his paper for James, DuBois traced the process by which ethics was "liberating" itself from ultramundane, theistic teleology that was "useless as a science." Scholasticism, with its "pernicious" substitution of dogma for faith, caused reason to be subjected to dogma, and ethics to be based on dogma instead of on facts. At the time of Descartes and Bacon, he went on, the separation of science from teleology and the conviction that only matter was capable of scientific treatment led to enormous advances in science, but left metaphysics bogged down in scholasticism. There it had stayed, he said, as unproductive from Kant to Royce as it had been from Abelard to Occam. Metaphysics would regain an equal place with science, he asserted, when it dropped inquiries into the categories of reason, space, perception, and authority of conscience, and systematically studied accumulated facts, as the physicist studied heat. With James and Royce, DuBois continued, an attempt had been made "to base ethics upon fact—to make it a *science*."* Its method was to separate the "what" from the "why" on the way to the creation of an all-embracing science, "the beacon light of a struggling humanity to guide its knowledge of the Infinite." (As a side issue, DuBois took a page or two to prove the necessary existence of objective reality, but James rejected the proof as begging the principal question of the whole idealist position.) Here then, according to DuBois, was "the cornerstone of a world structure—first the What, then the Why—underneath the everlasting Ought."

Even after DuBois abandoned his plans for a career in philosophy, these ideas showed their reflection in his work. James had expressed reservations about DuBois's analysis—his failure to show the method of "real teleology" despite his assumption of its existence, the impossibility of making a science out of ethics, and the "oracular & ambiguous" nature of the conclusion that "truth is the one path to teleology, teleology is ethics." Yet, despite these reservations,[52] DuBois continued to assume that the path to reform lay in the accumulation of empirical knowledge which, dispelling ignorance and misapprehension, would guide intelligent social policy. As he said succinctly in his diary: "The Universe is Truth. The Best ought to be. On these postulates hang all the law and the prophets."

As success in Hart's course turned DuBois toward history, his diary noted: "What we want is not a philosophy of history but

* James commented in the margin: "I doubt whether we do seek to make it a science—to me that seems impossible."

such a collection and . . . placement of facts physical and mental as to furnish material for a philosophy of man." For a Negro with a missionary sense, this suggested a study of the background of the Negro in America, a study of his "advance" since emancipation. The accumulation of adequate historical information for understanding the Negro, DuBois thought, would pave the way for a just social policy. At Berlin, Schmoller confirmed this basic analysis, but redirected DuBois's scholarly ambition to economics, and ultimately to sociology. In a letter to the Slater Fund trustees in 1893, DuBois outlined his program after his return to America: to get a place in a Negro university (Howard University in Washington was his first choice) and to build up a department of sociology for two purposes: "1. Scientifically to study the Negro question past and present with a view to its best solution. 2. To see how far Negro students are capable of further independent study & research in the best scientific work of the day."[53]

DuBois returned from Germany in the summer of 1894, his education complete (except for receiving his Ph.D. at Harvard in 1895). Conscious that he had received an education rare for any young American, black or white, he embarked on a mail campaign to secure a job. Eventually three offers came. He accepted the first, the chair in classics at Wilberforce University at Xenia, Ohio, at $800 a year. Shortly thereafter, the Lincoln Institute in Missouri offered $250 more, and even later, Booker T. Washington invited DuBois to Tuskegee Institute in Alabama to teach mathematics. DuBois stuck to his original commitment and, in the fall of 1894, started on a career of teaching and research, which, continuing for sixteen years, would include what he afterward characterized as "my real life work."[54]

THE SCHOLAR'S ROLE

DuBois made his way to Wilberforce in the hot August of 1894. Still quite lean, just below medium height and very erect, he wore a Vandyke beard which, together with his retreating hairline, gave him an air of maturity beyond his twenty-six years. He had a high silk hat and affected the gloves and cane of the German student; together they added to the severe elegance of his appearance.

Nominally appointed to the chair in Latin and Greek, he soon shared the load in English, brought German to the curriculum, and would have added sociology if the college authorities had permitted. He also held the official title of "Keeper of Marks." Occasionally he even administered the college's formal discipline. Here was the beginning of his career, he told an English friend: "Life was now begun & I was half happy."[1]

But Wilberforce betrayed his ambitious dreams. In the students he found "the same eagerness, the same joy of life, the same brains" as in New England and in Europe.[2] But the religious life of the college ran afoul of his distaste for dogma and for institutional worship. Equating educational success with "moral and religious tone," the school enforced regular attendance at church and forbade both "clandestine associations" between men and women and even casual meetings on the campus. Separate walks were provided.[3] Sunday school was a great trial to DuBois, for Scriptural literalism outraged his intelligence and interpretative teaching violated college policy. On his twenty-eighth birthday, the new professor, impatient for scholastic excellence, feared "mental imbecility," because a revival had virtually imprisoned him in his room for almost a week, his classes suspended by faculty action to give the spirit free rein, his German and Latin conjugations forgotten amid the "wild screams cries groans & shrieks" rising from the chapel below.[4] Between revivals, faculty politics offered a career to the ambitious and a diversion to the settled; it flourished so abundantly that even the official history of the college refers to it. Primarily a church school, supported by the African Methodist Episcopal Church, the college received state funds as well—a situation which encouraged the maneuvers of both church and state. In his notebook DuBois complained that the president bought security in his own job by the appointment of an influential bishop's incompetent son. Financial problems regularly distracted the college's attention: in DuBois's first year, the college faced a debt of $12,000, with $2,000 being demanded immediately.

Two years of this impatient apprenticeship, brightened only by his marriage to Nina Gomer, a young girl from Cedar Rapids, Iowa, whom he had met at the college, made DuBois anxious to leave. Exasperated by "incompetence and rascality," he writhed through trivial disputes and looked anxiously for a new job, free from daily pettifogging. As he wrote at the time: "I can fight giants, but snakes—ouch! 'Tis the petty sins of petty souls that disarm me in the very whirl of battle."[5]

Relief came when the University of Pennsylvania offered him a fifteen-month appointment as an assistant instructor in sociology to prepare a scholarly study of the Negro community of Philadelphia. (His salary came to $60 a month.) A task so well tailored to DuBois's training he accepted with alacrity and moved east with his wife.

The following year, when Atlanta University sought an experienced sociologist to direct its studies of the Negro, President Horace Bumstead, who had known of DuBois years before, turned to him as the man, black or white, best prepared for the task. The matter of formal religion raised some doubt about the appointment. DuBois remained noncommittal, and Bumstead decided that DuBois's life with a new wife in the slum area of Philadelphia in order to perform "beneficent work" gave sufficient evidence of genuine religion.

DuBois remained at Atlanta for thirteen years, from 1897 to 1910. There he enjoyed a position of academic security in a college run democratically by its faculty. His talent deferred to and respected, he could expect encouragement, within the limits of available funds, for his scholarly work. Distinguished Negroes like Booker T. Washington and James Weldon Johnson visited the university; notable white citizens such as Jane Addams and Franz Boas came to speak. He kept in touch by mail with other scholars: Clark Wissler advised him on anthropology; William James commended him for his book, *The Souls of Black Folk*; Max Weber urged him to arrange for a German edition of it.

From 1894 until 1910, the scholar's role committed DuBois to three major tasks: first, to assemble accurate sociological data as the basis for intelligent social policy toward the Negro; second, to present the Negro's problems in a favorable light to a larger non-scholarly audience through lectures, books, and magazine articles; and third, to take the lead in bringing culture to American Negroes.

A Foundation of Facts

DuBois's dissertation, *The Suppression of the African Slave-Trade to the United States of America, 1638–1870*, which was in press at the time of his appointment to Pennsylvania, was his first major scholarly production. Following the political and institutional orientation of his adviser, Professor Hart, DuBois surveyed the attempts to enforce the existing laws against the trade, or more precisely, the failure to enforce them. In DuBois's view, the slave trade could have been curtailed by three methods: by raising American moral standards, by enforcing legal prohibition of the slave trade, or by destroying the economic attractions of the traffic in men. All three failed, the first because the existence of slavery itself showed moral weakness at just the point at which moral strength was needed; the second because the laws were "poorly conceived, loosely drawn, and wretchedly enforced," and the third because no one was willing to attempt it. In a preliminary report DuBois had said that while Southern planters recognized slave labor as an economic good and the slave trade as its strong right arm, and while Northern capital continued unfettered by a conscience, "Northern greed joined to Southern credulity was a combination calculated to circumvent any law, human or divine."[6]

The final abolition of slavery he attributed partly to direct moral appeal and to political sagacity, but principally to the "economic collapse of the large-farming slave system." This economic emphasis came as rather a surprise, for it received little support in the text. In his report to the American Historical Association during his Harvard days, DuBois had concluded that abolition came from "an enlightened public policy, the common moral sense of a great people enforcing its sovereign will by majorities for Lincoln and by the point of the bayonet."[7] This conclusion fitted the material in his book better than the one he used. The summary published in the book appears to have been added after his work in economics at Berlin. DuBois apparently sensed that his economic explanation was inadequately proved, for in his preface he warned that because of the paucity of facts and statistics bearing on "the economic side of the study," the conclusions were subject to modification.

Actually the book was more a study in ethics than in either politics or economics. One reviewer noted that its hortatory tone revealed the advocate rather than the historian. Influenced by his understanding of James's pragmatism, by his own sense of mission, and by the tone of uplift prevalent in the period, DuBois could not escape the "ought" which he assumed underlay the "what" and the "why." Though the book was to be a contribution to the "scientific study of slavery," DuBois could not conceal his indignation at the "cupidity and carelessness of our ancestors." Even the Northerners, made of "sterner moral fibre than the Southern cavaliers and adventurers," swept away moral opposition because of the "immense economic advantages of the slave traffic to a thrifty seafaring community of traders." For DuBois, the obvious question suggested by the study was: "How far in a state can a recognized moral wrong safely be compromised?" And his answer, in words with the ring of *The Book of Common Prayer,* had little to do with scientific history: "It behooves nations as well as men to do things at the very moment when they ought to be done." Yet the book was a tremendous plum for the young scholar. The hortatory tone was perhaps unavoidable when DuBois took on a study with racially sensitive aspects; the narrowness of its legal and institutional research followed the current mode. These limitations faded next to the fact that he had prepared a solid piece of work with which Harvard inaugurated its *Historical Studies.*

Between his first book and his second, *The Philadelphia Negro: A Social Study*, DuBois changed the direction of his scholarship. The historian turned to sociology, and the moralist struggled toward the ideal of objective research. With Charles Booth's *Life and Labour of the People in London* and the cooperative volume, *Hull House Maps and Papers*, as his models, he conducted a fifteen-month survey of the 45,000 Negroes centered in the Seventh Ward of Philadelphia, a door-to-door inquiry on family status, morality, occupations, religion, social intercourse—any pertinent facts about the Negro which might pierce existing generalizations which, he said, were based on "fantastic theories, ungrounded assumptions, or metaphysical subtleties." He and his sponsors at the university regarded his study as the raw material from which would emerge the "solution" of Negro problems in a large American city. Without this groundwork of "intelligent and discriminating research," DuBois said, the labor of the statesman and philanthropist "must continue to be, in a large extent, barren and unfruitful."

DuBois did not equate "intelligent and discriminating research" with absolute truth, and with disarming candor he pointed out sources of error within his work: errors of the statistical method, "even greater error" from the imprecision of personal observation; above all, moral conviction and preconceived patterns of thought which "enter to some extent into the most cold-blooded scientific research as a disturbing factor." Outside the investigator more traps threatened: misapprehension, vagueness, forgetfulness, and deliberate deception on the part of the people being questioned. With so many possibilities of error, the shrewd judgment of the trained observer had to supplement what was statistically demonstrable. This was legitimate, if that judgment was guided by the "heart-quality of fairness, and an earnest desire for truth despite its possible unpleasantness." When DuBois finished the study, he was satisfied that his book could pass the most rigorous tests of reliability. He hoped that it would be only the first in a series of urban studies which, when taken together, would "constitute a fair basis of induction."

The even-handed allotment of blame to both races gave weight to DuBois's claim of relative impartiality. The Negroes he criticized for their sexual looseness, the inefficiency of their organizations for social betterment, the failure of the richer Negroes to assert their leadership and of the poorer to seek it, the venality of their political life, and the extent of criminal activity within the race. White Philadelphians, he said, made things worse by their color prejudice: they created obstacles to Negro employment both inside and outside trade unions; by regarding Negroes as a group rather than as individuals, they branded the entire race with the characteristics of its degenerate criminal class; they used the fear of ultimate intermarriage to curtail every prospect of Negro advancement.

Yet despite this fair distribution of blame and the "heart-quality of fairness" in the research itself, DuBois's "Final Word" arose more from his preconceptions than from his research. Negroes were to catch up on modern civilization by paying taxes, supporting schools, lowering the crime rate, seeking industrial opportunities, broadening their amusements beyond prayer meetings and church socials, and in general by emphasizing honesty, truth, and charity. At the same time, DuBois stressed "above all" the duty of the better classes of Negroes, frankly called the "aristocracy," to reach down to help the retarded masses. The whites had two duties: first, to enlarge Negro opportunities instead of harping constantly on the unreal problem of intermarriage; and second, to cooperate with the better Negroes by recognizing distinctions within the race. Here again was the DuBois of Fisk, appealing at once to the "best of you" in the white world and to the Negro elite in the black, seeking salvation through a Negro aristocracy encouraged by its white peers. His schoolboy insights now seemed confirmed by fifteen months of research in Philadelphia.

Actually, certain facts in the text threw serious doubt on the legitimacy of the role assigned to the Negro elite. For example, white leaders were urged in their own interest to stand behind the rise of the Negro aristocracy. Yet it was doubtful, and at best unproven, that a thriving Negro middle class, serving its race as professional and business men, would have served the whites' self-interest. Indeed, such a Negro group might emerge as direct competitors who would impinge on white businesses and services without any compensating guarantee of diminishing the Negro problem.

His advice to Negroes had pitfalls too. If the Negro elite induced Negroes to withdraw support from the city's corrupt political machine, this act would have deprived Negroes of those political jobs which, by DuBois's own account, came to them as compensation for the support of corruption. The loss of jobs would have been an immediate economic loss without any guarantee of a compensating gain: the honesty of city fathers gave no assurance of their friendliness to Negroes.

The two aspects of the work—the report on the research and the conclusions—were not essentially related. Empiricism wrestled with research, and each scored one fall. Yet in this type of survey, the author's "final word," which is recognized as a frank statement of his own views, is relatively unimportant. The factual evidence stands on its own, inviting every reader to make an independent appraisal. And here DuBois's great strength showed up. His block-by-block survey was exhaustive and imaginative. His patience and honesty are revealed on every page. It was undoubtedly this aspect of the work which, forty-five years later, led Gunnar Myrdal, the Swedish sociologist, to regard *The Philadelphia Negro* as a model study of a Negro community.[8]

Before and after the publication of *The Philadelphia Negro*, DuBois was working toward a theory of sociology. He rejected Herbert Spencer, whose "verbal jugglery," DuBois said, ultimately led to enigmatic abstractions like "consciousness of kind." According to DuBois's view, this school avoided real men and real things and concentrated on a "mystical" whole full of "metaphysical lay figures" which corresponded to its theories but bore little relation to observable fact.[9]

Schmoller had shown an alternative. In revolt against the deductive method of the Manchester school of economics, Schmoller, the "authoritative exponent" of the "modernized historical school,"[10] wanted to collect historical and factual material from which would emerge a science of economics which could point the direction for national policy. According to DuBois's notes on Schmoller's seminar, Schmoller assumed that the "observations of different persons always lead to the same result."[11] Therefore empiricism would eventually provide a concrete basis for policy: first the facts, then a program based on those facts.

In his theoretical writings, DuBois applied these principles to the Negro in America. Like Schmoller, he believed that research would reveal basic natural laws. Even chance, he thought, could ultimately be explained in terms of law, though free will might prove more recalcitrant. Since accurate research would prepare for future social reform, the first step was to engage the attention of scholars in systematic study of Negro life. This would fill a conspicuous gap in America's knowledge and at the same time serve as a specialized laboratory for study of man's social development in a microcosm. Two premises he regarded as inescapable in any analysis of the Negro problem: the existence of variations within the race and the acknowledgment of the Negro's ability to advance. To a Negro audience, he later added a third: a denial of the degeneracy of mulattoes. From there on, he believed in following the evidence. Even these premises, DuBois claimed, he held undogmatically: in seeking truth, he would never insist on them in the face of evidence to the contrary. He distinguished sharply between pure research—the accumulation of facts—and recommendations for reform, warning that any attempt to give research a double aim, that is, pure science *and* reform as an immediate rather than as an ultimate goal, would defeat both objects. A convinced rationalist, confident from his Harvard days of the congruity of reality and ethics, he never doubted the usefulness of this task. As he told the American Academy of Political and Social Science: "The sole aim of any society is to settle its problems in accordance with its highest ideals, and the only rational method of accomplishing this is to study those problems in the light of the best scientific research."[12]

In Philadelphia, and for thirteen years after his arrival at Atlanta, DuBois attempted to conduct some of that research. His best work achieved real excellence: for the 1910 census reports, he prepared a reliable commentary on the Negro farmer; for the *Bulletin of the Department of Labor*, he wrote an admirable short social study of the Negroes of Farmville, Virginia; for a German and for a Belgian publication, he prepared workman-like accounts of the Negro question and of the Negro worker; in the *American*

Historical Review, he published a significant paper in 1910 which suggested that, despite all the charges against Negroes in Reconstruction governments, "practically the whole new growth of the South has been accomplished under laws which black men helped to frame thirty years ago."[13] This last article appeared when Reconstruction legislatures were being described almost exclusively in terms of bribery, whiskey, and gold-plated spittoons. Later scholars have confirmed that DuBois had the better of the argument.

The Atlanta University *Publications*, the principal item in DuBois's scholarly bibliography for this period, are somewhat harder to appraise, for they have to be judged in the perspective of fifty years ago. Looking toward a "Program of a Hundred Years," he proposed to investigate various categories of Negro life —artisans, businessmen, college alumni, and criminals; churches and schools—at the rate of one a year for ten years. When this ten-year cycle had been repeated ten times, the accumulated material was to serve as an unerring guide to scholars, philanthropists, and statesmen. Under DuBois's direction, this program continued for sixteen years (he maintained a remote but active connection with the project even after his departure from Atlanta in 1910). Each volume included the resolutions of a conference held annually at Atlanta; the transcript of speeches delivered at the conference; and miscellaneous essays germane to the topic but not necessarily based on the year's research. The hard core of each volume, the tabulation and summary of the year's investigation, suffered from a method which, however unavoidable in view of DuBois's tight budget, could hardly have yielded a substantial scholarly report.

An analysis of one volume reveals the drawbacks of DuBois's technique. For *The Negro in Business* (1899), DuBois asked investigators (frequently his own former students) in various communities to list local businessmen. Questionnaires answered by these men were returned to Atlanta along with an interpretation by an "intelligent investigator of some experience." Of course, the replies to DuBois's questionnaires came from a sifted group— he felt lucky to get 150 replies out of 500 requests. Furthermore, no one made—under the circumstances, no one could make—an adequate check on the accuracy of the information which did come in. Still, this raw material was regarded as "substantially accurate," especially since doubtful estimates of capital invested were omitted when discovered. From this survey DuBois concluded that the existing range of Negro business activity showed a definite gain and attested to the Negro's progress in general. As an outgrowth of this encouraging report, a committee on resolutions at the conference which terminated each year's study urged other Negroes to enter business. The growth of a merchant class would be a "far-sighted measure of self-defense" which would make for wealth and mutual cooperation; but Negroes must be careful to avoid already overcrowded trades, for one-sided development "puts the mass of the Negro people out of sympathy and touch with the industrial and mercantile spirit of the age." The Negro masses were urged to patronize Negro stores, but businessmen were prudently warned not to count on that patronage. In summary, the committee said: "We *must* cooperate or we are lost. Ten million people who join in intelligent self-help can never be long ignored or mistreated."

A later generation has doubts about this methodology, for styles in scholarship change, and men see their grandfathers' ways as quaintly primitive. Yet the Atlanta *Publications* had impressive value. For one thing, the factual information caught the attention of the casual reader and led him on to DuBois's conclusions. Furthermore, as the reaction to DuBois's first two books had shown, scholarly material from the pen of a Negro raised the reputation of the race. In the *Nation*, the reviewer of *The Suppression of the African Slave-Trade* noted that it was a matter of "profound significance and great encouragement" that a member of a race a generation from being hunted could write a volume so creditable to himself, to his university, and to American historical scholarship.[14] An anonymous reviewer of *The Philadelphia Negro* in *Outlook* noted less special pleading in DuBois than in generously inclined white writers. Finally, whatever their limitations, the 2,172 pages of the series provided the best information on the Negro then available. In that era most writing about the Negro was done by untrained observers who, looking out of a Pullman window, saw pretty much what they expected to see; by writers who, in the solace of their libraries, had only their theories to guide them; or by Southerners who, knowing Sam and Auntie from the old days, spoke authoritatively about the whole race. DuBois's pioneering idea of introducing organized facts into the miasma of opinion and prejudice which passed for discussion of the Negro was novel and arresting. Even Columbia and Chicago, the great centers of academic sociology, were only a few years ahead of DuBois in making empirical inquiries the basis of their sociology. To be sure, a whole generation of American scholarship was turning against what DuBois called "metaphysical subtleties" in a search for fact which would give substance to theory, and the "Chicago school," in studying how group behavior resulted from the pursuit of distinctive, characteristic interests, had methodological refinements well beyond DuBois's Atlanta *Publications*. DuBois's significance is that he was probably the first sociologist in the South and certainly the first in the field of Negro studies to make empirical evidence the fulcrum of his work. Writing in 1951, Howard W. Odum listed twelve of DuBois's titles at the top of a chronological list of American sociological works in the area of race, ethnic groups, and folk.[15]

Educating White America

DuBois's scholarly reputation introduced him to popular audiences without shackling him by its demand for objectivity. His facts could be aimed at immediate goals instead of being poured into a reservoir that could be tapped only in some remote future. More important, his articles reached an audience untouched by his more scholarly work. In the pages of *Dial, Collier's, Nation, Booklover's Magazine, World Today, Outlook, Atlantic Monthly,* and *Independent,* DuBois spoke to just the educated element of the white American population to which he looked for Negro improvement. Usually he adapted historical or sociological material to demonstrate Negro progress, or to show that the whites' race prejudice prevented Negro advancement. Once in a while, he commented directly as a contemporary observer in defense of the Negro. Occasionally he divorced himself entirely from sociology long enough to release his pent-up indignation at the conduct of white America toward its black brothers.

Loyal to a theory of progress, DuBois interpreted the Negro's history since emancipation as a steady climb upward. In popular articles and lectures he ranged over Negro America, and the accumulation of evidence showed a race rising against impressive odds. From 1870 to 1900, he reported in 1904, illiteracy had declined almost 50 per cent, principally as a result of the Negro's own efforts: in one generation, thirty thousand black teachers had given two million children the rudiments of learning, and four-fifths of the expense of the Negro schools had been borne by Negroes themselves through direct and indirect taxes. As a result of education, the intelligence and efficiency of Negro workmen had brought them three hundred million dollars worth of property. In *Advance*, he pointed out that since the Civil War the Negro had established the principle of the monagamic home, earned a living as a free laborer, and begun to develop the "Exceptional Man—the group leader."*

DuBois knew Georgia best. Almost half of Georgia's Negroes were still farm laborers—a condition closest to slavery, he explained—but above them was a small and growing 14 per cent of independent landowners. At the economic and social peak, 20,000 artisans had freed themselves from rural tyranny, while 8,000 business and professional men enjoyed varying degrees of prosperity substantially above the rest of their fellows. He estimated that Negroes in the state had by 1909 already saved fifty million dollars, and that they had paid more in tax assessments of various kinds designed to support schools than the state had spent on Negro education—the Negro, in effect, he said, was helping to bear the burden of white education.

Now and then, he came upon one of the dozen autonomous Negro centers in Ohio and Indiana where in proud isolation a black community defied the prejudices of the white world. Occasionally a Negro community, like that in Durham, North Carolina, achieved the same situation by developing an unusual inner

* The "exceptional men" included Frederick Douglass, Alexander Crummel, William O. Tanner, Booker T. Washington, Paul Laurence Dunbar, and Charles W. Chesnutt.

organization, the closed circle of a group economy which made only incidental contacts with the surrounding white world. Here 5,000 Negroes gathered their puny resources to develop five manufacturing outlets and a loan association. DuBois reported on these communities with pride: he was eager to show white America what the Negro could accomplish by himself.

Even more important had been the spiritual uplift of the period. As he said in a fifty-year summary for the New York *Times* in 1909: "From contempt and amusement they have passed to the pity and perplexity of their neighbors, while within their own souls they have arisen from apathy and timid complaint to open protest and more and more manly assertion." Now the Negro was ready to fight in the van of progress not only for himself, DuBois said, but for the emancipation of women, universal peace, democratic government, socialization of wealth, and human brotherhood. Here, he thought, was a momentous transformation: from slavery to freedom, from four millions to ten millions, from denial of citizenship to enfranchisement, from unorganized irresponsibility to organized group life, "from being spoken for to speaking, from contemptuous forgetfulness on the part of their neighbors to uneasy and dawning respect, and from inarticulate complaint to self-expression and dawning consciousness of manhood."[16]

When the Negro lagged, DuBois was ready to blame the white man. The persistently high Negro crime rate he blamed on the economic effects of emancipation, the double standard of justice in the courts, the convict lease system (which, he said, made criminals of delinquents), the increasing brutality of white mobs which shattered black faith in white justice, and the exaggerated and unnatural separation of the best classes in both groups. It was only natural that Negroes should pilfer in an industrial society in which the earnings of thrift, efficiency, and genius were often stolen by the strong and crafty; why should Negroes not steal in communities where the "theft of truth" in newspapers and magazines drew no effective protest from those who considered themselves good? "A system which *discouraged* aspiration and endeavor *encourages* crime and laziness."[17] Negro voters in Philadelphia were venal, he admitted, but their petty bribes were merely bread and butter compared to the large-scale graft which benefited Philadelphia's

influential white citizens at the expense of public funds. When
DuBois acknowledged that, despite educational advances, Georgia
Negroes were still relatively ignorant, he placed the responsibility
on white men: the state had persistently starved its Negro schools,
and Atlanta had deprived Negroes of the use of its new Carnegie
Library. The South's policy of disfranchisement checked the Negro at every point: in his education and his work, in the accumulation of property, in the elimination of crime and disease, and
in the inculcation of self-respect and ambition. A Southern Negro
peasant bound by the perpetual debt of the crop lien system had
little incentive to save or to work efficiently.

In 1903 DuBois collected a group of his fugitive essays and
some new material into *The Souls of Black Folk*, his most successful volume.* James Weldon Johnson has said that it "had a
greater effect upon and within the Negro race in America than
any other single book published in this country since *Uncle Tom's
Cabin.*"† In its judicious fairness, skillful writing, and resourceful adaptation of scholarly material to a popular audience, it is
DuBois's best statement of the Negro's case to white America, and
despite a looseness of imagery which clouds meaning,‡ it is a
minor American classic.

All of DuBois's techniques appear in the book. Reining in
his sense of personal loss, he welcomes the death of his infant son
as an escape from bondage: "Well sped, my boy, before the world
has dubbed your ambition insolence, has held your ideals un-
attainable, and taught you to cringe and bow. Better far this
nameless void that stops my life than a sea of sorrow for you."
He reprints an account of the Freedmen's Bureau from the *Atlantic Monthly*. His Atlanta conference reports provide the material for articles on the Negro church and on the Negro college
graduate. His essay on Alexander Crummell emphasizes the role

---

* The book went through more than twenty editions, and in 1940 DuBois
reported that it was "still selling." A new edition was published in 1953 by
the Blue Heron Press.

† *Along This Way* (New York, 1935), p. 203. In *Tell Freedom: Memories
of Africa* (New York, 1954), pp. 224–26, a young South African colored man,
Peter Abrahams, describes the sense of purpose he received from a first reading of *The Souls of Black Folk*.

‡ E.g.: ". . . rolling hills lie like passioned women wanton with harvest."

of the individual leader on the progress and morale of the race. He draws on his own experiences to describe back-country Southern schools for Negroes. He even includes a short story, an exotic cross-racial tale reminiscent of George Washington Cable. The critical, but respectful, essay on Booker T. Washington, which did much to influence DuBois's later career, appears here.* In short, this is a cross section of the scholarly Dr. DuBois's appeal to white America.

The most striking characteristic of the book is not its emotional intensity, but its calm balance, the absence of devils and angels, the recognition of the genuine racial difficulties created by three hundred years of precedent. He speaks tolerantly of the Negro's slavery—"not the worst slavery in the world, not a slavery that made all life unbearable, rather a slavery that had here and there something of kindliness, fidelity, and happiness,—but withal slavery, which, so far as human aspiration and desert were concerned, classed the black man and the ox together." He points to the two major obstacles to Reconstruction—the tyrannical slaveholder who "determined to perpetuate slavery under another name," and the idler-freedman who "regarded freedom as perpetual rest." He recognizes "enough argument" on both sides to support the stereotypes of the shiftless Negro and the tyrannical white Southerner, enough certainly to create barriers to mutual sympathy.

The fairness of his approach, however, does not rule out a vigorous statement of the Negro's cause. DuBois might be "the last to withhold sympathy from the white South in its efforts to solve its intricate social problems," and he might acknowledge that a partly developed people could profit by the guidance of the best and strongest of their neighbors. But the best whites in the South do not rule, he asserts, and therefore a Negro without the ballot is left exposed to the "exploitation and debauchment of the worst." The operation of the crop-lien system not only robs the Negro of the fruits of his labor, but discourages thrift and ambition, though DuBois turns from occasional well-tended farms "with a comfortable feeling that the Negro is rising." He thinks

* See below, pp. 68–69.

that the physical isolation of Negro and white upper classes guarantees that "both whites and blacks see commonly the worst of each other." He states again his conviction that only through education, of white as well as of black, can color prejudice be conquered. At one point the tone of a threat enters his book: If Negroes do not possess an educated leadership, will they be satisfied with their lot, he asks the white South, or "will you not rather transfer their leading from the hands of men trained to think to the hands of untrained demagogues?"

Fairness, restraint, and scholarly reporting—these qualities in *The Souls of Black Folk* were useful as part of a long-range campaign to coax the white man into justice for the Negro. In moments of crisis, however, that method was too slow, and the pressure of the color line on a sensitive Negro, proud and emotional, led DuBois into direct statement of Negro demands, even into direct attack on the Negro's enemies. He turned to trip-hammer accusations—accusations based on his knowledge as a sociologist, to be sure, but drawn up by the hand of a propagandist.

In 1906, for instance, the Atlanta race riot, which in four days of fighting led to five deaths, was defended by John Temple Graves, editor of the Atlanta *Georgian*, as a spontaneous flare-up of white Atlantans against black rapists. DuBois replied heatedly. He blamed the riot on Hoke Smith and Clark Howell, two candidates for governor who, DuBois said, had spent two years trying to outdo each other in vilifying the Negro. (Actually this was truer of Smith, and of his backer Tom Watson, than of Howell.) He thought that a disgraceful police force and penal system had helped. When a lawless collection of white teen-age boys and irresponsible leaders attacked the Negro community, he said, the blacks broke the unwritten law forbidding Negro self-defense against white aggression, and bloodshed resulted. The horror of the outburst gave DuBois a chance of codify the Negro's protest against the South under the heading "lessons of the riot": 1. It was criminal procedure to stir up race hatred as a path to political preferment. 2. The way to stop crime, among Negroes and white men, was by just courts, an honest police force, and a reforming (not a money-making) prison system. 3. The achievement of a peaceful community was beyond hope when a half to a third of the population was ignorant, and defenseless to the attack of the worst elements of the city. 4. The only way a Negro could be sure his property would be defended was to put a ballot in his hand. 5. Radical action in the South was necessary to prevent more outbreaks: reduce the representation in Congress of any state which disfranchised one part of its population—the Fourteenth Amendment provided for this—and grant federal aid to the South's public schools in order to combat illiteracy and barbarism.

DuBois's treatment of the Atlanta riot showed a growing talent for propaganda as distinguished from scholarship. The logic of parts of his argument—the arbitrary introduction of the issue of federal aid to Southern education as a lesson of the riot, for example—indicated an advocate's sense of timing. After all, a reader might accept Graves's explanation of the riot and reject DuBois's without affecting, one way or the other, the value of DuBois's recommendations.

The roles of scholar and advocate need not be incompatible, especially when, as in DuBois's case, the scholar is convinced that truth is itself the best advocate. Yet the temptation is always present to mix scholarship and propaganda, to merge research and reform, drawing from research a recommendation for reform which it does not produce by itself. How far DuBois yielded to this temptation was revealed in an extreme form in his biography of John Brown, the abolitionist, which appeared in 1909. Published as part of a historical series edited by E. P. Oberholtzer, the book was largely a pastiche of quotations from earlier writers; it added nothing new except DuBois's notion that Brown's contacts with Negroes needed further analysis. Since few written records were available, DuBois merely speculated: "Even in the absence of special material the broad truths are clear." By the end of the book, DuBois's commentary on the legacy of John Brown to the twentieth century ("The cost of liberty is less than the price of repression") served as a bridge to a critique of race relations in 1909.

The biography, like the article on the Atlanta riot, illustrated the tension in DuBois's plans as a scholar. The cumulative weight of facts might eventually solve Negro problems, but waiting was slow, and DuBois was not a patient man.

Training the Negro

DuBois's burden behind the Veil was itself a full-time undertaking. His job at the university charged him with educating young Negro students. Beyond that, DuBois felt impelled to guide the thinking of the Negro masses and to hold high a more sophisticated racial ideal to the select upper fraction, the "Talented Tenth." This double life—writing to reach an educated white audience and guiding the intellectual life of the Negro—involved DuBois in a continuous readjustment of his focus, for as he himself observed in *The Souls of Black Folk*: "The would-be black *savant* was confronted by the paradox that the knowledge his people needed was a twice-told tale to his white neighbors, while the knowledge which would teach the white world was Greek to his own flesh and blood."

Only the expense of traveling seems to have restrained DuBois's willingness to address Negro groups anywhere, anytime. When he could not attend a meeting in person, he frequently sent a statement to be read. In a week's extension course in Atlanta, he traced the history of the Negro race from Africa to the present. He wrote a series of brief articles on a similar theme for the *Voice of the Negro*, an able monthly published in Atlanta for a small, but national, audience. After his return from Europe he had prepared for an unidentified audience a talk on German socialism and, for what seems to have been a Washington gathering, a commentary on Thomas Carlyle. His signed contributions to his own magazine, *Horizon*, contained political analysis and direct advice on elections.

To a group of school children in Indianapolis, he held up the privilege of membership in a race which would lead world civilization: "In time we are going to be the greatest people in the world, if only we do the work that is laid before us as it ought to be done."[18] In a graduation address for Washington's colored high schools in 1904, he denounced selfish slogans like "paddle your own canoe" and "the devil take the hindmost" as false views. Education, he said on a return visit the next year, communicated the ideals of civilization and the methods for achieving good. He warned that some men feared the Negro's manhood with its ambition, power, and unconquerable resolution.

To the Negro businessmen of Chicago in 1898 he urged intensive economic organization of the Negro market behind a tariff wall of racial pride. Instead of wasting resources in "crowded mobs called church picnics, in hideous clothes called fashionable," he demanded that Negroes stress thrift and business knowledge: a crusade for a penny savings bank, he said, "would mean more to us today than the right of suffrage."[19] To educated women he outlined the functions of mothers ("not quantity, but quality"), of homemakers, and of leaders in human intercourse. He even found time to urge a Pennsylvania school girl who was inattentive to her studies to meet her responsibilities to herself and to her race.

To students enrolled in colleges he assigned a special function. The Talented Tenth of the race, from whom the exceptional man would rise, they must "leaven the lump" and "guide the Mass away from the contamination and death of the Worst, in their own and other races," he said.[20] Somewhere, either at Harvard or at Berlin, perhaps at both, DuBois had run across Carlyle. In this British elitist DuBois found a text for young Negroes: disdain for a money civilization and zealousness for cultural richness among a choice band of heroes ready to lead the masses. He told the students to heed this gospel according to Carlyle: "the nobility of effort, long continued, wearying, never ending effort, the imperativeness of eternal strife, the divinity of sweat."[21] Fresh from inspirational training in colleges, they were to return to their communities, leaders in business and the professions, and, above all, leaders in bringing the blessings of civilization to the Negro millions. Preparation for a trade, the industrial education so sedulously pressed by Booker T. Washington, did not qualify them for broad leadership as DuBois understood it: they required a rich acquaintance with the heritage of civilization and a trained intelligence. After DuBois's arrival at Wilberforce, his lecture, "The Art and Art Galleries of Modern Europe," emphasized the relevance of Western artistic treasures to the spiritual heritage of Negro Americans.

At Atlanta DuBois gave the juniors and seniors a rigorous two-year course, loosely tied together under "sociology and history," in economics, political science, and staitstics. The year after his arrival, the university catalog, which spoke of making Atlanta the "center of an intelligent and thorough-going study of the Negro problems," indicated the breadth of its new professor's intention:

> It is intended to develop this department not only for the sake of the mental discipline but also in order to familiarize our students with the history of nations and with the great economic and social problems of the world. It is hoped that thus they may be able to apply broad and careful knowledge to the solving of the many intricate social questions affecting their own people. The department aims therefore at training in good intelligent citizenship; at a thorough comprehension of the chief problems of wealth, work and wages; and at a fair knowledge of the objects and methods of social reform.[22]

(It is the measure of the man that DuBois thought that he could impart a "thorough comprehension" of the chief problems of wealth, work, and wages.) College-bred men were needed "to leaven the lump" not only as teachers and sociologists, but, as DuBois told the graduating class at Fisk ten years after his own commencement, as scientific farmers leading to an "aristocracy" of "country gentlemen," as merchants rather than as mere money makers, as doctors, artists, and scientists. The legal profession seemed crowded, he said, and the ministry attracted too many "sap-headed young fellows, without ability, and in some cases, without character," though even there trained conscientious workers would find a place.[23]

In his students DuBois looked for the missionary devotion of his own youth. In a prayer at morning chapel, written, as he said himself, more for man than for God, he said: "There is no God but Love and Work is his prophet—help us to realize this truth O Father which thou so often in word and deed has taught us. Let the knowledge temper our ambitions & our judgments. We would not be great but busy—not pious but sympathetic—not merely reverent, but filled with the glory of our Life-Work. God is Love & Work is His Revelation. Amen."[24]

For the intellectual elite who met as the "American Negro Academy," DuBois had a rather more sophisticated message. In an address entitled "The Conservation of Races" which he delivered in Washington soon after his appointment to Atlanta, DuBois rejected the facile assumption of the unity of the human family and the American idea that it could through conglomeration cut across the racial determination of history. Racial differences mainly followed physical race lines, he argued, but mere physical distinctions did not define the deeper spiritual, psychical differences which, however much based on the physical, infinitely transcended it. Actually, as physical differences lessened, he said, the spiritual differences emerged with greater clarity: the English revealed their capacity for constitutional liberty, the Germans for science and philosophy, the "Romance" race for literature and art. Negroes too, he went on, possessed the "cohesiveness and continuity" of these racial groups, but their full spiritual message had still not emerged. The civilization of Egypt had given a hint of that message, he said, but the Negro race, like the yellow and Slavic races, was just starting.

To deliver their message, DuBois thought, American Negroes must stand not as individuals but as part of a race of two hundred million which had an advance guard of eight million in America. In DuBois's view, American Negroes could not reach this fruition by absorption in white America; they had to stand as a unit possessed of "stalwart originality which shall unswervingly follow Negro ideals."

Was the Negro American a Negro or an American? DuBois answered that he was American by birth, citizenship, political ideals, language, and religion; thereafter, he was a Negro, part of a half-sleeping race now awakening. Through racial organizations —colleges, newspapers, business groups, schools of literature and art, intellectual clearinghouses like the American Negro Academy —we Negroes, DuBois said, must "conserve our physical powers, our intellectual endowments, our spiritual ideals; as a race we must strive by race organization, by race solidarity, by race unity to the realization of that broader humanity which freely recognizes differences in men, but sternly deprecates inequality in their opportunities of development." The Academy, he hoped, would stand in the vanguard, a mouthpiece for scattered Negro leaders who saw the need for progress through less whining and more dogged work, through the conquest of disease, crime, and impurity—vices which, unless themselves conquered, would conquer the black race. DuBois wanted the Academy to aim high for the best goals, a strong manhood and a pure womanhood, rearing a racial ideal for the glory of God and the uplift of the Negro people.[25]

Training Negroes and educating white America—these tasks made the scholar's role a busy one for DuBois for sixteen years, the period from his late twenties to his early forties. The years did not show: his hairline was now in almost full retreat, but the swift, impatient movements and the trim, agile build were those of a youthful man. If he was older than his years when he went to Atlanta, he was younger when he left in 1910. Mrs. DuBois, whom her husband saw as "beautifully dark-eyed" and thorough as a German housewife, stayed at home while he traipsed around the country. Basically a homemaker, she did not share her husband's scholarly interests. They had had two children: the older, their son Burghardt, who died while still an infant; their daughter Yolande, who was in the early stages of growing into a comely young lady and who was to present DuBois with a much-treasured granddaughter. DuBois himself was not the type to stay much at home. His travels took him away at frequent intervals, and when he was in Atlanta, he spent long hours in his office. He rarely ventured off the campus, for Southern custom closed much of Atlanta's life to him, and he would not accept the rest on humiliating terms. He never entered a streetcar, never attended the theater or concert hall. When white friends visited him in Atlanta, they had to seek him out at his study. What social life he had was with selected Negroes who taught at neighboring colleges—one of these, John Hope, became his closest friend over the years and eventually gave him sanctuary from later troubles. His monthly gatherings with these friends, generally stag affairs, gave DuBois a brief relief from the intensity of living the Negro problem. The conversation almost invariably came around to one aspect or another of the color line, but at least the gathering created a moment of relaxation among peers with whom DuBois could unbend. An alumnus of Atlanta, James Weldon Johnson, was astonished in 1904 to find that DuBois's brooding, intransigent public demeanor could dissolve into joviality, even frivolity. But few white men, or women, ever saw this DuBois. They saw only the vigorous sociologist— cold, austere, dedicated.

III

FROM TOWER TO ARENA

Midway in his fourteen years at Atlanta, DuBois started to descend from the tower to the arena. His program as a social scientist was not working out as planned: his published work fell short of his own standards and failed to influence the white world in any important way. At the same time, he was convinced of the need for immediate action. The social and economic condition of the black man was retrogressing and, DuBois believed, Booker T. Washington, feted and admired, was betraying the Negro into permanent servility.

To meet the new situation, DuBois readjusted his program. While still at his post in Atlanta, he increased the stridency of his appeals to white America, organized the "Niagara Movement" to mobilize aggressive Negro opinion, and started a magazine, *Horizon*, to instruct his people in the most effective political use of their numbers. But his new program was unsuccessful. White journals for the most part closed their pages to him, the Niagara Movement crumbled, and *Horizon* became an unbearable expense. In the meantime, his "radical"* activity compromised his position at Atlanta.

In 1910, at the lowest point of DuBois's career, a group of white liberals rescued him by summoning him to edit *Crisis*, the magazine of a new organization, the National Association for the Advancement of Colored People (NAACP). The job promised nothing in the way of security, and it drew DuBois, by then past his fortieth birthday, away from the work for which his years of training and experience best suited him. Yet the challenge was more than he could resist; the invitation was a welcome "Voice without reply."[1] With his acceptance of this position, DuBois entered his great years.

---

* The word has no economic implications. The "radicals" were Negroes who agitated for full social and political equality; the "conservatives" fell in with Washington's accommodationist views.

The Failure of Scholarship

DuBois's Program of a Hundred Years was the perfect symbol of his goals. It embodied his almost blind faith in pure science as a source of truth and as a technique for Negro advancement. It attracted his ambition, for through it he would gain prestige in the white world as a successful scientist, and in the Negro world he would be hailed as the prophet of his race.

But there were pitfalls in this program. White philanthropy might be uninterested in supporting his work. His scholarly work might not command prestige in the white world, and white scholars might appear less committed to science than to perpetuating stereotypes about the Negro. Finally, in the Negro world DuBois's role might not evoke respect and gratitude but hostility. All these dangers were very real, and they eventually crippled his whole program.

DuBois's great faith in humanity's allegiance to truth led him to expect that many people would be eager to give financial support for research on Negro problems. In 1900, the year of the twelfth census, he proposed a federal appropriation of between $250,000 and $500,000, to be supervised by a mixed committee of Negroes and white men, to survey the Negro's occupations, wages, land, property, taxation, and education; perhaps suffrage and crime could be added. "For half the cost of an ironclad to sail about the world and get us in trouble," he said, "we might *know* instead of *think* about the Negro problems."[2] But this castle stayed in the air, and the Atlanta study the next year survived on a paltry $250. DuBois promised that twice the expenditure would double the usefulness of his work, but the university could not, and the nation did not, spring at the chance. President Bumstead might on occasion grant DuBois an additional $100 and wish him well in his attempt to raise more funds outside the college, but usually the Atlanta administration was forced into retrenchment. As early as 1904 the executive and finance committee of the trustees delayed publication of the previous conference report until a donation for that specific purpose could be found. Discouraged, DuBois said that he would be willing to settle for a mere ten-page report—most reports ran well over a hundred pages. In 1908 Bumstead's successor, Edward T. Ware, as sympathetic to DuBois's work as Bumstead had been, suggested that the conference be discontinued. Only a grant of $1,000 from the Slater Fund saved the work from suspension.

When funds were hard to get, the administration became cautious: controversial material might antagonize a potential benefactor. On one occasion, in 1907, Bumstead instructed DuBois to submit future copy to the administration before publication, and then three days later he urged a change in a sentence which dealt with Southern laws against intermarriage: "In a matter of such delicacy as this," he said, "I do not think we ought to take any risk, especially when by so slight a change all risk is averted and nothing of value lost."[3] The timidity of the administration was even more striking when Ware asked: "Is there any controversy connected with raising money for the purchase of Frederick Douglass's Home which would make it unwise for us to invite our students to participate?"[4] In short, even for his unique program, DuBois found sparse support. Caution ruled editorial policy, and chronic deficits threatened to end the series at any time.

The critical reception accorded to the Atlanta *Publications* varied. Sometimes a perfunctory summary of the book appeared; more often, especially in newspapers and nonscholarly magazines, enough praise to adorn a subsequent report. Frank W. Taussig, the economic historian, said—apparently in answer to DuBois's request for a testimonial—that in his judgment no better work was being done anywhere in the country and that "no better opportunity is afforded for financial support on the part of those who wish to further the understanding of the Negro problem."[5] DuBois himself was never under the illusion that his work met the most exacting standards of pure science. He only insisted that it was as thorough as limited resources permitted and "well worth the doing," especially since aside from the Census Bureau and the Department of Labor, only Atlanta University seriously studied the facts of the Negro's condition.* But other scholars had more doubts. Reviewing *The Negro Church* for the *Political Science Quarterly,* Walter L. Fleming, the historian, observed: "Mr.

---

* In 1940 DuBois asserted that every book on the American Negro published from 1910 to 1925 drew on the Atlanta studies for material.

DuBois's theories and opinions may be correct; they are certainly worthy of attention; but they are not well supported by any known facts, nor by the mass of valuable material here collected. . . . Indeed the effect of this intermingling of facts and theories in this monograph is somewhat confusing and contradictory."* A reviewer of the *Negro Artisan* for the *Yale Review* commented that, inevitably in such volumes, much appeared that was "miscellaneous, scrappy, unimportant, and dubious." With patronizing archness, more galling because of the admixture of praise, he continued: "Perhaps the volume, excellent as it is, illustrates the fact that the characteristic gift of the author, as of the race he adorns, lies rather in the field of literature than of exact science." Commenting on the same report, another reviewer questioned DuBois's crucial premise, the Negro's capacity to absorb modern civilization. DuBois, he said, did not give the "faintest suggestion" that the Negro's inherited racial nature might present an "all-pervading and fundamental" barrier to his adaptation to modern conditions.[6] A variation on this racial theme had appeared anonymously in the *Nation* the previous year: "Mr. DuBois's thought and expression are highly characteristic of his people, are cultivated varieties of those emotional and imaginative qualities which are the prevailing traits of the uncultivated negro mind."[7]

Part of the appeal of a scholarly career had been DuBois's observation that educated men, or at least scholars, were above prejudice on the Negro question. His discovery that this was not universally true, that prejudice appeared even in men of apparent good will, appalled him. He could forgive Thomas Nelson Page, whose Southern background, according to DuBois, made it difficult for him to shed prejudice. But DuBois found the same virus in intelligent Northerners as well. Few persons in the United States, he said, did more to retard the solution of the Negro problem than Lyman Abbott, editor of the *Outlook*. Walter F. Willcox of Cornell's Department of Political Economy and Statistics told DuBois in 1904 that he was "agnostic" about the relative importance of

---

* Review of Dubois, ed., *The Negro Church* (Atlanta, 1904), *Political Science Quarterly*, XIX, 702–3 (December 1904). This judgment must be read in the light of the anti-Negro bias in Fleming's own work.

persistent racial characteristics and of the pressures of the color line in holding the Negro back. DuBois's blistering reply scoffed at judgments based on observations from the window of a railroad car and continued: "If you insist on writing about & pronouncing judgment on this problem why not study it? . . . There is enough easily obtainable data to take you off the fence if you will study it first hand and not thro' prejudiced eyes."[8] Later the same year DuBois objected to a report of the Committee on the Economic Position of the Negro, of which Willcox was chairman, on the grounds that its statistics underestimated the number of Negro servants who supported families of their own. DuBois conceded that he could not prove the error in Willcox's work, but he was sure from his own knowledge that the report was wrong. As DuBois saw it, science in the hands of white scholars was deserting its calling: "It has made itself the handmaid of a miserable prejudice. . . . It has supprest evidence, misquoted authority, distorted fact and deliberately lied."[9]

While DuBois was losing rapport with white scholars, he was also finding fewer outlets for his popular articles on the Negro question. In his peak year he had placed articles in ten different magazines.* But as early as 1904 Bliss Perry of the *Atlantic* urged DuBois away from the race question. *Collier's* rejected DuBois's bid for a regular column of commentary on the rise of the darker nations, and when it printed one of his articles, it appeared above an advertisement for Peerless Brand Evaporated Cream and across from Sanitol Tooth Powder. When *McClure's* published what DuBois called the "small narrow anti-Negro propaganda of Thomas Nelson Page" and DuBois asked for a hearing from the other side, S. S. McClure disclaimed any desire to open his pages to controversy—a rather anomalous statement for the most brilliant of the muckraking editors. The following year he rejected an article, "Black Social Equals," as "rather an unwise thing to print." Among the magazines of general circulation, only the *Independent* remained hospitable. Yet in the very years of DuBois's

---

* They were the *Atlantic Monthly, Dial, World's Work, Harper's Weekly, Annals of the American Academy of Political and Social Science, Independent, Bulletin of the Department of Labor, Southern Workman, Outlook, Missionary Review of the World.* He appeared twice in the *Dial.*

declining influence with white readers, Thomas Dixon was making his fortune with his trilogy of white supremacy, *The Leopard's Spots, The Clansman,* and *The Traitor.*

The accumulation of rebuffs—financial difficulties at Atlanta, differences with white scholars, and a declining market for his articles—gnawed at DuBois's earlier faith in the scholar's role. His discouragement was deepened by events unrelated to himself, for his stay at Atlanta coincided with the dark night of Negro freedom. In 1890 Mississippi resorted to a cumulative poll tax and an "understanding-the-Constitution" provision in order to disfranchise the Negro, and when the Supreme Court, in Williams *v.* Mississippi (1898), raised no objection to these technically proper, "nondiscriminatory" clauses, other states were encouraged to go and do likewise or better. By 1910 the Negro was no longer a voting element in the South. After years of struggle, in which DuBois took part through protest meetings and petitions to the legislature, Georgia finally in 1908 passed the amendment which for all practical purposes disfranchised Negroes. Even in the councils of the Republican party, Southern Negroes were being frozen out; both parties were to be the preserve of white Southerners. The Negro was the victim of increasing violence. In 1906 there were two major race riots, one in Atlanta and another in Brownsville, Texas. Lynchings were decreasing in number, but, according to C. Vann Woodward, the percentage of Negro victims was growing and, according to Walter White, the lynchings were increasing in brutality and were reaching into the North. In 1908 a lynching occurred at Springfield, Illinois, the capital of Abraham Lincoln's state.*

In their economic life the Negroes' condition was hardly better. Organized labor closed its ranks to Negroes and fought their strike-breaking activities. As early as 1902 DuBois's survey of the Negro artisan, despite its optimism for the future, reported that the Southern laborer and employer, having united to disfranchise the Negro, had also united to hold him down economically. Even unorganized labor narrowed the vector of Negro jobs as much as it could; when the Negro attempted to regain his job by working for less,

---

* An influential account—it started the chain of events leading to the National Association for the Advancement of Colored People—is William E. Walling, "The Race War in the North," *Independent,* LXV, 529–34 (September 3, 1908).

he was rewarded by the white worker with hatred, and sometimes with violence. Negroes seemed to be losing in one community the progress achieved in another, and their permanent advance was blocked off by the absence of an efficient apprentice system and by the opposition of new unions. The industrial schools such as Hampton and Tuskegee failed to prepare their students adequately: with little differentiation between what was taught to teachers and to carpenters, the industrial schools followed the patterns of an earlier age, unaware of either changing industrial conditions or the presence of labor unions. Because of white control of franchises and licenses, Negro tradesmen were frequently denied the opportunity to serve even their own people. Negro farmers still lived at the margin of existence, and the agrarian grievances which gave rise to Populism were the beginning rather than the sum of their troubles. DuBois had always looked to education as the way out of these problems, yet his own survey of Negro public schools showed that they had deteriorated during the twenty years before 1910.

In the first decade of the new century Negro disfranchisement removed the votes in state legislatures and in city councils which might have opposed a cavalcade of segregation ordinances govering transportation, state institutions, working conditions, residences—practically any place in which the two races came in contact other than as master and servant. Color, it seemed, was being transformed into caste.

The inescapable fact for DuBois was that apart from, in spite of, or because of his work at Atlanta, the Negro was not making any marked improvement in America. Neither optimism nor the idea of progress could conceal stark events: disfranchisement, the Atlanta riot, the lynching episodes.

To make matters worse, DuBois's reputation among Negroes was suffering a partial eclipse. His defense of his ideas evoked scorn in much of the Negro press. After seeing a review copy of *The Souls of Black Folk,* with its moderate criticism of Washington's ideas, the *Colored American,* previously respectful to DuBois, warned that all his "vainglorious posturing and pompous attitudinizing" would avail him nothing.[10] His criticism of industrial education in *The Negro Artisan* led the *Southern Workman,* the

editorial spokesman for both Hampton and Tuskegee, to withdraw its respectful admiration of DuBois and to adopt a hostile
tone. Among prominent white men, DuBois's rank was subordinated to Washington's: DuBois's appeal to Jacob Schiff, a white
philanthropist, for support for a monthly magazine was apparently
referred to Washington at Tuskegee for clearance; the influential
Garrison-Villard family for years would hear no evil about Washington; even Hart regretted DuBois's share in a controversy with
Washington. The contrast between the poverty at Atlanta and the
apparent opulence at Tuskegee dramatized the relative prestige
of DuBois and Washington.

Thus DuBois's program fell short of every purpose. As pure
science it failed to measure up to DuBois's own standards and drew
unfavorable notice from some white scholars. The retrogression
of the Negro's lot made the value of any learned contribution from
Atlanta seem negligible. On the personal level, the program had
gained attention for DuBois on both sides of the Veil, but his prestige was overshadowed by a competitor whom DuBois was bound
to despise.

The Fight Against Booker T. Washington

Booker T. Washington's vogue among influential white men
and his prestige among Negroes made an outspoken statement of
the Negro's cause urgent. As DuBois saw it, Washington was leading his people into a blind alley: in exchange for paltry support
of industrial education, Washington was bartering away the claim
to political and civil rights; indeed he was even surrendering their
manhood. Every concession Washington won from the white man,
DuBois thought, yielded essential ground which would have to be
retaken by hard fighting.

Though nominally a debate over educational systems, the
Washington-DuBois controversy actually arose from DuBois's attack on Washington's whole program. Washington focussed on
the Negro masses. He favored industrial education because he
thought that technical skills would make Negroes invaluable and
therefore welcome in an industrial economy. In seeking support
for industrial education, Washington was willing to postpone po-

litical and social rights, and in appealing to white philanthropy, he maintained a friendly, accommodating attitude toward all white men, Southerners and Northerners alike. He felt that the temporary suspension of political and social rights was not too high a price for the attainment of this economic shelf.

Washington first gained wide attention by a speech at the Atlanta Exposition in 1895. On that occasion Washington urged members of his race to cast down their buckets among the friendly white Southern people and to share the common purpose of raising the South's economic level. He offered the white South a peaceful reservoir of Negro labor for the burgeoning Southern industries. In return he expected Southern support for industrial education. Social equality, he rejected; political and civil rights, he postponed. Many white leaders, North and South, hailed the speech as a basis for a rapprochement between Negroes and whites, and overnight Booker T. Washington became a national figure. When his autobiography, *Up from Slavery,* was serialized in *Outlook* in 1900 and published in book form in 1901, his national position was confirmed.

In a subsequent autobiography, *My Larger Education* (1911), Washington made explicit his acceptance of the dominant industrial movement of the age. With praise for industrialists like Andrew Carnegie who were contributing generously to Tuskegee and to similar schools, Washington repeated the familiar aphorisms of nineteenth-century American progress: advancement through self-help, thrift as a path to riches, the importance of responsibilities over rights. In a speech to a Negro audience, Washington even made Christianity the servant of industry: "Nothing pays so well in producing efficient labor as Christianity."[11]

Washington's soothing statements to white audiences won him prestige as the spokesman of his race. Because of his influence with white men and his access to white capital, prominent Negroes supported him and sought his favor. Much of the Negro press fell into line: it shouted down criticism of Tuskegee and its principal and branded DuBois as a jealous upstart.

As J. Saunders Redding says:

From white America's point of view, the situation was ideal. White America had raised this man [Washington] up because he espoused a policy which was intended to keep the Negro docile and dumb in regard to civil, social and political rights and privileges. Having raised him to power, it was in white America's interest to keep him there. All race matters could be referred to him, and all decisions affecting the race would seem to come from him. In this there was much pretense and, plainly, not a little cynicism. There was pretense, first, that Washington was leader by sanction of the Negro people; and there was the pretense, second, that speaking in the name of his people, he spoke for them.[12]

Washington's ideas did not go unchallenged. To educated Negroes, particularly those who lived in cities outside the South, the traditionally servile position of Negroes in America was abhorrent. Some, whose skin was pale enough, passed over into the white race and, by leaving the area where they were known, cut themselves loose from their past. Others drew into their own tight little group, avoiding contact with the poorer, less educated elements which they thought were responsible for awakening anti-Negro feelings, especially in the North. One articulate group, however, the heirs of Frederick Douglass, channeled their resentment at second-class citizenship into an active fight for equality. Some, like Kelly Miller of Howard University and Charles W. Chesnutt, the novelist, spoke with quiet voices. Some, like Harry C. Smith, the editor of the Cleveland *Gazette,* were more insistent. A few, like Ida B. Wells-Barnett, the chairman of the Anti-Lynching League, and William Monroe Trotter, who with George W. Forbes edited the Boston *Guardian,* threw restraint to the winds in their attacks on American discrimination and on Booker Washington's soft words. (Trotter had been a contemporary of DuBois's at Harvard, but they had hardly known each other.) In the early years of the century, DuBois gradually moved into the position of leader of this articulate group.

The notoriety of the Washington-DuBois controversy has obscured the similarity of their views for at least six or seven years after the Atlanta speech. The picture of Washington created by partisans of DuBois has shown him as toadying to the whites, acknowledging Negro disfranchisement without a murmur, and selling out Negro aspiration for a mess of economic pottage. Actually Kelly Miller was probably right in 1903 when he wrote that Washington "would not disclaim, in distinct terms, a single plank in the platform of Douglass."* Though he ordinarily spoke in cautious diplomatic terms, he did on occasion take a position against white prejudice, even without the prodding of the Negro press. He spoke out boldly against the "grandfather" clause in the Louisiana constitution of 1898, and though unwilling to associate himself publicly with the move, he asked Francis J. Garrison, William Lloyd Garrison's son, to help raise money to aid responsible colored men in Louisiana in testing it in the courts. The previous year, in Atlanta, he had condemned the violence which had culminated in the lynching of a Negro named Sam Hose, and, in private, he had expressed his fear of associating on a public platform with a Negro whose reputation of toadying to the whites might have compromised his own position. Off the record, he offered to help DuBois to press an action against the Pullman Company for alleged discrimination. In 1903, just before the publication of *The Souls of Black Folk,* he joined DuBois in protesting to the Rhodes Trust the exclusion of Negro candidates from consideration in the Atlanta area.†

Furthermore, until the publication of *The Souls of Black Folk,* Washington maintained cordial personal relations with DuBois. In 1900, Washington, apparently at DuBois's request, recommended him for a position as superintendent of the Negro schools in Washington, D.C., and the following year, DuBois accepted a social invitation to Washington's summer camp in West Virginia. At the 1902 Atlanta conference, Washington praised DuBois's work as a "monument to his ability, wisdom and faithfulness."[13] Until the break in 1903 Washington and his white backers continued to

* Kelly Miller ("Fair Play," pseud.), "Washington's Policy," Boston *Evening Transcript,* September 19, 1903. Guy B. Johnson speaks aptly of Washington as "in some respects a greater leader of white opinion than he was of Negro opinion." *American Journal of Sociology,* XLIII, 63 (July 1937).

† In an excellent article, August Meier uses his research in the Washington papers as the basis for saying that "the Tuskegean had for his goals full equality and citizenship rights." "Booker T. Washington and the Rise of the NAACP," *Crisis,* LXI, 70 (February 1954). He cites further evidence of Washington's efforts against segregation and disfranchisement in his recent article, "Toward a Reinterpretation of Booker T. Washington," *Journal of Southern History,* XXIII, 220–27 (May 1957).

urge DuBois to join the staff of Tuskegee. Though Washington equivocated, compromised, and frequently kept silent, he differed with DuBois on method rather than on final goals. And even in the choice of method, they shared some ground.

Conversely, DuBois had at various times moved closer to the Tuskegee ideology than his partisans would admit. In a letter to the New York *Age,* he had greeted Washington's Atlanta speech as the basis for a real settlement if the South would open the doors of economic activity to the Negroes and if the Negroes would co-operate with the white South in "political sympathy."[14] (Such accord was reminiscent of DuBois's talk to young Negro leaders at Fisk.) In the mid-nineties, when Washington was telling a Brooklyn audience that it was more important that the Negro be *prepared* for voting, office-holding, and the highest recognition than that he vote, hold office, and be recognized, DuBois was scoffing at the Negro's "wail" of complaint against his lack of privilege: "Bah —what of that! what does man who has the world in his grasp care for the meteors that escape him—and what does the monarch of the sphere, of the 7 stars and solar years care if some little stars of the universe shine not for him? Turn your back on evils you can not right, & press to work that is calling so loudly and clearly."[15]

DuBois's speech on the "Meaning of Business" in 1898 reflected the mercantile spirit of the age so characteristic of Washington's teachings. Business organization and economic development must claim the major energies of the people, he said. The task was therefore to accumulate capital and to use it wisely: "The day the Negro race courts and marries the savings-bank will be the day of its salvation."[16]

On universal suffrage DuBois was no more outspoken than Washington. When Georgia considered the Hardwick bill for effective Negro disfranchisement in 1899, DuBois endorsed educational and property qualifications for voting, thus protecting the ballot for the few at the expense of the many. DuBois was more insistent than Washington in applying the standard equally to both races, but on the basic issue of universal suffrage, neither took a particularly democratic view.

DuBois always regarded industrial education and college work as complementary. About 1899 he outlined a plan of cooperation between the investigative conferences at Hampton and Atlanta. In the same year he assured Washington of his "best sympathy for the Tuskegee work" and predicted that eventually it would "undoubtedly bear fruit."[17] In 1901, he publicly praised Tuskegee's ten-year battle against the crop-lien system, one-room cabin, and poor and short-termed public schools. The next year, in inviting Washington to the annual Atlanta conference, DuBois emphasized his anxiety to minimize the break between colleges and industrial schools and to cooperate with Tuskegee. Even in *The Negro Artisan* (1902), where his comments were more explicitly critical of industrial education, he was also on record as a member of the resolutions committee which stated: "We especially commend Trades Schools as a means of imparting skill to Negroes, and manual training as a means of general education. We believe the movements in this line, especially in the last ten years, have been of inestimable benefit to the freedmen's sons."[18]

This atmosphere of mutual cordiality, however, was deceptive, for the pressures which led to the explosion in 1903 had been building up for three years. In 1900 DuBois spoke very generally of the Negro who forgot too easily that "life is more than meat and the body more than raiment." Such a person was likely to be "a traitor to right and a coward before force."[19] The following year, in reviewing Washington's autobiography for the *Dial,* DuBois ascribed two great achievements to him: gaining the sympathy and cooperation of the white South and learning so thoroughly "the speech and thought of triumphant commercialism and the ideals of material prosperity" that he gained equal consideration in the North. Opposition to his ideals of material prosperity at the expense of social and political advance, DuBois explained, arose from the "spiritual sons of the abolitionists" and from a large and important group in Washington's own race "who, without any single definite programme, and with complex aims, seek nevertheless that self-development and self-realization in all lines of human endeavor which they believe will eventually place the Negro beside the other races. While these men respect the Hampton-Tuskegee idea to a degree, they believe it falls short of a complete programme. They believe, therefore, also in the higher education of Fisk and Atlanta Universities; they believe in self-assertion and ambition; they believe in the right of suffrage for blacks on the same terms with whites." These opponents were silenced, he said, only by "Mr. Washington's very evident sincerity of purpose. We forgive much to honest purpose which is achieving something. We may not agree with the man at all points, but we admire him and cooperate with him as far as we conscientiously can. It is no ordinary tribute to this man's tact and power, that, steering as he must amid so many diverse interests and opinions, he to-day commands not simply the applause of those who believe in his theories, but also the respect of those who do not."[20]

The tone of the essay aligned DuBois with this latter group, in which he included some of the most important Negro intellectuals —the educator Kelly Miller, the poet Paul Laurence Dunbar, the physicist Henry O. Tanner, and the novelist Charles W. Chesnutt. Even in the role of critic, DuBois remained fair: the criticisms of Washington were vigorous, but Washington's own position was presented with understanding.

The essay on Washington in *The Souls of Black Folk* the following year still retained much of DuBois's balanced appraisal of Washington—respect for the "most distinguished Southerner since Jefferson Davis" together with sharp criticism of his overemphasis on industrial education. DuBois praised the Tuskegee leader's achievements in forging bonds which linked the North, the South, and the Negro and in making progress for the Negro possible in education and industry. But he feared that Washington's success made increasingly impossible the Negro's ultimate achievement of full status as a citizen. Washington, DuBois said, asked the Negro to give up, at least for the present, three things: political power, insistence on civil rights, and higher education of Negro youth. "As a result of this tender of the palm-branch, what has been the return?" DuBois asked. In the ten years since this policy had been "triumphant," DuBois said, three things had occurred: the disfranchisement of the Negro, the legal creation of a distinct status of civil inferiority, and the steady withdrawal of aid from institutions for the higher training of the Negro. DuBois did not attribute these developments directly to Washington's teachings, but, DuBois said, "his propaganda has, without a shadow of a doubt, helped their speedier accomplishment." However much Wash-

ington's program calmed the fears of the white South and commanded the respect of Northern industrialists, DuBois opposed it
for committing the Negro to a hopelessly subordinate status. "So
far as Mr. Washington preaches Thrift, Patience, and Industrial
Training for the masses," DuBois said, "we must hold up his hands
and strive with him, rejoicing in his honors and glorying in the
strength of this Joshua called of God and of man to lead the head-
less host. But so far as Mr. Washington apologizes for injustice,
North or South, does not rightly value the privilege and duty of
voting, belittles the emasculating effects of caste distinction, and
opposes the higher training and ambition of our brighter minds,—
so far as he, the South, or the Nation does this,—we must un-
ceasingly and firmly oppose them."

A substantial gulf had come to separate the two men. But the
gulf was not new. Why did the differences develop into open war-
fare at the time? It is hard to say. Perhaps the favorable reception
of DuBois's early work gave him sufficient security to challenge
the champion. Perhaps the hammering attacks on Washington by
Trotter in the Boston *Guardian* and the more restrained criticism
elsewhere appealed to DuBois's pride in his race. Perhaps Atlanta's
failure to share in the white philanthropy at Washington's command convinced DuBois of the hostility behind Washington's
diplomatic cordiality. Perhaps DuBois already had suspicions that
his path of scholarship would not lead to advancement of the
Negro and that a more aggressive policy of agitation was required.
All these factors undoubtedly contributed in varying degrees to
the decision, and DuBois's publication of a collection of his fugitive essays seemed like the appropriate occasion for a firm challenge.

Behind the conflict in ideas were two discordant personalities.
Both possessed titanic ambition. Washington, thick-set and slow
moving, had the assurance of a self-trained man. A shrewd, calcu-
lating judge of people, he had the soft speech and the accommodating manner that made him equally at home among sharecroppers
and at the President's table. A master of equivocation, he made
platitudes pass as earthy wisdom, and he could take back unnoticed with one hand what he had given with the other. DuBois,
slight, nervous in his movements, never forgot for a moment

his educational background. Proud and outspoken, he held aloof from the Negro masses, but felt at home with a small company of his peers with whom he could be witty and convivial. Washington had the appearance of a sturdy farmer in his Sunday best; DuBois, with his well-trimmed goatee, looked like a Spanish aristocrat. Where Washington was accommodating, DuBois was fretful and aggressive. The conflicting personalities of these two men supplied the rallying points for two groups of articulate Negroes. James Weldon Johnson observed years later that one unfamiliar with the twelve-year period after 1903 could not imagine "the bitterness of the antagonism between these two wings."[21]

Once the fire had broken out within the race, it created its own fuel. On the one hand, Washington was frightened by the attacks and apprehensive for his role as leader. On the other hand, the adverse criticism which greeted DuBois's moderate essay may well have provoked his proud spirit. His comments against Washington grew ever more vehement until mutual recriminations blocked compromise. In the Negro press the partisans of both parties egged DuBois into even blunter criticism. The *Colored American* chided DuBois as a "hanger-on at a place created by white people"; seeing little chance to sell *The Souls of Black Folk* on "its own bottom," DuBois tried to sell it by a sensational attack.[22] The *Southern Workman,* noting that "pessimism is never helpful," found DuBois unfair to Washington: the latter had his eye on the Negro masses, DuBois on the few more favored than the rest yet shut out from social and political equality with the white man.[23] At the same time the Cleveland *Gazette* labeled DuBois's essay a "proper estimate,"[24] and the *Guardian,* which had been singing DuBois's praises even before the essay appeared, gladly welcomed its new ally. DuBois responded to this last bit of adulation directly. After the "Boston riot," a meeting in July 1903 at which heckling of Washington led to Trotter's arrest for disorderly conduct, DuBois wrote to Clement Morgan: "While I have not always agreed with Mr. Trotter's methods, I have had the greatest admiration for his singlehearted earnestness & devotion to a great cause and I am the more minded to express this respect publicly when I see him the object of petty persecution & dishonest attack."[25] DuBois thus aligned himself with the "radicals."

Once committed to battle, DuBois continued to attack. Under a thin veil of praising Washington as part of the "advance guard of the race," he subordinated Washington's work as an educator and moral leader to his skill in political maneuver. He referred to the "marvelous facility" with which Washington "so manipulated the forces of a strained political and social situation as to bring about . . . the greatest consensus of opinion in this country since the Missouri Compromise." Washington, DuBois continued, "kept his hand on the pulse of the North and South, advancing with every sign of good will and generosity, and skillfully retreating to silence or shrewd disclaimer at any sign of impatience or turmoil."[26] Few readers could miss the object of DuBois's remarks the following year: What are personal humiliation and denial of civil rights against a chance to earn a living, or filthy Jim Crow cars next to bread and butter? he asked sarcastically. "Earn a living; get rich, and all these things shall be added unto you. Moreover, conciliate your neighbors, because they are more powerful and wealthier, and the price you must pay to earn a living in America is that of humiliation and inferiority."[27] One of his addresses to the Washington, D.C., colored school children included a warning against the humiliating program which sought "to train black boys and girls forever to be hewers of wood and drawers of water for the cowardly people who seek to shackle our minds as they shackled our hands yesterday." "Loose yourselves," he told them, "from that greater temptation to curse and malign your own people and surrender their rights for the sake of applause and popularity and cash."[28] Moving directly into the camp of the enemy, he spoke at Hampton in 1906 and attacked the "heresy" of industrial education: "Take the eyes of these millions off the stars and fasten them in the soil and if their young men will dream dreams, let them be dreams of corn bread and molasses." He admitted the necessity of training most men to provide the world's physical wants, but he begged the teachers attending the summer session at Hampton to release their most able students for higher education, "the training of a self whose balanced trained assertion will mean as much as possible for the great ends of civilization."[29]

Even before *The Souls of Black Folk* appeared, Washington had called a conference of outstanding Negroes to consider the present condition and future of the race. The conference purportedly sought a reconciliation of views, but DuBois told Kelly Miller that he was afraid the meeting would become a "B. T. W. ratification meeting."[30] Yet DuBois accepted the opportunity to confront Washington with his equivocal stands on such questions as civil rights, and organized a caucus of the opposition. He proposed that these men stand on the following platform: full political rights on the same terms as other Americans; higher education of selected Negro youth; industrial education for the masses; common school training for every Negro child; stoppage of the campaign of self-deprecation; careful study of the real condition of the Negro; a national Negro periodical; thorough and efficient federation of Negro societies and activities; raising of a defense fund; judicious fight in the courts for civil rights. "Finally the general watch word must be, not to put further dependence on the help of the whites but to organize for self-help, encouraging 'manliness without defiance, conciliation without servility.' "[31] As the meeting approached, a circular letter, probably put out by DuBois, warned that "the main issue of this meeting is *Washington*, refuse to be side-tracked."[32]

Washington never lost mastery of the conference. He controlled the invitations and travel allowances. Lyman Abbott and Andrew Carnegie were on hand to praise him abundantly. After he and DuBois had spoken, a committee of three was selected to appoint a larger committee as the steering group for the Negro race in America. The committee of three included both principals, and the third member, Hugh M. Browne, was so responsive to Washington that DuBois was overruled on every major point, including the membership of the permanent Committee of Twelve for the Advancement of the Interests of the Negro Race—a sort of Negro general staff. When Washington was named chairman of this group, DuBois resigned to avoid responsibility for statements over which he would have little personal control.[33]

The failure of the 1904 conference solidified DuBois's opposition to Washington. In January 1905, DuBois's article in *The Voice of the Negro*, "Debit and Credit (The American Negro in account with the Year of Grace 1904)" listed in its debit column "$3,000 of 'hush money' used to subsidize the Negro press in 5 leading cities."[34] This was the first open attack on the "Tuskegee machine," the elusive organization through which Washington influenced Negro life in America by his power over appointments, both political and educational, by his manipulation of white capital, and by his control over a part of the Negro press. William H. Ward of the *Independent* and Oswald Garrison Villard of the New York *Evening Post* urged DuBois either to withdraw his statement or to substantiate it with factual proof. But though evidence in the Booker T. Washington papers backs up DuBois's charge, the charge could not be proved: advertisements from Tuskegee in friendly journals were hard to brand as bribery, and proof of direct bribery—if it existed—lay hidden in the files of givers and takers. Privately, on a confidential basis, DuBois assembled a substantial portfolio to convince Villard, but Villard legitimately rejected this hearsay evidence as insufficient; he retained his faith in Washington's "purity of purpose and absolute freedom from selfishness and personal ambition," though he admitted that Emmett J. Scott, Washington's confidential secretary, had been "extremely injudicious."*

Washington's program gave DuBois an anvil on which to hammer out his own ideas. At the core of DuBois's philosophy was the role assigned to the Talented Tenth because, like all races, DuBois said, the Negro race would be saved by its exceptional men, trained to the knowledge of the world and man's relation to it. As teachers, ministers, professional men, spokesmen, the exceptional few must come first: "To attempt to establish any sort of system of common and industrial school training, without *first* (and I say *first* advisedly) without *first* providing for the higher training of the very best teachers, is simply throwing your money to the winds." DuBois did not deprecate the importance of industrial training,

* The list of charges and the correspondence relating to it are in the Oswald Garrison Villard Papers, Houghton Library, Harvard University. August Meier's article, "Booker T. Washington and the Negro Press: With Special Reference to the *Colored American Magazine*," has put beyond historical question the fact that Washington attempted to buy support in the Negro press. *Journal of Negro History*, XXXVIII, 67–90 (January 1953). In a friendly biography of Washington, Samuel R. Spencer, Jr., acknowledges that "in some cases" Washington and his staff encouraged the printing of Tuskegee press releases "by occasional 'contributions' to Negro editors." *Booker T. Washington and the Negro's Place in American Life* (Boston, 1955), p. 163.

but "it is industrialism drunk with its vision of success, to imagine that its own work can be accomplished without providing for the training of broadly cultured men and women to teach its own teachers, and to teach the teachers of the public school." DuBois pointed to the thirty college-trained teachers on Washington's own staff as an effective argument for training in the liberal arts.[35]

DuBois's theory of the Talented Tenth was the striking product of his own total experience and training. It singled out a select minority, enriched it with the finest education, and then bade it lead the masses. They were to be the thinkers, educators, ministers, lawyers, editors, political leaders. To the ears of DuBois's opponents, this theory, from the mouth of one who was undoubtedly a member of the Talented Tenth, had a selfish, self-serving ring, and its echoes of the heroic vitalism of Carlyle and Nietzsche do not recommend it to modern ears. Booker Washington was able to score constantly against DuBois by charging that DuBois was interested only in a handful of Negroes, while Washington concerned himself with the masses. There was some truth in Washington's charge, but not much. An essential part of DuBois's idea was that the tenth was to be trained as the servants of the other 90 per cent. Their special privileges were justified by the benefits which they could confer on their fellow men, and DuBois never asked for special privileges on any other terms. DuBois himself had had as fine an education as any man in America; was he not using his entire energy to raise his people? With a thousand, or ten thousand, Negroes similarly trained, similarly devoted to duty, how long would American Negroes remain in poverty and degradation?

The training of the Talented Tenth was a means to an end: political and civil rights equal to those of other Americans. In 1899, DuBois had acknowledged the propriety of proscribing ignorance and bribery; by 1901, skeptical of Georgia's avowed intention to disfranchise the ignorant, he asked in an unpublished article: *"Do you propose to disfranchise ignorant white people? Do you propose to leave the ballot in the hands of intelligent Negroes and protect them in its exercise?"*[36] Three years later he withdrew his acceptance of partial Negro disfranchisement and argued in favor of universal suffrage free from arbitrary educational requirements, for, he said, in losing the ballot, Negro workingmen faced a hostile South unprotected and powerless. In March 1905, DuBois and four other Negroes petitioned President Theodore Roosevelt to instruct his Attorney-General to help in testing the validity of state constitutions which deprived the Negro of his vote by constitutional trickery and to support the passage of the Morrill bill, then pending, which forbade racial discrimination of any kind in vehicles in interstate commerce.

To help in the fight to secure Negro rights, DuBois committed himself to a program of direct agitation. He denounced Negro silence during the previous decade: the absence of complaint had permitted white America to assume that the Negro was satisfied. If Negroes sat "in courteous and dumb self-forgetting silence" until others came to their rescue, he said, degeneration and destruction might come first. In a preoccupied world, people had to take care of themselves.[37]

Agitation and Organization

From 1903 until 1910, DuBois took some time from his duties at the university to devote himself to his new program of direct agitation. As professor of sociology, he continued to train part of the Talented Tenth and to issue sociological reports. But as spokesman for the "radical" wing of the Negro race, he took on new responsibilities.

To mobilize articulate Negroes ready to fight for their rights, DuBois in 1905 sent out a summons for the first convention of what became known as the Niagara Movement.[38] Several of DuBois's "radical" associates had for some time been urging him to organize a national committee of Negroes representing their views. Two of them, F. L. McGhee and C. C. Bentley, drew up a plan for the new group: a nation-wide organization with committees assigned to definite Negro problems, local organizations of militant Negroes, and an annual convention to plan and to generate enthusiasm. In response to DuBois's appeal, twenty-nine professional men from thirteen states and the District of Columbia met at Niagara Falls, Ontario. These were to be the nucleus of the "very best class of Negro Americans." For DuBois, the movement's executive officer, the Niagara Movement was to serve two functions: in the white world, its annual manifestoes would periodically call attention to the Negro's complaint; among Negroes, the movement would whip up indignation against the injustices of white America. Both purposes hinged on Booker T. Washington: the steady barrage of protest would contradict his soothing assurances to the whites, and the movement would offer dissident Negroes a medium for opposition to him.

A "Declaration of Principles," largely written by Trotter and DuBois, was dramatically "submitted to the American people, and Almighty God" after the first convention. It indicated the broad sweep of the Negro "radical" protest with which DuBois now associated himself. Demands for suffrage and civil rights headed the list, followed by complaints against "peonage and virtual slavery" in the rural South and against the prejudice "helped often by iniquitous laws" that created difficulties in earning a decent living. Two classes of men deserved public excoriation, it said: employers who imported ignorant Negro American laborers in emergencies, and then afforded them "neither protection nor permanent employment" (an elaborate circumlocution for "strike breakers"); and labor unions which excluded "their fellow toilers, simply because they are black." Free and compulsory education through the high-school level was set as a universal minimum, and college training, instead of being the "monopoly" of any class or race, should, the statement continued, be open to talent. Trade schools and higher education were both listed as essential. In the courts the Negro wanted upright judges, juries selected without reference to color, and equal treatment both in punishment and in efforts at reformation. Some of DuBois's old complaints appeared: "We need orphanages and farm schools for dependent children, juvenile reformatories for delinquents, and the abolition of the dehumanizing convict-lease system." Any discrimination along the color line was said to be a relic of "unreasoning human savagery of which the world is and ought to be thoroughly ashamed." The Niagara group expressed astonishment at the increase of prejudice in the Christian church, and labeled the third-class accommodations of

Jim Crow cars as an attempt "to crucify wantonly our manhood, womanhood, and self-respect." They pleaded for health—the opportunity to live in decent localities with a chance to raise children in "physical and moral cleanliness."

To right the wrongs, the small band urged national aid to education, especially in the South, a return to the "faith of the fathers," and legislation to secure proper enforcement of the War Amendments. Rejecting the "cowardice and apology" of the current Negro leadership, it called for "persistent manly agitation" as the road to liberty, for "to ignore, overlook, or apologize for these wrongs is to prove ourselves unworthy of freedom." To accomplish its ends, the Niagara group appealed for the cooperation of men of all races.

The past decade, the Niagara band said, had shown "undoubted evidences of progress": the increase in intelligence and in the ownership of property, the decrease in crime, the uplift in home life, the advance in literature and art, and the demonstration of executive ability in religious, economic, and educational institutions. However, in the face of the "evident retrogression of public opinion on human brotherhood," only loud and insistent complaint could hold America to its professed ideals.[39]

After its initial meeting, the organization gained membership slowly for about two years. The original members tried to interest their friends, and they in turn passed the word along. The 29 at Niagara Falls in June increased to 150 from thirty states by December; by April of 1907, 236 members and 144 associate members were on the rolls. But the appearance of strength was deceptive, for by November 1907, the membership owed $2,650 in back dues, and the organization had hardly sufficient funds to pay postage, much less to initiate court actions to protect Negro civil rights. In 1909 dues were lowered from five dollars a year to two in an attempt to prevent the accounts from falling further into arrears, but still the legal department pressed for funds, and the treasurer's report for 1909 was glum.

The Niagara Movement never solved its basic organizational problems. It had no headquarters. DuBois, as perennial executive secretary, gave the group whatever continuity it had, but his strenuous efforts to hold the membership together by mail never caught up with the need. Committees and departments were located in their chairmen's heads—perhaps a thousand miles from an essential colleague. In larger Negro communities, like Boston, members met fairly regularly for discussion or for a joint protest against some local grievance. In smaller communities correspondence was a thin substitute for face-to-face contact. The annual convention was intended to rally esprit, but expense, inconvenience, and unsteady interest held down attendance.

The narrow base of membership in the organization—principally educated Negroes from business and the professions, the self-appointed spokesmen for the Negro masses—diminished its general appeal. The elite character of the movement, a sort of exclusive club the present membership of which passed on new applicants, was felt even by friendly contemporary observers: the editor of the Jersey City (New Jersey) *Appeal,* a Niagara booster, warned DuBois that he "would do well to get closer to the people, I mean the masses as well as the classes."[40] Mary White Ovington, a white New York social worker, whose account of the second convention at Harper's Ferry for the New York *Evening Post* in 1906 left little doubt of her partiality, urged DuBois to let her discuss the Negro and the labor problem at the 1908 gathering: "I should like to hammer that side of things into some of the aristocrats who are in the membership."[41]

Even within the narrow range of the Talented Tenth, the Niagara Movement could not command unanimous support. For one thing, it faced the active hostility of Washington and those responsive to him. Just after the first Niagara convention, Washington urged Charles W. Anderson, Collector of Internal Revenue in New York City and a Washington intimate, to secure a man "who would get right into the inner circles of the Niagara movement through the Brooklyn crowd and keep us informed as [to] their operations and plans."[42] Furthermore, the Niagara Movement competed with at least three other comparable organizations —the Afro-American Council, the Negro American Political League, and the American Negro Academy—and all effort to unify the four groups led nowhere. Some fear of Niagara "radicalism" held down membership: one member resigned when he moved to the South. The white president of Storer College at Harper's

Ferry, the host to the second convention, although saying that he did not think the Niagara convention had injured his institution, withdrew his invitation to the movement to return another year until his trustees had a chance to express themselves. That year the movement went to Boston. A Springfield, Massachusetts, Congregational minister declined membership because, although in "most hearty sympathy with the aims of the Niagara Movement," he was unable to bring himself into accord with its methods.

The tight directorate of Niagara leadership lost itself in a sea of bickering. In 1907 the organization came near to dissolution when a feud between Trotter and Morgan in Massachusetts grew from a local coolness to a cause of nation-wide dissension and led DuBois to threaten resignation when the executive committee failed to support his decision between the two. DuBois contributed little to internal amity, for he was likely to regard his own program as the only one worthy of acceptance. Years later a participant in the 1906 convention recalled that "in the whole meeting DuBois insisted on having his way and had it as usual."[43] The presence of DuBois and Trotter in a single group was a fairly safe insurance against amity.

In 1911 DuBois still wrote hopefully of making the Niagara Movement an annual conference without fees, but by that time the force of the movement had long since spent itself. The reaction of the Negro press ranged from distrust to friendly indifference. The New York *Age,* guided from Tuskegee, poured continual abuse on DuBois and his colleagues,* while the Cleveland *Gazette* maintained an amiable though reserved attitude. As Niagara's membership dwindled, even DuBois's own magazine, the *Horizon,* gave it little space.

In the intervals between annual conventions, DuBois continued the Negro's protest over his own name. While the *World's Work* printed his analysis of the 1906 Atlanta riot and its five "lessons," the *Independent* carried a frenzied clamor:

Doth not this justice of hell stink in Thy nostrils, O God? How long shall the mounting flood of innocent blood roar in Thine ears and pound on our hearts for vengeance? Pile the

---

* See, for example, New York *Age,* October 15, 1908: "The pessimistic folly of these senseless radicals does not reflect the sentiment of Negro brains."

pale frenzy of blood-crazed brutes, who do such deeds, high on
Thine Altar, Jehovah Jireh, and burn it in hell forever and forever!

Forgive us, good Lord; we know not what we say!

Bewildered we are and passion-tossed, mad with the mad-
ness of a mobbed and mocked and murdered people; straining
at the armposts of Thy throne, we raise our shackled hands and
charge Thee, God, by the bones of our stolen fathers, by the
tears of our dead mothers, by the very blood of Thy crucified
Christ: What meaneth this? Tell us the plan; give us the sign!

Keep not thou silent, O God!

Sit not longer dumb, Lord God, deaf to our prayer and
dumb to our dumb suffering. Surely Thou, too, are not white,
O Lord, a pale, bloodless, heartless thing![44]

As DuBois warmed to this new form of protest, his tone became
more strident and waspish, indifferent to the resentment he might
create in white opinion. In an address on "Negro Ideals," to the
Ethical Culture Society in New York, he spoke casually of the
Negro blood which made wonderful the genius of Lew Wallace,
Alexander Hamilton, and "many other Americans who may wish
to have it forgotten."[45] In "Black Social Equals," the article rejected by *McClure's*, he added former Senator George H. Pendle-
ton of Ohio and Henry Timrod, and he traced the large American
mulatto population to the easy sexual mores of the slave period, a
taunt to the white South which had been passing laws against intermarriage to maintain the purity of its race. As a defiant valedictory to his career at Atlanta, he wrote an article for the *Independent* defending the individual's right to marry without inter-
ference. While he held that marriage between races was likely to
unite incompatible personalities, irreconcilable ideals, and different grades of cultures, he branded legal prohibitions of intermarriage as "wicked devices to make the seduction of women easy
and without penalty." There was no adequate scientific proof of
the "necessary physical degeneracy" of nonwhite races, he said,
"nor has the will of God in the matter of race purity been revealed
to persons whose credibility and scientific poise command general
respect."[46] He told an audience in Atlantic City that if he had
appeared anywhere but last on the program, he would have been

too surprised to speak. He addressed a YMCA audience in New York City "with no feeling of pleasure," because the segregated policies of the YMCA did not square either with Christianity or with manhood.[47]

DuBois was turning away from his white neighbors, for what he thought were sufficient reasons. In education, he felt that with the older philanthropic generation of Cravaths and Wares and Armstrongs passing, the Negro could no longer expect white allies to give positive help to Negro advancement.* In society at large, DuBois began to see that prejudice against the Negro was not merely the result of ignorance but had real economic roots. The conviction was growing in him that politicians and capitalists deliberately cultivated race prejudice for their own ends. Politicians out of job who attributed all the white man's problems to the presence of the Negro, he said, consciously appealed to race prejudice to restore themselves to power. The Atlanta riot he saw as "a sort of first-fruits of this newer economic race danger." At the same time, unscrupulous capitalists were tempted to "transmute race prejudice into the coin of the realm" by pitting black workers against white: white workers being held to the depressed standards of black labor, while black workers were kept in line by the threat of replacement by the whites. Thus the workers of each race, regarding the other as the chief cause of unfair treatment, were trapped into mutual antipathy, and low wage scales in the South held down labor all over the nation. Yet despite this analysis of the problem, DuBois could not surrender his earlier faith in education. The obvious corrective, he said, was still trained intelligence, and he urged federal aid to public schools wherever literacy fell below certain minimum standards.[48]

DuBois's direct appeals to the white world through the Niagara resolutions and his new agitative articles had little apparent effect: the Niagara Movement was, by and large, ignored by the white press, and the tone of DuBois's articles barred his work from every major publication except the *Independent. John Brown,*

---

* A personal rebuff may have reinforced this view. In 1908 DuBois was apparently accepted as a member of the Massachusetts chapter of the Sons of the American Revolution, but the organization's national headquarters revoked the membership on a technicality.

more a part of DuBois's propaganda than of his scholarship, sold only 665 copies in the seven years after its publication in 1909.

To supplement the Niagara Movement, DuBois and two associates, F. H. M. Murray and L. M. Hershaw, launched *Horizon,* which appeared monthly from January 1907 until July 1910. (Just over a year before, DuBois had tried to publish a magazine, called the *Moon,* by himself, but it had lasted only a few months.) *Horizon* ran to eight or ten pages, about the size of the *Reader's Digest* but with larger type and cheaper paper. Expenses were held to a minimum, for Hershaw owned a printing shop and the three partners produced the copy for the magazine by themselves, each in a separate signed section. Yet the cost was heavy, and the magazine attracted few advertisers and not enough subscribers to make ends meet. Outlets through local dealers were a matter for individual negotiation, an expensive and time-consuming procedure. The magazine lasted three and a half years only because the partners, and especially DuBois, were willing to make up the deficit out of their own pockets.

Much of DuBois's section of the magazine served the purposes of the Niagara group: publicity for its meetings, publication of the texts of successive addresses to the nation, taunts directed at Washington* and at discriminatory white groups such as the Episcopal

---

* One is worth quoting at length—an anecdote entitled "Constructive Work."

"The White Man looked contemptuously down upon the Black Leader who smiled back affably. 'Get out of here,' yelled the White Man as he kicked the Black Leader down stairs and tossed a quarter after him. The Black Leader pirouetted and bumped and rolled until he landed sprawling in the dirt. The dark and watching crowd were breathless, and one of them grasped his club and bared his arm. Slowly the Black Leader arose and his Eager Supporters assiduously brushed off his pants. Then the Black Leader squared his shoulders and looked about him. He cleared his throat and the throng hung upon his word breathless, eager, while the one man clutched his club tighter.

" 'My friends,' said the Black Leader, 'the world demands constructive work: it dislikes pessimists. I want to call your attention to the fact that this White gem'man—I mean gentleman—did *not* kick me nearly as hard as he might have: again he wore soft kid boots, and finally I landed in the dirt and not on the asphalt. Moreover,' continued the Black Leader as he stooped in the dust, 'I am twenty-five cents in.' And he walked thoughtfully away, amid the frantic plaudits of the crowd. Except one man. He dropped his club and whispered:

" 'My God!' "

Church. Beyond that, as a token of the Negro's responsibility for his own advancement, DuBois revived his appeal for Negro emancipation from the Republican party, not, as in his Fisk days, to unite with Southern Democrats to produce a new South, but to ally the Negro with the more radical Northern wing of the Democratic party and to rebuke the Republicans.

As the election of 1908 approached, DuBois backed slowly into the Democratic party and even campaigned for the Democrats in Ohio. Previously when it had appeared that only national action could prevent universal Negro disfranchisement in the South, DuBois had entertained some hope for Republicans, as the petition to President Roosevelt had indicated. In DuBois's estimate of "Debit and Credit" for 1905, he praised the party's statement opposing special discrimination in the election franchise. Individual Republicans attracted his favor. He sent Governor Robert M. LaFollette of Wisconsin a cordial invitation to the 1905 Atlanta conference; he shared in the adulation, widespread among Negroes, for Senator Joseph B. Foraker of Ohio, a persistent defender of the Negro's cause. As late as 1908, he wrote of himself as a believer in Republican principles.

But DuBois never went the whole way with the Republicans. The Democratic South having destroyed the basis for Negro–white political cooperation, DuBois had watched Roosevelt hopefully. By the end of 1906, he realized that he had hoped in vain. Roosevelt had made a few token concessions to the Negro, DuBois said, but in general, he was trying to exclude the Negro from governmental service and was making a frantic effort to appease the white South. After the discharge of the Negro soldiers involved in the Brownsville riot in 1906, DuBois had repudiated Roosevelt and later had extended this repudiation to William H. Taft, the heir to presidential power, partly because of Taft's role as Secretary of War in the Brownsville affair and partly because he was nominated at a Republican national convention which seated Southern "lily white" delegations (delegations which excluded Negroes, who had since the Civil War been a major element in the Republican party in the South).

With the election of 1908 approaching, how could 300,000 Negro votes carry maximum political weight? Between the disfranchising Democrats and the "lily white" Republicans, what choice was there? Prohibitionists no longer attracted him, because although he believed in local option, he regarded state prohibition as undesirable and impossible to accomplish. A vote for the Socialists was merely thrown away. All doors seemed closed. In February 1908, he urged his subscribers to stay home on election day if their only choice was between Taft and Bryan.

By April, however, he started a gradual move into the Democratic camp:[49] Negroes should normally support Republican candidates, but the Republicans, feeling assured of the Negro vote by the payment of "six minor political offices thrown us as a sop at the command of a traitorous and cringing Boss," were, under the leadership of Roosevelt and Taft, acquiescing in the loss of Negro rights. Then, from July to October, DuBois devoted his columns in the *Horizon* to a series of "talks" frankly designed to lure the Negro voter into the Democratic camp.

The Republican party, DuBois told his small audience, had forfeited its claim to the Negro's vote. Never opposed to slavery, the party had supported Negro enfranchisement in Reconstruction times only to maintain itself in power. Later, when it no longer needed black votes, it had deserted the Negro and had "winked ponderously at the Crime of '76." Nor had its record improved: with full control of all branches of the national government, the Republican party tolerated Negro disfranchisement; ignored discrimination in interstate commerce; acquiesced in the punishment of alleged Negro criminals without due process of law, under circumstances of unspeakable atrocity and barbarism; gave formal sanction to "lily whitism"; urged Negroes to eschew higher education in favor of education fitting them to be laborers, servants, and menials; dismissed a Negro regiment from the army when a "few blacks were suspected of treating the South as the South treated them." In the fact of this record, "the Negro plank of the Republican platform has become a standing joke," and Negro voters were "looked upon as fools, too amiable to bolt, and too venal to be feared."

So much for the Republicans. The Democratic party, according to DuBois, offered most to the race and to the nation. It stood for the strict regulation of corporate wealth. It supported organized labor which, DuBois thought, was embracing an increasing proportion of the Negro working force. The Democrats stood for freedom and independence for brown and black men in the West Indies and the Philippines, a point on which DuBois (and other Negroes) felt strongly because the racist appeals of American imperialists were giving national currency to notions of inferior and superior races which heretofore had been restricted largely to the South. Democrats opposed a high tariff, which the Negro consumer paid without compensating advantages as a producer. Finally, Democrats spoke against all special privilege, he said, and "every influence and move toward greater democratic freedom, wider popular power, and abolition of special privilege is, whether intended or not, an inevitable step toward the emancipation of black men as well as white."

DuBois insisted that the Democratic party deserved a trial, at least a trial, as the evil containing the larger element of good. Since the Civil War, he wrote, two irreconcilable elements, a "radical socialist Democracy at the North" and an "aristocratic caste party at the South," at opposite poles on free trade, imperialism, caste privilege, and regulation of corporate wealth, had shared power in the Democratic party. The South maintained the alliance, he said, because while the Negro voted Republican solidly and blindly, the only possible anti-Negro vote was Democratic; the North, because it needed Southern votes to win a national election. "The Negro voter today therefore has in his hand the tremendous power of emancipating the Democratic Party from its enslavement to the reactionary South," DuBois argued, for the Negro could deliver New York, New Jersey, Ohio, Indiana, and Illinois to the Democrats "with ease" and could make their triumph possible in a dozen other states.* As DuBois saw it, Democrats needed active Negro support before they dared alienate the Solid South; votes thrown to Bryan would symbolize Negro emancipation from vassalage to the Republican party.

When election day came, however, there was no visible Negro defection from the Republicans. Taft's easy victory over Bryan disappointed DuBois, but hardly surprised him.

---

* When DuBois repeated this analysis four years later, the Indianapolis *Freeman* warned: "Forget it. Balance of power is a [double]-edged sword." September 28, 1912.

DuBois's overtures to the Northern Democratic party indicated a significant new direction to his thought. The scrappy evidence available from his youth reveals DuBois as economically rather conservative. Speaking of Populist radicalism after his return from Europe, he had denied that "the conclusions of ages of conscientious research are to be cast away in a moment just because some long beard from the wild & woolly west wants to shirk paying his just debts."[50] In an essay he pointed to Schmoller's work in the statistical bureau at Stuttgart and to the abrupt check that both political and economic liberalism had received in Germany under the rising Prussia as "fortunate" occurrences that had tamed Schmoller's youthful radicalism. His discussion of German Socialists led him to speak of "these two almost opposing arguments of Democracy and Socialism."

Yet by the first decade of the twentieth century, perhaps under the influence of Miss Ovington, DuBois veered toward the Socialist party. As early as 1904 he admitted that, while not a Socialist, he shared many Socialist beliefs. Three years later in the *Horizon*, he tempted the Negro along the same path:

> I do not believe in the complete socialization of the means of production—the entire abolition of private property in capital—but the Path of Progress and common sense certainly leads to a far greater ownership of the public wealth for the public good than is now the case. I do not believe that government can carry on private business as well as private concerns, but I do believe that most of the human business called private is no more private than God's blue sky, and that we are approaching a time when railroads, coal mines, and many factories can and ought to be run by the public for the public. . . .
>
> In the socialist trend thus indicated lies the one great hope of the Negro American. We have been thrown by strange historic reasons into the hands of the capitalists hitherto. We have been objects of dole and charity, and despised accordingly. We have been made tools of oppression against the workingman's cause—the puppets and playthings of the idle rich. Fools! We must awake! Not in a renaissance among ourselves of the evils of Get and Grab—not in private hoarding, squeezing and cheating, lies our salvation, but rather in that larger ideal of human brotherhood, equality of opportunity and work not for wealth

but for Weal—here lies our shining goal. This goal the Socialists with all their extravagance and occasional foolishness have
more stoutly followed than any other class and thus far we must
follow them. Our natural friends are not the rich but the poor,
not the great but the masses, not the employers but the employees. Our good is not wealth, power, oppression, and snob-
bishness, but helpfulness, efficiency, service and self-respect.
Watch the Socialists. We may not follow them and agree with
them in all things. I certainly do not. But in trend and ideal
they are the salt of this present earth.[51]

In urging the Negro into the Northern Democratic party and
in praising socialism, DuBois was groping toward a new alliance.
The Democrats seemed to be moving in the right direction: independence for American colonies, regulation of corporate wealth,
opposition to special privilege, a friendship for organized labor,
and a low tariff. Socialists had the right long-range goals. DuBois
wanted to emancipate black men from their traditional alliances
with rich philanthropists and with the Republican party—two
alliances reinforced by Booker Washington—and to turn the Negro
toward liberal and Socialist groups whose programs would serve
the Negro's own interest. In approaching these groups, the Negro,
DuBois thought, had to make a realistic use of his political
strength. Such alliances might in the end point a way for the
Negro.

The Low Ebb of a Career

Despite its apparent diversity, DuBois's program of agitation
from 1903 to 1910 possessed a remarkable unity. But by 1910 the
prospects for this program, and for DuBois, seemed dim. As a
matter of fact, both DuBois's careers—as a scholar and as an agita-
tor—came to a dead end. As a result of criticism which he had
stirred up among white philanthropic sources, Atlanta University
faced continuing difficulties in finding outside support. Ware
would not suggest that DuBois leave, but DuBois could readily
recognize the burden which his presence imposed on the college.
His work in class yielded satisfaction, but teaching was not his
primary interest; as a scholar, he wrote primarily for the outside

world, not for the classroom. In the outside world, his brusque handling of racial intermarriage, the traditional raw nerve of the "Negro question," and his frankness in analyzing the economic roots of race prejudice showed that he despaired of help from richer white men. His attack on Washington (the figure of compromise between the two races) and his angry reiteration of Negro grievances deprived him of a substantial white audience. Toward the end of the decade, he was working on a novel, *The Quest of the Silver Fleece,* which tried to argue the Negro's case in fictional form. But when it appeared in 1911 few read it. White America would not listen; this group DuBois, in effect, surrendered to Washington.

How then would the Negro rise? DuBois's general answer was: through the intelligent use of his own resources—a national racial organization speaking with a single clear voice; a Negro vote skillfully managed as a bargaining weapon among competing parties; and an accurate appraisal of his own self-interest, which in concrete terms meant receptivity to socialism and political friendliness to the Northern Democrats.

Yet his plan for Negro self-help fared badly too. DuBois led an army in tatters. The Niagara Movement, the proposed defender of the race, failed, indeed did not even provoke widespread opposition, and finally disintegrated. Unable to grow, it frustrated DuBois's hope for an autonomous Negro organization standing on its own feet to fight for Negro rights. Despite the movement's brave words, the influence of Booker Washington showed no decline, though the steady pressure of Negro "radicals" had forced Washington to speak out for Negro rights with more vigor than was his wont. This was scant solace for the cause. DuBois's own magazine, *Horizon,* faced chronic financial troubles. After the first year its advertising rates were cut fifty per cent, but still the revenue was insufficient to meet the cost of publication. In 1908 DuBois appealed for a hundred "guarantors" to contribute $25 a year to the cost of running the magazine. In April 1910, DuBois wrote desperately to his partners urging them to help keep the magazine going at least until the summer meetings of the Niagara Movement. But he acknowledged that even that might be impossible. The magazine finally expired in July 1910. As DuBois saw it, Negro

America was unwilling to support a single uncompromising journal. By the end of 1909, Scott, Washington's secretary, was gloat-
ing: "One by one the old enemies are 'coming into camp.' "[52]

If the white liberals of the NAACP had not offered DuBois a
fresh start in 1910, he would presumably have remained at Atlanta.
He might have continued as a teacher, warmed by the excitement
of young minds and by the awkward gratitude which is the reward
of even ordinary teachers. He might have continued unobtrusively
to send forth college-trained men and women. But few outside the
university would have known about him. Already squeezed by
financial pressure, the Atlanta *Publications* would probably have
suffered a decline in quality already apparent in the contrast between *The Philadelphia Negro* and *John Brown*. At Morehouse
College, DuBois's friend, John Hope, met similar financial pressure by capitulating to Washington and admitting him to the
board of trustees. A similar surrender at Atlanta, which DuBois
acknowledged as a possibility,[53] would have cut the ground from
under his whole professional life.

In *Darkwater* DuBois traced a steady parade of triumphs from
Great Barrington to New York, every stage the culmination of his
highest ambitions, every step forward a victorious battle against a
white world reluctant to recognize ability in a black skin. Actually
the facts do not bear out this account. DuBois's progress from
obscurity in the Berkshires to a position of national prominence
is an impressive tribute to his talent. The Negro race would
eventually come around to his views, and the editorial experience
on *Horizon* and the organizational trials of the Niagara Movement
would serve him well as background for his later years. But in 1910,
when he stepped from Atlanta to a new career in New York, it was
not a climax of triumphs, but a rescue from a series of recent failures.

ENTENTE WITH WHITE LIBERALS

The National Association for the Advancement of Colored People gave DuBois an entente with white liberals who had enough money to sustain an organ of protest and enough allegiance to American democracy to tolerate the "radical" Negro point of view. With the relatively secure financial backing that the *Horizon* lacked, the *Crisis,* the Association's monthly magazine, gave DuBois a secure editorial chair and an independent forum.

The initial inspiration for the Association came from a group of whites outraged by the Springfield lynching in 1908. William English Walling's denunciation of the outrage in the *Independent* called for a "large and powerful body of citizens" to revive the spirit of Lincoln and Lovejoy. In response to the article, a group including Miss Ovington and Charles E. Russell, a prominent Socialist writer, approached Oswald Garrison Villard to write a "call" for a national conference on the Negro on the centennial of Lincoln's birth, 1909. Villard complied, and a notable array of fifty-three professional men and women summoned "all believers in democracy to join in a national conference for the discussion of present evils, the voicing of protests, and the renewal of the struggle for civil and political liberty."[1] The list of signers included some leading white social reformers of the day: Jane Addams, John Dewey, William Dean Howells, John Haynes Holmes, Hamilton Holt, Henry Moscowitz, Charles H. Parkhurst, J. G. Phelps-Stokes, Lincoln Steffens, Stephen S. Wise, William H. Ward, Lillian D. Wald, and Mary E. Woolley. Five Negroes besides DuBois joined in the "call": William L. Buckley, a New York school principal; the Reverend Francis J. Grimke, whom DuBois had listed among the critics of Washington in 1903; Bishop Alexander Walters of the African Methodist Episcopal Church, the president of the Afro-American Council; Dr. J. Milton Waldron, treasurer of the Niagara Movement; and Ida B. Wells-Barnett, chairman of the Anti-Lynching League.

White influence predominated in the conferences and in the organization that emerged. At the early meetings the presiding officers were invariably white, and of the twenty-four published speeches only five were given by Negroes. The Constitutional League, primarily a white organization and in its fight for civil rights a progenitor of the NAACP, was merged with the new group, and John E. Milholland, its president, assumed the post of vice-president of the Association. Although many prominent Negroes were on the newly incorporated Association's "general committee," only one Negro—DuBois—appeared on the first slate of officers in May 1910. The excess of white influence made some of the Negroes present wary. Two prominent "radicals," Trotter and Mrs. Wells-Barnett, had little faith in their white allies, and one woman (perhaps Mrs. Wells-Barnett) cried out in one meeting: "They are betraying us again—these white friends of ours."[2] But DuBois, one of the original incorporators, was quietly encouraged by the net results of the meetings: "The vision of future cooperation, not simply as in the past, between giver and beggar —the older idea of charity—but a new alliance between experienced social workers and reformers in touch on the one hand with scientific philanthropy and on the other hand with the great struggling mass of laborers of all kinds, whose conditions and needs know no color line."[3]

DuBois had been making contact with this group of liberals for many years. Ward, the editor of the *Independent*, had regularly published even DuBois's most fiery tracts, such as "A Litany at Atlanta." Miss Ovington had spoken at Atlanta in 1904, had reported the second Niagara convention for Villard's *Evening Post*, and may even have become a member of the Niagara Movement. DuBois had become a director of Milholland's Constitutional League in 1907. Jane Addams had brought DuBois to Chicago to speak at Hull House. In 1907 DuBois had supported Moorfield Storey's Anti-Imperialist League.* DuBois's relations

* DuBois's private venture in "imperialism" never seems to have gotten off the ground. The DuBois papers contain a prospectus for the "African Development Company" with DuBois listed as secretary. Ten thousand shares were to sell at a par of five dollars. The purpose of the company was to buy and develop land in East Central Africa for the cultivation of coffee and other

with Villard continued to be more equivocal. A deep personal hostility divided them, but by 1910 Villard's views on the race question had moved close to DuBois's and to those of other liberals. An editorial in Villard's *Evening Post* criticized Washington's role as "political boss of his race" and urged Negroes to fight immediately against present discrimination to prevent the "tightening of chains that must some day be broken if this is to be a republic in more than name."[4]

The alliance of liberals who made up the new Association gave breath to DuBois's stifled hopes at Atlanta. With support for his scholarship dwindling, with the *Horizon* losing money on each issue, and with the Niagara Movement collapsing, the offer from the Association, then only several months old, opened up white support previously denied to him. On the other side, the Association turned to him because his record of agitation together with his academic experience made him the ideal candidate for editor of the *Crisis* and director of research. Legally the *Crisis* was the property of the Association, and in the public eye it would be regarded as the spokesman of the Association. Because of this intimate relationship, DuBois's hostility to Washington aroused the fears of some directors, but this obstacle was removed after DuBois agreed not to make the *Crisis* the organ of attack on Tuskegee and promised to represent no clique and to "avoid personal rancor of all sorts"[5]—a pledge only partly kept.

Working with Progressives

In his inaugural address in 1913, a classic statement of progressivism, Woodrow Wilson spoke of returning America to its first principles. The method was the spread of knowledge—"science" he called it—and the spirit was to be the "hearthfire of every man's conscience and vision of the right."[6] Wilson was speaking of the New Freedom; he could as easily have been talking about the program of the Association.

---

products. The promoters assured investors that they already had contracts with certain native chiefs for "valuable concessions of land." This venture is mentioned nowhere else in DuBois's writings. It may have been just an elaborate joke.

Though the initial statements of the Association were a bit vague, they clearly aligned the new group with the Progressive movement. Progressives were intent on removing hindrances to the free development of the individual; the Association focussed on the great impediment to Negro individuals—discrimination, especially segregation. To fight this discrimination, the Association proposed education, legal action, and organization: education of the American people in their abuses of Negro rights; appeals to courts and legislatures to remove obstacles blocking Negro progress; and organization into a single articulate group of those Americans, white and black, whose democratic faith abhorred the color line. The new organization started simply as a national office that released public statements on Negro matters. The board of directors met monthly for policy decisions, and in the intervals DuBois, Miss Ovington, Villard, and Joel E. Spingarn, a professor at Columbia University, gave part of their time to routine matters. As the membership grew, NAACP branches, first in the Northeast and then all over the country, bridged the gap between the national office and the members. The branches supplied the national office with information and in turn served as rallying points and distributing centers for material prepared in New York. A natural division of labor developed, the New York office handling national questions and the branches dealing with local matters. All concentrated on the spread of information. The Association, like the progressives, assumed that when Americans knew of injustice, their intelligence and moral principles would demand reform from legislatures and courts.

To this program DuBois gave ready assent. He wanted no special treatment for the Negro, merely an equal chance. He was glad to link the Negro's progress to progressivism, to free the Negro from concentration on his own progress and unite him with every cause of world uplift, with the "people who are revolutionizing the world."[7] Even before the first issue of the *Crisis* appeared, he called upon a Negro audience to escape its provincialism and to give moral and financial support to the new group. The following year he mailed out a characteristic appeal to a thousand of the most prominent Negroes in the United States, urging them to join the Association and to secure three additional subscribers to the *Crisis* in order to link colored people themselves with the drive for their own freedom.[8] The Association—and the *Crisis*—would speed the arrival of democratic justice: "Evolution is evolving the millennium, but one of the unescapable factors in evolution are [*sic*] the men who hate wickedness and oppression with perfect hatred, who will not equivocate, will not excuse, and will be heard."[9] The lead editorial in the first issue of the *Crisis* presented his apocalyptic vision: "Catholicity and tolerance, reason and forebearance can to-day make the world-old dream of human brotherhood approach realization; while bigotry and prejudice, emphasized race prejudice and force can repeat the awful history of the contact of nations and groups in the past. We strive for this higher and broader vision of Peace and Good Will."[10]

Though jealous of the *Crisis'* independence, DuBois recorded and supported the work of the Association. He joined in the Association's campaign against lynching and suggested methods other than publicity for fighting it: better administration of present laws, court action in all possible instances, new legislation, and federal intervention when the states were incompetent to deal with outrages. In 1910, when Chicago, Philadelphia, Columbus, and Atlantic City were considering the establishment of segregated public schools, he condemned the move as "an argument against democracy and an attempt to shift public responsibility from the shoulders of the public to the shoulders of some class who are unable to defend themselves."[11] In 1913 he joined Storey and Villard in a written protest to Wilson against the growing practice of segregation in governmental agencies in Washington. They condemned the humiliating stigma of segregation, especially when inflicted by the federal government itself, and reminded Wilson pointedly that the Negro also expected to share in the New Freedom.

In politics DuBois continued to urge the Negro to use his ballot with maximum effect in every election—an uncommitted vote, available to the highest legitimate bidder willing to pay, not in the coin of the realm or in minor jobs, but in genuine effort for Negro advancement. In 1916 DuBois, Spingarn, Villard, and A. H. Grimke, president of the Washington, D.C., branch of the Association, sent a letter to Charles Evans Hughes, the Republican candidate for the presidency, asking for a specific statement on lynching, disfranchisement, and appointments to office. (Hughes never committed himself.) The following year, drawing on his own experience, DuBois urged Negroes everywhere in the South to register and vote on every possible occasion, even though the white primary deprived their vote of its significance. He promised that the Association planned to challenge the white primary through the courts.

Occasionally DuBois extended his attack on segregation into fields which the Association discreetly left alone. When a proposed reunion of the Methodist churches South and North provided for a separate Negro branch with its own bishops, DuBois questioned the relation of the church to the teachings of Jesus Christ. He mocked two Baltimore churches which moved uptown to the "wealthy and exclusive and socially elect," where learned prelates would ask the echoing pews how the church could teach the working man.[12] Actually, though the ideals of Christianity made discriminatory churches a favorite whipping boy, DuBois really regarded them as too moribund to respond to any appeal to a Christian ethic. In Billy Sunday and the torpedoed "Lusitania," he saw the depths to which white Christianity had fallen: Sunday approximating the "whirling dervish, the snake dancer and devotee of 'Mumbo Jumbo'," the "Lusitania" publicizing the cheapness with which a Christian nation regarded human life.*

In spite of the parallels between DuBois's editorials and the activities of the Association, his entente with progressivism never ripened into an alliance. On the national front, both Theodore Roosevelt and his Progressive party and Woodrow Wilson and his progressive Democratic party failed to respond to Negro overtures, and other reform groups held the Negro at arm's length. In the Association, tension between DuBois and his white colleagues developed almost immediately and never disappeared.

The hopes kindled by white reformers led DuBois first to the Progressive party. In 1912, hoping to commit the Progressive party

---

* *Crisis*, X, 81 (June 1915). DuBois's hostility to Christian churches had a long life. See, for example, his strictures on the Catholic hierarchy, *Crisis*, XXX, 120–21 (July 1925).

to Negro rights, DuBois drafted a tentative civil-rights plank which Joel Spingarn presented to the platform committee. But Roosevelt, whose bid for Southern electoral votes required a "lily white" party in the South to attract white support, adopted an equivocal stand on the Negro—recognition in the North and exclusion in the South—and so the Progressive party as a whole remained silent. DuBois turned reluctantly to Woodrow Wilson.

He found Wilson's background disquieting. Wilson, left to himself, would welcome a "world inhabited by flaxen-haired wax dolls with or without brains." But at least, DuBois thought, he was a "cultivated scholar" who might treat the Negro with "far-sighted fairness."[13] Thomas E. Watson's attack on Wilson as "ravenously fond of the negro"[14] lent support to the hope that Wilson might at least be as fair to Negroes as Cleveland had been. When Democratic leaders actively solicited Negro votes in the North, DuBois drafted a statement for Wilson's signature, but when Villard presented it to the candidate, Wilson rejected it and released a more moderately phrased letter which promised "absolute fair dealing" and "not mere grudging justice, but justice executed with liberality and cordial good feeling."[15] With only this general commitment, DuBois still urged Negroes to "take a leap in the dark."*

When Wilson's administration was five months old, DuBois praised Wilson's fiscal program, but warned that not all problems were economic. As the administration grew older, neither Wilson's "high purpose" nor the achievements of his first years compensated, in DuBois's judgment, for his "shifty and unmeaning platitudes" behind which segregation was introduced into the Post Office and Treasury departments while lynching went unrebuked.[16] Still unappeased in 1916, DuBois repudiated Wilson, and when Hughes failed to make a specific statement during his presidential campaign, DuBois urged a vote for Allan L. Benson, the Socialist candidate, or no vote at all: if Negroes could not make their political will felt positively, at least they could pre-

* *Crisis*, V, 29 (November 1912). Of DuBois's support for the Democrats, William H. Hart of the Howard Law School commented: "Father, forgive him for he knows not what he does." Washington *Bee*, October 12, 1912.

vent any single party from assuming that it had the black vote
tied up without compensation.

The rebuff from organized labor was discouraging, but less
final. At Atlanta DuBois had not taken a strong position on
unions. If anything, his attitude was mildly hostile; his comments in *The Negro Artisan* were neutral, but the following year,
he wrote to Walter Hines Page about the desirability of "curbing
the power of trade unions."[17] When he joined the Association's
staff, however, he seems to have raised his hopes. Though he
warned that when organized workers fought for an Irish or a
German clique which was content to let others starve, "they deserve themselves the starvation which they plan for their darker
and poorer fellows," he carried the union label on the *Crisis*, even
though it meant that no Negro could print it. He knew that he
was somewhat eccentric in this stand; most Negro leaders opposed
unions, if only because of the extent to which unions discriminated against black labor. He guessed that the mass of Negro
workers similarly regarded white workers as enemies rather than
as prospective friends. But since he believed that unions had been
responsible for all of labor's gains, he looked beyond present discrimination, beyond the Negro's immediate interest, to the millennium when white workers would share their gains with their
black brothers.[18] But in this decade organized labor, as represented
by Samuel Gompers' American Federation of Labor, kept the barriers against the Negro as high as it dared.

Other reform groups gave scarcely more reason for hope. At
Atlanta DuBois had avoided cooperation with the women's suffrage movement lest his motives be misunderstood. Yet he put the
force of the *Crisis* behind the movement, for any great human
question concerned Negroes as well as whites, and this particular
one touched the Negro question even more closely: an argument
for female suffrage needed only slight revision to include all adults
regardless of race or sex. Furthermore, DuBois said, votes for
women meant votes for black women, who "are moving quietly
but forceably toward the intellectual leadership of the race."[19]
But the color line kept cropping up in feminist discussions all
through the decade. In 1915 one feminist leader said that colored

women should have the vote on the same basis as colored men—
hardly a stand calculated to command Negro applause. In 1911
DuBois's editorial, "Forward Backwards," said that the Prohibitionists ignored the Negro for eleven months, then demanded his
support under pain of further disfranchisement; when Negroes
refused, they were branded as "not worthy of the ballot."[20]

A real barrier set Negro advancement apart from other social
reforms. Since each reform movement spoke for a minority seeking to gain majority support, it could hardly gamble for uncertain Negro support at the expense of certainly alienating one section of the nation, and probably more. Wilson had been elected
with Southern votes and depended on a Congressional majority
heavily buttressed by Southerners. In the election of 1912, when
Roosevelt had to break into the solidly Democratic South in order
to win the presidency, a forthright statement on the Negro would
have reduced the Southern section of his party to a shambles. The
advocates of women's suffrage propagandized in a nation largely
hostile or indifferent to Negro suffrage; to have hitched their program to the race question would have recklessly multiplied their
problems. In the labor movement, long-range policy might point
to the wisdom of Negro–white solidarity, but in the meantime
work voluntarily shared with Negroes would cost some white workers their daily bread. In almost every movement for social reform,
DuBois thus found the race question limiting his hopes for the
progressive alliance.

Even the Association itself never commanded his unequivocal
support. Almost a year after joining the Association's staff, on the
very day he urged the thousand "best colored people in the United
States" to join, he was planning to continue the Niagara Movement as an annual conference without fees. His relations with
the Association remained diplomatic rather than organizational,
and even as the Association passed from white dominance to joint
control and finally to Negro dominance, DuBois persisted in regarding the *Crisis* as a continuation of the *Horizon*: a personal
journal, connected with the Association only slightly more intimately than the *Horizon* had been with the Niagara Movement.
When he received a bid to England to speak in behalf of African
natives, he reported the invitation in his magazine by saying that

the president of the African National Native Congress "wrote THE CRISIS as follows. . . ."[21] When in 1915 his salary, previously paid out of Association funds, came from the income of the magazine, he claimed that the Association had never spent a cent of its funds for the magazine, and that he had assumed exclusive financial responsibility though the Association had held legal ownership. His comment that "there is both precedent and moral right that legal ownership rightly follow such financial risk"[22] indicated clearly that in allowing the *Crisis* to remain in the Association's hands, he felt that he was exercising restraint in dealing with an ally. Miss Ovington even spoke of the *Crisis* as a "rival" to the Association.[23]

DuBois's failure to work in harness with his colleagues threatened to destroy the group in 1914. The previous year, after a heated board meeting, DuBois wrote to Villard, then chairman of the board, asking for "reasonable initiative and independence in carrying out my part of the work." He admitted the right of any member of the board to criticize his work, but he rejected the notion that Villard was his superior and denied Villard's right "to imply in his criticism that any independence of action is a breach of discipline or a personal discourtesy."[24] Villard replied tartly, not to DuBois but to Spingarn, who came to fill the uneasy role of liaison officer. As executive of the Association, the chairman of the board, he said, "must exercise certain authorities over the paid employees of the Board, whether they be editors or clerks."[25]

By the fall of 1914 the uncomfortable tension in the Association offices led DuBois to ask Spingarn for a frank explanation. Spingarn replied with an unexpected broadside. As DuBois's closest friend in the Association, Spingarn warned him that a sharply antagonistic atmosphere surrounded DuBois not only at the Association offices, but in the whole colored world as well: even some of DuBois's closest friends felt resentment as well as affection toward him. Spingarn conceded that part of this was caused by DuBois's devotion to principle, but he noted that even men who shared DuBois's principles could not escape the idea that DuBois mistook obstinacy for strength of character: choosing to wreck the cause rather than lose some preferred point, he magnified every personal difference into a question of principle. On occasions when DuBois thought he had won a point through strength of character or successful argument, his white friend told him, he had actually won for the same reason that parents capitulate to spoiled children in company—simply to avoid a scene. DuBois's colleagues were less willing than he to wreck the cause. Many people who wanted an end to this needless bickering, Spingarn said frankly, saw DuBois as the only discordant element in what was developing into a smoothly running organization and thought that the elimination of DuBois was essential to the work of the Association. Spingarn warned DuBois that he must either espouse the cause wholeheartedly as his own or—the alternative was unstated but clearly implicit—leave.[26]

An unchastened DuBois acknowledged a temperament difficult to endure, but he disclaimed responsibility for the friction. His great and only ambition was to make the *Crisis* a spectacular success, but to do so, he needed a free hand unfettered by the slights and unkindnesses of Villard, who, DuBois had hinted to a Boston audience, was trying to make the Association a one-man organization. The real cause of the bickering, he told Spingarn, was Villard's unconscious race prejudice which called for paternalism rather than cooperation in dealing with a Negro, even in the same office.[27]

This storm lowered the humidity but did not clear the air. The board continued to debate the status of DuBois and of the *Crisis* for most of the next year. In January 1916, Spingarn, now chairman and always the peacemaker, worked out a compromise statement: the *Crisis*, as the official organ of the Association, should chronicle its progress, but the editorials, as the "expression of the personality which gives them shape," could hardly hope to satisfy all members. The board could only insist that the editorials never sink to the "level of petty irritations, insulting personalities or vulgar recriminations."[28] This nod in every direction seems to have quieted, if not satisfied, all factions.

At the root of these disagreements was more than a clash of personalities, though undoubtedly DuBois's stubbornness, arrogance, and irascibility, bred by forty years of the color line, contributed their share. The Association was in many respects a

typical progressive cause: an attempt by men of good will to re-
cover basic American democratic traditions through publicity,
legislation, and court action. Its laissez-faire bent required the
removal of barriers that held the individual back from his own
full development through his own powers. It knew no grouping
between the individual and the nation. It knew no color line.
Villard told one correspondent that the Association desired "to
help one race quite as much as the other."[29] If DuBois were to
join the Association's chorus, he had to sing this tune. Yet fundamentally DuBois sang in a different key: he was a Negro, fighting
for Negroes, committed to Negro self-help in the Niagara Movement and the *Horizon*, distrusful of white men. His view had not
changed since his talk to the American Negro Academy in 1896:
Negroes must channel their physical powers, intellectual endowments, and spiritual ideals through the whole Negro group to
make their characteristic gift to civilization. Periodically his Negro racism broke through: in 1913 he observed in the *Crisis* that
"the most ordinary Negro" is an instinctive gentleman, but "it
takes extraordinary training, gift and opportunity to make the
average white man anything but an overbearing hog."[30] DuBois
never came to a feeling of community with his associates. Though
as a practical matter he lent himself to the NAACP's program, he
never fully accepted it as his own. It took the Association a quarter
of a century to grasp the significance of their differences.

DuBois's own program, the main lines of which were drawn
together in 1915 in an article, "The Immediate Program of the
American Negro,"[31] attested to the division between him and
the Association. One part paralleled the Association's program,
though DuBois was more explicit in condemning the barriers
created by the "oppression of shrewd capitalists," the "jealousy
of trade unions," and the "shackles on social intercourse from
the President and the so-called church of Christ down to boot-
blacks." Yet this merely negative program of fighting obstructions
was not enough. Negroes needed to work out their own projects
for moving ahead, not assuming that "God or his vice-[regent] the
White Man" would do it for them. "Conscious self-realization
and self-direction," DuBois said, "is the watchword of modern

man, and the first article in the program of any group that will survive must be the great aim, equality and power among men." Negroes had to plan their own building and loan associations, cooperatives for production and distribution, and blueprints for systematic charity. They should embark on a planned migration from "mob rule and robbery" in the South. In art and literature, DuBois said, the black man must set loose the tremendous emotional wealth and "dramatic strength" of his problems; in politics, he must organize—the next year DuBois would speak of a Negro party.

For all this, DuBois said, organization was essential. He thanked God that most of the Association's support came from black hands, but he called for a still larger proportion, and added: "We must not only support but control this and similar organizations and hold them unswervingly to our objects, our aims, and our ideals." Negro objects, Negro aims, Negro ideals—not the shared goals of a biracial group fighting for democratic equality. The distinction was important, and would grow in importance.

Over the years DuBois had become aware of the dilemma of Negro separatism. Striving for integration (a long-range goal) and striving for security (a short-range goal) frequently drove DuBois in opposite directions, and he tells in *The Souls of Black Folk* how the conflict split his personality: "One feels ever his two-ness—an American, a Negro; two souls, two thoughts, two unreconciled strivings; two warring ideals in one dark body, whose dogged strength alone keeps it from being torn asunder." He made there what was perhaps his first reference to "that curious double movement where real progress may be negative and actual advance be relative retrogression." Three years later he pointed out that Negroes were forcing their way into white labor markets, but they were doing it at the price of increased anti-Negro prejudice. He wondered if perhaps the Negro's "only path of escape" was to organize a closed Negro business community—this would "provincialize" the Negro and perhaps also increase prejudice against him, but it would produce income.[32] When the same sentiment appeared in *The Negro in the South*—a book of four lectures, two by DuBois and two by Washington—E. H. Clement of the editorial staff of the Boston *Evening Transcript* assumed that DuBois had come to accept segregation. DuBois denied this interpretation: he was opposed to physical segregation, but he was "perfectly willing" to accept "spiritual segregation and an economic segregation on the spiritual side"—that is, Negroes were to live alongside their white fellow men, but were to trade at their own stores and serve themselves. He was quite sure that this arrangement was "going to be the rule for some time."[33]

From 1910 until after the first World War, DuBois continued to pick his way through this thorny problem. Each decision reflected an *ad hoc*, pragmatic test rather than a sustained point of view. He accepted segregated YMCA branches, for example, because the Negro's urgent need for social and recreational opportunities overbalanced the endorsement of segregation implied by the use of segregated facilities. In general, his alliance with white progressives seems to have drawn him back briefly to the policy of slow integration. In 1911 he said that the absence of intense racial separateness in the North gave more hope for a "slower but larger integration" than the intense Negro self-consciousness and cooperation in the South.[34] The same year he warned that the acceptance of separation indicated a willingness to "sacrifice the foundations of democracy for peace."[35] On the other hand, he could speak of "Blessed Discrimination" which provided concrete economic advantage—the *Crisis*, for example, was "capitalized race prejudice."[36] Significantly, this last comment came latest: DuBois moved irregularly toward the acceptance of segregation which gave some economic compensation. In 1917 he told his readers: "We see more and more clearly that economic survival for the Negro in America means . . . that he must employ labor, that he must organize industry, that he must enter American industrial development as a group, capable of offensive and defensive action, and not simply as an individual, liable to be made the victim of the white employer and of such of the white labor unions as dare." American Negroes, he said, were singularly well endowed to work out efficient industrial cooperation; they were all in approximately the same economic group, and they shared a mounting group loyalty and an imperative need for a change in their industrial life.[37] Two years later his editorial, "Jim Crow," suggested his indecision: he insisted that Negroes work

with their own people in art, industry, and social life to build
a "new and great Negro ethos," yet he condemned segregation
as impossible and impolitic. In these years DuBois avoided saying
right out that chance advantages justified approval of segregation. For the present he preferred to speculate on both policies,
recognizing always a dilemma calling for "thought and forebearance."[38]

To achieve his complex ends, an appeal to truth and to the
conscience of America were DuBois's familiar weapons, and he
continued to use them in this decade. In 1910, when Washington
gave Europe an unusually sanguine picture of Negro conditions
in the South, DuBois joined with thirty-one other Negro Americans in protesting Washington's report as a violation of truth:
"It is one thing to be optimistic, self-forgetful and forgiving, but
it is quite a different thing, consciously or unconsciously, to mis-
represent the truth."[39] And the hard core of truth had to include
disfranchisement, 2,500 lynchings in the previous twenty-five years,
and unprotected women.

But the road to truth was far from smooth, and America's conscience seemed remarkably obdurate. DuBois was a sensitive
Negro in white America, where the experience of discrimination
touched the Negro at almost every facet of his life.* Caught in
the vise of his emotion, he could not respond directly to what
went on around him. He recorded the poignancy of being a Negro in America: the "real tragedy" was "the inner degradation,
the hurt hound feeling" which caused joy "at the sheerest and
most negative decency."[40] A prejudiced white man confirmed the
Negro's expectation of American discrimination, but a non-
prejudiced white did not necessarily undo the damage, for far
from showing a brighter picture, he might by contrast merely point
up the gloom. Spingarn's ability to reach behind DuBois's wall of
reserve made him a "knight," but the occasion of Spingarn's ill-
ness in 1918 led DuBois to lament how few were the men who
could work *with* Negroes as well as work *for* them. The tone of
DuBois's columns in the *Crisis* vacillated between hopefulness

* See Abram Kardiner and Lionel Ovesey, *The Mark of Oppression* (New
York, 1951), for a psychiatric discussion of the extent to which the color line
affects Negro personality.

and despair, for he saw at the same time how far the Negro had come and how far he still had to go in achieving an equal place in American society. An editorial appointment, a philanthropic gift, a biracial sociological meeting in the South would raise hopes that in a month could be crushed by a lynching or by the spread of prejudice into a new area. The resolutions of the Southern Sociological Congress in 1913, which, according to DuBois, was the first occasion in American history when Southern blacks and whites had met under Southern auspices to discuss the race problem, contained "scarcely a word" which the *Crisis* could not endorse. But even this small step forward was balanced by the conduct of the Atlanta *Georgian* which, he said, tried to foment a lynching. In an early issue of the new magazine DuBois had hailed recent court decisions as the "glimmerings of a new dawn," but seven months later when the Newburyport, Massachusetts, *Herald*, reprinted an editorial, "The Negro Vote as an Annoying Factor," from the Nashville *Tennessean and American*, the *Crisis* mourned that the soul of New England, as well as the Middle West, was being poisoned by Negro haters in the South. DuBois was convinced—and the conviction weighed heavily on him—that race prejudice in the United States was a "deliberately cultivated and encouraged state of mind."[41]

Sometimes after recurrent exasperation, or under severe provocation, DuBois abandoned reason and cajolery and turned frankly to a threat of force. After a bloody lynching at Coatesville, Pennsylvania, in 1911, he warned that Negroes had had enough: they had crawled and pleaded for justice, he said, and they had been "cheerfully spit upon and murdered and burned." "If we are to die," he went on, "in God's name let us perish like men and not like bales of hay."[42] When Negroes in Gainesville, Florida, failed to resist an attacking white mob in 1916, an editorial, "Cowardice," insisted that they should have fought in self-defense to the last ditch if they killed every white man in the country and were themselves killed in turn. A striking generalization followed: lynching, he said, would stop in the South "when the cowardly mob is faced by effective guns in the hands of people determined to sell their souls dearly."[43] Later the same year, in reply to a young woman who wanted more refinement and fewer overtones of violence in the *Crisis*, DuBois reminded her that no human group had "ever" achieved its freedom "without being compelled to murder" thousands of oppressors. Though he hoped that this would not be true for American Negroes, *"it may be necessary."*[44]

DuBois's threats of violence were only the most extreme manifestations of his divergences from his white associates. While the Association cautiously assailed legal barriers, DuBois's shots ranged freely over the church, industrialists, labor unions, philanthropic foundations, and even hit his white liberal colleagues. When he went one step further and suggested the possibility of separate, independent Negro development, perhaps through an Association more tightly geared to "our objects, our aims, and our ideals," he left white liberalism far behind. In DuBois's view, the path upward was blocked by hurdles uncleared by progressivism.

But though programs diverged and tempers wore thin, the entente with the Association held. The Association could ill afford to lose DuBois's superb editorial talents on a successful magazine. His columns of editorials sparkled; his news columns contained the fullest available record of information about colored men here and abroad. As the years went on, the *Crisis*, largely because of DuBois's prestige, attracted young Negro writers whose articles, short stories, and poems complemented his own contributions. The Association could not afford to sacrifice the prestige of his mounting reputation. When he appeared as a principal speaker at the International Congress of Races in London in 1911, for example, his success there reflected credit back on his organization. Conversely, the *Crisis* gave DuBois a secure berth which, without hampering his writing and his nation-wide lecturing, gave him both an opportunity and a continuing obligation to plan the emancipation of the Negro.

Joining the Great Crusade

After the first World War started, Wilsonian idealism and wartime opportunities for the Negro caused a resurgence of DuBois's hopes for his alliance with white progressives.

At the outbreak of the war in 1914, DuBois's support went

immediately to the Allies. Although the war occurred because of the "wild quest for Imperial expansion among colored races," he said, Negro sympathy should go especially to England, since no nation was fairer with darker people, and to France, the "most kindly" of all European nations in personal relations. Departing from the general American pattern of sympathy for invaded Belgium, DuBois, recalling the Belgian Congo, felt that Belgium deserved every pang she got. Russia had never drawn the color line, he thought, and Japan had created respect for the darker races in the Russo-Japanese war. The triumph of the Allies, DuBois thought, would leave things no worse, and perhaps it could improve them, for the fighting skill of colored men might bring new ideas of the essential equality of all men. Germany, he said, in exalting race prejudice, made the prospect of its victory seem like the "triumph of every force calculated to subordinate darker peoples." Hence, in DuBois's view, it was better for Negroes to give sympathy to those nations that might postpone, if not make unnecessary, a world war of races.[45]

Six months later, his essay, "The African Roots of War," in the *Atlantic Monthly,* mocked the "mere habit" of regarding the Balkans as the storm center of Europe and named Africa as a prime cause of "this terrible overturning of civilization." In Europe, DuBois said, the progressive democratization of wealth and of political power was yielding a new "democratic despotism"—an alliance of exploiting capitalists and skilled workers who shared the wealth wrung from backward nations. The rich grew richer, he said, and although they permitted political democracy, they also encouraged a deepening hatred toward the darker races. The skilled white worker did not yet have his full share of the exploited wealth, but that was a matter of negotiation, DuBois explained; the loot was ample for all. The war, he charged, was the result of the conflicting jealousies of "armed national associations of labor and capital whose aim is the exploitation of the wealth of the world, mainly outside the European circle of nations." At home, where the worker was appeased by state socialism and intimidated by public threats of colored labor, the fruits of exploitation fell mainly to the aristocracy of labor, while the ignorant and restless were forming a "large, threatening, and, to

a growing extent, revolutionary group in advanced countries."
DuBois could see some future threats to peace: a victors' quarrel
over the spoils, a revolutionary protest of the lowliest workers,
and a colored revolt against foreign domination. To avert these
disasters, he said, racial prejudice and slander must end; "Stead-
fast faith in humanity must come"; forceable economic expansion
over subject peoples and religious hypocrisy must stop; African
people must have land, modern education and civilization, and
home rule.[46]

After America's entry into the war, DuBois's analysis touched
Wilson's concept of the Great Crusade at many points. Both
shared a faith in self-determination of peoples, both put substantial weight on the value of locally responsible democratic government as a means of maintaining peace. Both saw the war as
a possible solution of the problem of war itself, provided that the
world could engage in a marked moral revolution.

More important for DuBois, perhaps, the war produced opportunities for arguing the Negro's cause. Just after the American
declaration of war, Negro leaders, DuBois among them, gathered
in Washington to promise support, but also to demand the right
to train as fighting men under Negro officers, the end of lynching,
universal suffrage, universal and free common school training, the
abolition of the Jim Crow railroad car, repeal of segregation ordinances, and equal civil rights in public institutions. The following year thirty-one Negro editors echoed many of the same demands, and added a new one: acceptance of Negro help where
needed (a reference to restrictions set up both by employers and
unions).

DuBois warmed to the war slowly as he saw chances for the
Negro to move ahead. When talk of not drafting Negroes was
current, DuBois noted jubilantly that Negroes would take over
white jobs in factories, learning lucrative trades which would contribute to their security. Once in the front-line trenches, white
soldiers would never again become competitors because, DuBois
said ominously, "THEY WON'T COME BACK."[47] Later on, as the catalog of Negro gains grew—recognition of citizenship in the draft,
higher wages, better employment, appointment of Negro Red
Cross nurses, the overthrow of some segregation ordinances, a

strong word from Wilson against lynching, Newton D. Baker's cooperation in setting up Negro officer-training schools (segregated, but finally turning out a thousand Negro officers)—he gave more positive support to the war effort, for he regarded these gains as the beginning of a permanent surge rather than as the crest of a wave which would shortly spend itself and recede. By the end of 1917 he had scarcely a doubt that after fifty-four years the tide against the Negro had turned and that from then on the Negro would see "the walls of prejudice crumble before the onslaught of common sense and racial progress."[48] The darker races had risen, and the Negro's progress was assured, not all at once perhaps, but certain. The death of "Pitchfork Ben" Tillman, one of the most prominent Southern spokesman for white supremacy, ended an era, DuBois thought, and gave hope for the coming of a greater leader who would unify white labor and the small farmer, and would welcome the Negro as an ally. Finally, in July and August of 1918, more than a year after America's entry, he gave unequivocal support to the war: this was the Day of Decision, the time to put down the menace of German militarism and to inaugurate the United States of the World. Though Negroes had a special interest, he said, they forgot their grievances and "close[d] ranks" with white fellow citizens and their allies abroad. "We make no ordinary sacrifice," he said, "but we make it gladly and willingly with our eyes lifted to the hills."* The following month, in "A Philosophy in Time of War," he spoke unequivocally of "our war" and "our country" which, though not perfect, was at least better than Germany: "The survival of the Best against the threats of the Worst." The Negro's first duty, he said, was to fight the war without hesitation or protest; to send soldiers and

---

* *Crisis*, XVI, 111 (July 1918). In the Negro press one read the charge that DuBois's conversion to the war effort was not unrelated to the War Department's tentative consideration of commissioning him as a captain attached to the General Staff to advise on Negro matters. DuBois rejected this notion of a "corrupt bargain." The *Messenger*, a radical journal, had suggested earlier that DuBois and others like him go to France if they were so anxious to make the world safe for democracy. "We would rather make Georgia safe for the Negro." Now it said that "Close Ranks" would "rank in shame and reeking disgrace" with the Atlanta compromise. Even the Washington branch of the NAACP did not like it. Cf. *Crisis*, XVI, 216, 218 (September 1918); *Messenger*, I, 31 (November 1917) and III, 9–10 (May-June 1919).

stand behind them. By this support Negroes were to serve both patriotism and interest, for by serving their country they would gain justice from a grateful America.[49]

After the war, the very height of DuBois's hopes set the measure of his disillusionment. His Easter editorial in 1919 asked for the payoff for the Negro's loyalty: Negroes had helped to save the world; they could have "wrought mischief and confusion, patterning themselves after the I.W.W. and the pro-Germans." But not one Negro, he said, was arrested as a traitor or "even" as a conscientious objector. With clean hands the Negroes looked for the fair play which they had given.[50] Instead, race riots, mounting discrimination by trade unions, and shameless treatment of Negro soldiers abroad rewarded Negro loyalty. Shocked, hurt, angry, DuBois raised again the threat of violence, and when his rage subsided, little was left of his alliance with white liberalism.

Sent by the Association to France, primarily to gather material for a history of the Negro in the war, DuBois returned steaming with wrath both at the Army's discrimination and at his own race leaders—like Emmett Scott and Robert Russa Moton, Washington's successor at Tuskegee—who failed to protest. DuBois has never published the full results of his investigation, but he has said enough about assignment to labor battalions, contemptuous white officers, systematic undermining of Negro relations with the native French population, and slow promotions to indicate the nature of his protest.

The conduct of the AFL during the war ended for DuBois the chimera of solidarity with organized labor. He directly charged Gompers with engineering the East St. Louis race riot in 1917.[51] Though he still believed that trade unions had advanced the worker from chattel slavery to the threshold of industrial freedom, he warned that white philanthropy's whole scheme for settling the labor problem in the previous twenty years had rested on playing black against white, a "mischievous and dangerous program" which had received additional impetus from the unions themselves. In the present labor movement as represented by the federation, he asserted, "there is absolutely no hope of justice for an American of Negro descent." Still he held back the full force of his attack, separating his assault on the AFL from a rejection of all white workers: one could not expect workers stunted by heredity and century-long lack of opportunity to possess the larger sense of justice which could be expected from the privileged classes. But this easy judgment on the masses did not apply to the leadership: the recent AFL convention, labeling Negro labor as "scab," he said, showed that the AFL yielded the Negro his status as a man reluctantly, denying him every privilege it dared.[52] DuBois's tone suggested almost an ultimatum to organized labor: it must grant the Negro worker full equality, or suffer the full force of DuBois's disfavor.

Nothing did more to contribute to the depths of DuBois's despair than the "Red Summer" of 1919, which "ushered in the greatest period of interracial strife the nation has ever witnessed." John Hope Franklin has counted about twenty-five urban race riots in the United States from June to the end of the year, the most serious in Chicago where a reign of terror, a "miniature war," following the murder of two Negroes led to a casualty list of thirty-eight killed, five hundred and thirty-seven injured.[53]

In May, before the Chicago riot, DuBois had returned to his old strident tone: the *Crisis* and thousands of Negroes, having been "drafted" into a great struggle, now returned to call a spade a spade in a land still shameful. Right in having fought to save democracy abroad, the Negroes were "cowards and jackasses" if they settled for less at home, he said. "Make way for Democracy. We saved it in France, and by the Great Jehovah, we will save it in the United States or know the reason why."[54] In September, after the riot, he warned Negroes that it might be necessary to raise the terrible weapon of self-defense and added that the line between aggression and self-defense was hard to draw.[55]

While this latter issue was in press, Representative James F. Byrnes of South Carolina, speaking on the floor of the House of Representatives, deplored Negro "incendiary utterances," particularly from a leader like DuBois, who had been "heretofore regarded as conservative" and whose position among his people had enlarged his "capacity for evil." Since recent issues of the *Crisis* had been so full of prejudices and appeals to passion that they could have "no other result" than to incite to deeds of violence, Byrnes said, the Justice Department should consider the editorials carefully under the terms of the Espionage Act.* Though at first DuBois's answer to Byrnes was simply thanks for allowing seventy-five million people to read what normally would have reached only a million, the following month, perhaps under pressure from the board of the Association, he said flatly in a "Statement" that although Negroes did not countenance violence except in self-defense, still they fought—an equivocation left for each to interpret as he wished.[56]

By 1920, when the idealism of the war years and the anger of the months following had both burned themselves out, a disillusioned DuBois commented: "Fools, yes that's it. Fools. All of us fools fought a long, cruel, bloody and unnecessary war and we not only killed our boys—we killed Faith and Hope."[57] As he surveyed the position of American Negroes, he found them still in bonds after the high hopes of the war. But at least they had gained "Self Knowledge" and "Self Control"; they had learned that there was "no royal road" to their emancipation. "It lies rather in grim, determined, everyday strife."[58]

The Loudest Voice in the Race

During the decade from 1910 to 1920 the balance of power among Negro leaders shifted from the "conservative" to the "radi-

---

* As a matter of fact, the Department of Justice had warned DuBois the previous year against the "tone" of some of the articles in the *Crisis*. As a result of the warning, the Association board added the chairman of the legal committee to the *Crisis* board and ordered all material, "of whatever nature," to be read by him before publication. It stated its policy that during the war the *Crisis* was "to confine itself to facts and to constructive criticism." In a report the following year, the Justice Department cited "Returning Soldiers" in the May 1919 issue as "objectionable," but reported that it had found "nothing of a radical nature" since July, 1919. In 1920 New York's Lusk Committee cited the *Crisis* in a report on revolutionary radicalism, though it certainly selected some surprising editorials as the basis for its charge. See *Congressional Record*, LVIII, part 5, 4303 (August 25, 1919); NAACP board minutes, May 13, 1918, June 10, 1918; *Investigation Activities of the Department of Justice* (66th Congress, 1st Session, *Senate Documents*, XII, No. 153) (Washington 1919), p. 185; New York State Legislature, Report of the Joint Committee Investigating Seditious Activity (Lusk Committee), *Revolutionary Radicalism* (4 vols.; Albany, 1920), II, 1318–21.

cal" wing, and as the most articulate "radical," DuBois stood at
the head of a conquering legion. The terrain had changed: 1915
was not 1895; DuBois had acquired some heavy artillery in the
Crisis and the Association; and the death of Washington gave the
"conservatives" a chance to capitulate gracefully.

In 1895 the typical Negro was a Southern farmer, working a
small acreage on shares, remote from urban influence and proper
educational facilities. Both in law and in practice, the position
of the Negro was slipping. The disfranchisement movement was
spreading that very year from Mississippi to South Carolina, and
an average of 141 Negroes had been lynched each year for the
previous four years. Always the philosopher of the possible, Washington formulated his Atlanta compromise in the context of 1895.
His method of conciliation, along with his annual Tuskegee
conferences and his pilgrimages to farmers' meetings, was designed to soothe racial tensions by allaying white apprehension
of aggressive Negro demands, by guaranteeing a stable Negro labor
force in the South, and by bargaining for security and education
for the Negro.

By 1915 Washington's world had changed and was about to
change even more rapidly. The Negro was leaving the farm and
going to the city; more important, he was moving North in substantial numbers. He was impelled to these migrations both by
the "push" of Southern agriculture and the "pull" of Northern
industry: the failure of Southern farms, because of crop losses,
floods, and the boll weevil, forced tenant farmers to seek new
means of support; industrial opportunities in the North, especially during the war when the abrupt end to immigration cut
off the foreign supply of unskilled labor, invited Southern Negroes to a new life.[59] From 1910 to 1920, when the increase of
Negro population in the South was negligible, the northeastern
states gained by 40 per cent and the north central states by 46 per
cent. The number of Negroes in Detroit multiplied seven times
in the period, and in Chicago, which in 1910 already had a substantial Negro group of 44,000, went up to 109,000. Philadelphia,
one of the great Northern Negro centers, had to find room for
almost 60 per cent more. For this sizable group, Washington's
ideas no longer had meaning: these Negroes had turned their

backs on farming and on handicraft industry, and instead of prudently casting down their buckets where they were, as Washington had suggested, they had snatched their pails and run to a new
life. Gathered in urban ghettoes, especially Northern ghettoes,
they had strength of numbers and the right to vote—powerful
weapons for their own defense. Significantly enough, the protest
against Washington's philosophy had come from educated Northern urban Negroes—DuBois, Trotter, Morgan, Forbes, Chesnutt,
Mrs. Wells-Barnett.

While these changes were occurring, Washington's position in
the race had altered. Respected, even at the height of his power,
as a bearer of "good gifts rather than glad tidings,"[60] he had suffered a stunning defeat in 1912 when his friends were turned out
at the White House, depriving Washington of his position of de-
cisive influence over Negro governmental appointments. Other
elements of control also slipped away: the administration of the
Julius Rosenwald Foundation funds for advancing rural elementary education for Southern Negroes was transferred from the
Tuskegee staff to a separate office of administration in Nashville.
The Negro press, long a bulwark of Washington's influence,
showed signs of kicking over the traces. Harry C. Smith of the
Cleveland *Gazette* had always been independent, but apparently
even Fred Moore of the New York *Age* became recalcitrant in
yielding to the Republican orientation of the Tuskegee machine.
As the decade advanced, metropolitan newspapers could count on
circulation and advertising for the income which ten years before
had come from Tuskegee.

More important, the pressures of discrimination were inducing Washington himself to speak out bluntly. His optimistic
statements in Europe in 1910 and his advice to Negroes as late
at 1914 to "quit thinking" of the parts of the city where they
could not live and beautify the sections in which they did live
showed the persistence of the accommodationist role. But in
1912 Washington protested privately to President Taft against
the drive for "lily white" Republicanism in the South;[61] and in an
article in the *Century* magazine, he answered the question "Is the
Negro Having a Fair Chance?" with a shuffling, but still unmis-

takable No.* A statement for the *New Republic* in 1915, to which Washington's death gave the appearance of a valedictory, condemned segregation as an injustice inviting other injustices, embittering the Negro, and dissolving the moral fiber of the white man[62]—quite a departure from his statement in 1895 that whites and blacks could in social matters be as separate as the fingers of one hand. By the time of his death Washington had moved substantially toward "radicalism."

He also appears to have tempered the force of his attack on DuBois and the "radicals." Writing to Villard in 1911, Washington seemed ready for peace: he spoke of a discussion with Storey in which they planned together for the cooperation of all forces for racial uplift. He added that he had had "several frank talks" with the editor of the New York *Age*, and that the *Age* would modify its tone in speaking of the Association.† Washington also promised to use his influence with other colored papers.[63] This gesture showed Washington's willingness to grapple at least with the advance demands of the "radicals" and, in effect, to bring himself closer to their views.

The changing conditions of Negro life which diminished Washington's power enhanced DuBois's position. As Negroes left the rural South, residence in Northern cities made them receptive to more advanced views. While maintaining their own independence, the Cleveland *Gazette* and the Chicago *Defender* did locally, or in several cities, what the *Crisis* was doing for a national audience, and their soaring constituencies were prepared to absorb uncompromising statements of the Negro position. DuBois caught the significance of these new areas in supporting "radical" thought. After a trip to the West Coast in 1913, he speculated on the notion

* Washington, "Is the Negro Having a Fair Chance?" *Century*, LXXXV, 46–55 (November 1912). On the basis of this article, the Chicago *Defender* assumed that Washington had reversed his previous position and congratulated him on his conversion. November 9, 1912.

† The *Age* had said of a forthcoming Association convention: "The big pow-wow, called the National Association, etc., having pow-wowed out in New York, that is fortunately impatient of whining problem solvers, will be held this year up Boston way, where the people like big talk from empty heads." Reprinted in *Crisis*, II, 16 (May 1911).

that the state of Washington might become a major Negro area, for already the four thousand Negroes in Tacoma and Seattle meant "much more to themselves and the world" than a hundred thousand in Alabama and Georgia because they had education and ambition.[64] (The admiration was reciprocated: the Seattle *Searchlight* and, further south, the Los Angeles *Liberator* and *New Age* gave DuBois unusually favorable press notices.)

The *Crisis* and the Association gave DuBois a springboard to power. In the Negro world DuBois was the symbol of the Association and of its work. White officers came and went. Before 1920, when James Weldon Johnson joined the staff, the Association never had an executive secretary who made his will felt as an independent force. As a result, local branches all over the nation identified the work of the Association with the personality of the vigorous editor whose views they received every month. Unaware of frictions in New York, they saw behind the *Crisis* and the Association a single figure—the austere, uncompromising, scholarly Dr. DuBois, unapproachable and unafraid. Even in 1910, the Cleveland *Gazette* said that "all loyal and intelligent Afro-Americans" recognize DuBois as the real leader of the race.[65] His connection with the NAACP gave him the local contacts useful for national speaking tours. In the seven months ending April, 1911, he reached 21,000 people in fifty-eight lectures. His 1913 trip carried him seven thousand miles in thirty states, and he returned in a glow. Having found the urban Negro (significantly, the *urban* Negro) "pulsing and alive with a new ambition and determinedness," he "thanked God for this the kindliest race on his green earth, for whom I had the privilege of working and to whom I had the pride of belonging."[66]

The mounting circulation of the *Crisis* was a tribute to his influence, and with each gain he set his goals higher. In April 1911, his 10,000 subscribers made him anxious for 25,000; a year later he had reached 22,000, and another three years later 35,000. In 1919, when the Association had seventy thousand members from thirty-four states, the *Crisis* reached its pinnacle of 104,000 subscribers.

DuBois moved confidently into his position of leadership. Indeed he could hardly resist a Messianic interpretation of his own

role. Occasionally he voiced it quite explicitly: his attack on
Indianapolis schools should not produce resentment against him,
he said, for he was not attacking, but merely making "straight the
way of the Lord."[67] In a Thanksgiving proclamation, mimicking
the form of executive declarations, he announced: "We, THE
CRISIS, By the grace of God, Guardian of the Liberties of ten
dark millions in this land and of countless millions over seas,"
established a day of rest and thanksgiving.[68] Aloof from the
throng, DuBois equated his monthly judgments with truth, not
vulnerable to attack from others whom he presumed to be less
informed. With urbane superiority, he urged three unnamed Negro monthlies in 1913 to stop throwing mud, for the Negro had
enough to fight about without engaging in unseemly squabbling.
The following year DuBois engaged in some squabbling of his
own: an almost blanket attack on the whole Negro press as de-
ficient in facts, wretched in English, and soft in the defense of
freedom. Yet when this produced a torrent of rage from insulted
editors, he calmly denied any partisan role: "Here as in so many
other cases THE CRISIS has but frankly voiced current criticism and
the personality of the editor has little to do with it."[69] And, in-
credibly enough, he probably believed it.

The early issues of the *Crisis* gave startling confirmation to the
charge from "conservatives" that DuBois's concern for Negro
rights touched the upper classes more intimately than the lower,
that he was more interested in the few than in the many. Three
striking examples appeared in the first fifteen months of publication. In the opening issue he noted that when discrimination
comes, "it comes with crushing weight upon those other Negroes
to whom the reasons for discrimination do not apply in the slight-
est respect, and thus they are made to bear a double burden."[70]
Sometimes the unstated implications went far beyond what DuBois
meant to say: "To treat all Negroes alike is treating evil as good
and good as evil."[71] In 1912 he published a two-page photograph
of the colored midwinter assembly in Baltimore in which he appeared prominently in a large gathering of Negroes in evening
clothes. Even as DuBois later recognized the rise to social respectability of more and more of his people, he undermined his
praise by patronizing tolerance: "Many a colored man in our day

called to conference with his own and rather dreading the contact
with uncultivated people even though they were of his own blood
has been astonished and deeply gratified at the kind of people
he has met—at the evidence of good manners and thoughtfulness
among his own."[72]

The role of a "brown Brahmin"[73] came as no new departure
for DuBois. The more surprising fact is that from this super-
cilious podium he succeeded in making himself the loudest voice
in the Negro race. The Great Barrington observer and the Boston outsider now had a national forum from which to lash and
encourage his people. Month by month the *Crisis* bestowed praise
or let loose its wrath. A Negro audience was chided for laughing
as Othello strangled Desdemona. Young college graduates were
urged to take on the mantle of leadership slowly lest they lose it
in an overwrap of self-importance—DuBois had changed his views
since his own college days. He gave counsel, unsolicited, to businesses and colleges. The Negro church was a favorite whipping
boy: its undue premium on "finesse and personal influence," he
said, made the way of "upright and businesslike" candidates for
higher positions difficult. Still choked with pretentious, ill-trained
men, many dishonest and otherwise immoral, it needed an overwhelming reform, he said, in order to create a place "where colored men and women of education and energy can work for the
best things regardless of their belief or disbelief in unimportant
dogmas and ancient and outworn creeds."[74] DuBois's estimate of
the bankruptcy of white Christianity made this program seem
especially urgent.

The spectrum of moods from month to month gave variety not
only in the subject matter of the *Crisis*, but even to its point of
view. Yet DuBois's thought remained consistent on one point:
his insistence on full Negro rights left him continuously opposed
to the Tuskegee philosophy of compromise and retreat. While
Washington lived, it would have been difficult to argue that
DuBois had eclipsed him. After DuBois left Atlanta, the contest
went on for five years until Washington's death in 1915, and
finally the balance tipped in DuBois's favor, for Washington's
successor lacked the personal appeal on which the Tuskegee
founder had capitalized.

DuBois's restraint over the five-year period had been, for him, remarkable. On several occasions he prodded Washington a bit, but this was nothing like the monthly peppering that he and his partners on the *Horizon* had delivered. But when Washington finally died in 1915, the *Crisis* obituary gave DuBois the last word in the long battle. He called his dead opponent the greatest leader since Douglass and the most distinguished man to come out of the South since the Civil War. He listed his achievements: alerting the American Negro to the necessity of economic development, emphasizing technical education, paving the way for black-white understanding. But at the same time DuBois punctured each item of praise: Washington never recognized the links between industry and politics, he did not understand the "deeper foundations of human training," and his program for Negro-white relations rested on caste. Negroes acknowledged a debt, DuBois said, but "in stern justice, we must lay on the soul of this man a heavy responsibility for the consummation of Negro disfranchisement, the decline of the Negro college and public school, and the firmer establishment of color caste in this land."[75]

With the death of the chief protagonist, the famous battle lost much of its point. The time had come for reconciliation, especially since so much of the conflict had centered on personality rather than on policy. Washington's position had demanded that he dominate any Negro group in which he took an overt part, and the 1904 meeting had shown that he could keep the initiative from passing even to a well-organized opposition. At his death the "conservatives" were left without a comparable leader; Moton, the new principal of Tuskegee, had to grow into rather than step into the shoes of the master, and, in any case, Moton was moderate in his views.[76] Sensing the moment for tact, DuBois urged the Association's officers to call off a meeting scheduled for Lincoln's birthday, 1916, to avoid the appearance of staging a counterattraction the day after a memorial service that had been arranged in Washington's memory. The same year, with Moton still uncommitted, the Association called a conference of Negro leaders—of all views, from Trotter to Scott—for a frank discussion of the principal Negro goals. Though conducted under the auspices of the Association, the Amenia conference (1916) was carefully dissociated from the NAACP's official policy. With a minimum of oratory it arrived at generally acceptable resolutions: that all forms of education were desirable for the Negro and should be encouraged, that political freedom was necessary to achieve highest development, that Negro advancement needed an organization and the practical working understanding of Negro leaders, and that old controversies were best forgotten. Finally, the conference "realizes the peculiar difficulties . . . in the South. . . . It has learned to understand and respect the good faith, methods and ideals of those who are working for the solution of the problem in various sections of the country."[77] The unanimity of the conference stood as a real victory for DuBois's wing of the race, a victory achieved by respecting necessary methodological differences in the South. Ironically, the resolutions contained little which would have evoked Washington's criticism in the last years of his life.

The achievement of this unity through the initiative of DuBois's organization left him as the new major voice of the race. After America's entry into the war, the extent of his victory became apparent when both the Washington conference of leaders in 1917 and the statement of the thirty-one Negro editors the following year repeated the principal items on DuBois's program and even used his words to express the will of the whole Negro people. DuBois wrote the second manifesto, and may have written the first as well. The program of the "radicals" had now been accepted as the dominant philosophy of the articulate race leaders.

By the end of the decade DuBois could feel confident of his own position. The *Crisis*, though it fell off from its peak postwar circulation, exercised a notable month-to-month influence, especially among Negroes. His position was recognized by the white world as well. His pen was feared, and even quoted in the *Congressional Record*. The New York *Sun* called him the "leading factor in the race question" since Washington's death,[78] and *Current Opinion* said he was regarded as the principal Negro spokesman in America.[79] The "note of lyric intensity" in *The Souls of Black Folk* gained mention in the *Cambridge History of American Literature*.[80] DuBois had reached the pinnacle of his power, exercising the influence which made him worthy to be ranked with Douglass and Washington.

Yet DuBois never became the race's leader, even in the sense in which Washington had filled that role. His voice carried farther than any single contemporary Negro's, but it never could ring with command. It was more like the loudest voice in a large, and sometimes quite dissonant, chorus. In a pluralist society it is doubtful that any single person may be said to be *the* leader. In the same period, who could speak for white America, Wilson or Warren G. Harding? Henry Ford or John Dewey? Though Negro life had not yet approached the variety of the white world, enough differentiation had long since occurred to make impossible the acceptance of one voice for ten millions.

Furthermore, at the moment when DuBois's influence reached its apex, other Negro leaders, even those who shared his general point of view, were competing for power. However much DuBois attempted to keep in touch with Negro life, other "functional leaders" reached the masses of Negroes with more immediacy: in religion, social welfare, politics, and labor, local leaders acquainted with a limited constituency and its problems carried more weight than a distant editor. DuBois's ideas might reach these leaders and affect them, but, to reach the masses, his ideas passed through local filters. DuBois might write the Washington manifesto of the Negro editors, but the measure of its influence depended on its local reception, and that was in the hands of local editors. He might address himself to labor problems, but labor leaders, such as A. Philip Randolph, were to hold the reins on policy. If DuBois set himself against the bulk of Negro leadership, it was he and not they who would fall.

Even within the region of his influence DuBois handicapped himself by righteous, tempestuous arrogance. His self-assured comments on the Negro press and the Negro church needled the precise group through which his influence would be felt. He could be repaid in kind. In 1918, when DuBois was tentatively offered a captaincy the month after his "Close Ranks" editorial, the Washington *Eagle* noted that a storm of protest among Negroes in that city swelled into a "cyclone of wrath and denunciation." Though it wished him well in the Army, the *Eagle* explicitly refused to console him in his time of trouble since he never had any sympathy for those similarly misfortuned.[81] This was the "mingled affection and resentment" against which Spingarn had warned him. The years did not mellow him. In 1925, when Kelly Miller, long on the fringes of "radical" thought, paid a tribute to the Association's work, DuBois said petulantly that he had wondered for years how long it would take Miller to come around to such a statement. The less educated elements of the Negro population might put up with DuBois's arrogance as the concomitant of his intellectual eminence. But men of comparable intelligence and training—Alain Locke was a Rhodes scholar—were not ready to accept DuBois's conception of himself at its face value.

One final reservation must be made. DuBois's ideas carried less influence in the South than outside. Despite the agreement at Amenia, the uncompromising aggressiveness of DuBois's program was unacceptable to Southern mores, and therefore not an expedient technique for Southern Negro leaders. Gunnar Myrdal has documented the extent to which the "peculiar difficulties" in the South color the race's program there.[82] Enormous variations may be hidden under "methodological differences"—after all, both Anglicans and Lutherans are trying to get to heaven.

Even with all these reservations—the inability of one leader to represent the entire race, the competition with other functional leaders, the handicap of his personality, and the inappropriateness of his philosophy in the South—the essential fact remains that no other Negro in 1920 spoke with as much authority or influence. In limited areas a local leader's role might eclipse DuBois's. But no one else could speak so effectively to a national audience.

The irony was that though he spoke with authority, the complexity of Negro progress made a consistent policy all but impossible.

V

PAN-AFRICA AND SOCIALISM

As DuBois lost touch with white American liberals, he sensed other forces at work in the world. Dark-skinned men growing restive under white domination, workers weary of an economic system which gave them slavery and their masters luxury—such discontented groups, he thought, would challenge American and European capitalists. Alert to opportunity, he urged Negroes to attune their aspirations to the struggle of the oppressed everywhere. To lose their self-centered provincialism, he said, Negroes must learn about Indian nationalism, about public ownership of utilities, and about the North Dakota Non-Partisan League; they must become acquainted with the "one new idea of the World War"— the Bolsheviks' notion that only those who work shall vote and eat.[1] As a first step, he said, some people in every colored community should learn French or Spanish. Then to acquaint themselves with the oppressed everywhere, Negroes must travel abroad, or at least send their best minds and most interesting personalities, by public subscription if necessary. Men everywhere were breaking their shackles; the Negro must join them to help and be helped. For more than ten years, this conviction pushed its way to the front of DuBois's thought.

Writing month after month on current events, he did not, of course, abruptly end one period of intellectual change and begin another. He might drop a hint, then wait twenty years before picking it up for further development. His praise of self-sufficient, segregated Negro communities came at the flood tide of the Niagara Movement. He was making advances to socialism in 1907, although in early 1908 he affirmed his attachment to the principles of the Republican party. Africa had an almost mystical fascination for him even on his twenty-fifth birthday, but thirty years elapsed before the fascination produced a program of action. Even as the hope for alliance with workers and colored men dominated his thought in the 1920's, a minor theme, self-sufficiency for the Negro community, was rising in a crescendo which by the early

1930's would make it dominant. Conversely, as new ideas came to prominence after the World War, the old ones did not disappear: the essence of his lecture, "Race Relations in the United States," for the American Academy of Political and Social Science in 1928 could have been written twenty-five years before. His ideas changed constantly, but the major changes came gradually, with a considerable overlap.

Throughout this diversity, however, the failure of the Great Crusade to emancipate the Negro produced one relative constant in DuBois's thought: a sour view of the white world. Once or twice, he wrote in praise of cooperation and courtesy. He respected the efforts of the Commission on Interracial Cooperation at Atlanta. He would on occasion admit that conditions had improved: the search for decent homes in the 1920's was a form of "higher friction," a real advance over the campaign against lynching from 1910 to 1920. But he admitted that he was "one of the greatest sinners" in feeling intense prejudice against white men. Expecting prejudice, he anticipated it and, he admitted quite frankly, perhaps even caused it.[2] As he grew older, a white face was "a sign of inherent distrust and suspicion."[3] In *Darkwater*, published in 1921, he wrote, almost as a boast, that since an incident in Nashville during his college days, he had never knowingly raised his hat to a Southern white woman. Occasionally he could laugh at prejudice, as when a steamship line listed him as Colonel DuBois because it misinterpreted its agent's symbol for colored. But more often his reaction to white America took the form of sardonic humor, and even of cruelty. He listed ten clichés recommended to white students in Southern colleges as "quite sufficient for all possible discussions of the race problem."[*] He took what he himself called a "mean, almost criminal and utterly indefensible joy" in hearing of a mob that lynched a white man. "We're sorry we're glad," he said. "We wish we were big enough to be dissolved in

---

[*] *Crisis*, XXIV, 107 (July 1922). These are the ten phrases: "1. The Southerner is the Negro's Best Friend. 2. Slavery was Beneficial to the Negro. 3. The Races will Never Mix. 4. All Negro Leaders Are Mulattoes. 5. The Place for the Negro is in the South. 6. I Love My Black Mammy. 7. Do you want your sister to marry a Nigger? 8. Do not disturb the friendly relations between the races. 9. The Negro must be kept in his place. 10. Lynching is the defense of Southern womanhood."

tears. . . . But we're not; we're just plain tickled at this blood-soaked land."[4] If more needed saying, he said it in *Darkwater*:

> The white world's vermin and filth:
> All the dirt of London,
> All the scum of New York;
> Valiant despoilers of women
> And conquerors of unarmed men;
> Shameless breeders of bastards,
> Drunk with the greed of gold,
> Baiting their blood-stained hooks
> With cant for the souls of the simple;
> Bearing the white man's burden
> Of liquor and lust and lies! . . .
> I hate them, Oh!
> I hate them well,
> I hate them, Christ!
> As I hate hell!
> If I were God
> I'd sound their knell
> This day!*

The scholarly world did not escape his scorn. In the course of his research for *Black Reconstruction*, he condemned the persistent historical tradition about the Civil War which whitewashed the South and smeared the Negro with lies. The conspiracy was so strong, he said, that the occasional book with a contrary thesis —such as Charles E. Russell's *Blaine of Maine*—was invariably railed at or ignored. The conclusions of Edward B. Reuter's

---

* *Darkwater: Voices from Within the Veil* (New York, 1921), pp. 53–54. In reviewing *Darkwater* for the *Nation*, Villard concluded his essay with these words: "If time can but mellow him; if the personal bitterness which so often mars his work can disappear; if a truer Christian spirit than now shines through his writings can guide him; if he desists from his recent dangerous advocacy of meeting force with force, and can bring himself to walk more in the manner of the Nazarene—the possibilities of his future usefulness seem great indeed." *Nation*, CX, 727 (May 29, 1920). Privately Villard wrote: "I think I pity Dr. DuBois almost more than any man in America, but I do not want to work with him; nor do I believe in his editing of *The Crisis*." In this letter Villard refused to review *Darkwater* for the *Crisis*. If the review were unfavorable, he feared, it would subject him to abuse and attack by Dr. DuBois: "I have had experience and I know" (Villard to Jessie Fauset, February 24, 1920, Villard papers).

widely read book, *The American Race Problem*, fit in with "dominating prejudices, correctly pessimistic," DuBois noted, because Reuter was not a human being and was not acquainted with human beings.[5] Six years after praising Thomas J. Woofter's study, *The Basis of Racial Adjustment*, as singularly fair and thoughtful, DuBois coined a new term, "Woofterism," to describe the technique of a later work: a collection of facts, themselves accurate, which tells only part of the truth.[6] In all this rancor, the Association escaped—and escaped with praise—only because in its membership, its board of directors, and its executive officers, the Negro had come to predominate.

A few select friends knew another DuBois, the jovial DuBois whom Johnson had seen at Atlanta, happy and witty among his own. Once in a while DuBois lifted the Veil long enough for white America to see—and be ashamed. White men, he said in a column in the *Crisis* in 1923, have the "impudence" to think that Negroes gaze hungrily at white society, yearning to enter. Where could white men find a group of people "more utterly beautiful, and filled with the joy of living and sweetness of spirit" than the "coterie," a group of upper-class New York Negroes with whom he had just spent an evening? "They were black, brown, yellow, orange, mauve, pink, and white; their hair wavered from gold to midnight in waves and curls and masses of every conceivable intricacy. Their limbs curved and moved with a grace well nigh inimitable and their soft and laughing eyes and voices held a fineness of love and beauty that I doubt if any group of white folks ever surpasses. I sat and feasted my eyes."[7]

The "coterie" might see a genial DuBois; his secretaries might too. But not white men: even Spingarn saw only the formal exterior. Even when DuBois showed his genial side to white America, it was to show "blithering idiots" how little he wanted "their drab and artificial company."[8]

No Response from Colored Peoples

Years of observation had made DuBois responsive to the problems of oppressed peoples everywhere. Abroad for graduate work, he had seen the Poles divided under three alien rulers. In *The Souls of Black Folk* he had spoken of the color line as the basic problem of the twentieth century. In 1907 he had predicted a day of reckoning for Belgian overlords in the Congo. He had joined in American anti-imperialist sentiment and had exulted in retrospect about yellow Japan's victory over white Russia. In 1912 China's revolution had appeared to him as a symbol of the world's enlarged color problem, and after a lecture tour to the West Coast the following year he had regretted that colored Californians did not recognize the Japanese as protagonists in the "silly but awful" world-wide fight of color against color.

DuBois's view of imperialism as the prime cause of the World War convinced him that peace could come only by removing the cause of war, that is, by granting land, modern education, and home rule to native populations in a "new peace and new democracy of all races: a great humanity of equal man." To help in that transformation, awakened Japanese, awakening Chinese, and young European-trained Indians were already working. Who would speak for Africa? Who better, DuBois asked, than the grandchildren of the African slaves, especially the ten million blacks in the United States?[9]

For about a decade after World War I, DuBois sought to provide that voice. After the peace conference in 1919, he withdrew his earlier approval of England and predicted that unless England cut free her dependencies, the world would have to meet a tyranny "as portentous as the God-defying dreams of Germany."[10] At the beginning of 1920, he welcomed insurrections in Jamaica, the new "Ethiopia of the Isles," as a response to the same sentiments which were giving rise to Pan-Africanism.[11] In April 1920, he condemned the Secretary of the Navy, Josephus Daniels, for "illegal and unjust seizure" of Haiti, and set "Freedom for Haiti" as the greatest single question in the presidential election that fall.[12] When Franklin D. Roosevelt, the Assistant Secretary, spoke of holding Haiti's vote in the League and of having written the Haitian constitution himself, DuBois hoped for the disappearance of the "impossible Wilson and his lackeys."[13] America's hold on the Philippines, Haiti, and Puerto Rico made him think that perhaps it was "safer inside a beast and next his vitals than out-

side and under his hands and feet."[14] Only the Negro vote of
America, he warned, could prevent Liberian concessions to the
Firestone Plantations Company from leading to "all the hell that
white imperialism has perpetrated heretofore in Africa and Asia."[15]
He told the 1930 convention of the Association that the end of
extraterritoriality in China, Egypt's political independence and
India's demand for it, and Ethiopia's entry into the League formed
part of that world movement of colored men to which the Association's program was related.[16]

DuBois's concern for Africa was not merely a tactical gambit.
A deep racial kinship bound him to the Dark Continent. He
revered the "essence of Africa," its "initial strife" which had begun
all culture: the development of the village unit in religion, industry, and government; the realization of beauty in folklore,
sculpture, and music.[17] He cited Franz Boas, the white anthro-
pologist, as his authority for saying that Africa possessed the art
of smelting iron while Europe was still using stone tools.[18] Africa
could teach the West the great truth that efficiency and happiness
did not necessarily go together in modern culture. Though Africa
might be behind in specific cultural areas, he argued, its over-all
line of development was contemporary, not prehistoric. Africa
needed modern communication systems, but its knowledge of
human souls had been deepened by its isolation. Its children were
courteous and happy, alien to the impudence on Broadway, or
Lenox Avenue.[19]

His sentiment for Africa needed no empirical evidence: "The
spell of Africa is upon me. The ancient witchery of her medicine
is burning my drowsy, dreamy blood. This is not a country, it
is a world—a universe of itself and for itself, a thing Different,
Immense, Menacing, Alluring. It is a great black bosom where
the Spirit longs to die. It is a life so burning, so fire encircled that
one bursts with terrible soul inflaming life. One longs to leap
against the sun, and then calls, like some great hand of fate, the
slow, silent, crushing power of almighty sleep—of Silence, of im-
movable Power beyond, within, around. Then comes the calm.
The dreamless beat of midday stillness, at dusk, at dawn, at noon,
always. . . . Africa is the Spiritual Frontier of human kind."[20]
This was the language of enchantment, even of mysticism. Nor

was it a casual fancy. Almost a decade later he affirmed that in
some respects the Negro was drawn closer to dark men outside
America than to his white fellow citizens.[21]

If ten million American Negroes were to speak for this Africa,
DuBois, as the recognized leader of the American Negro, was prepared to speak for ten million American Negroes. In 1917 he suggested a new African state formed from German possessions and
from the Belgian Congo; the following year he wanted to include,
if possible, Uganda, French Equatorial Africa, Angola, and Mo-
zambique. Before the peace conference assembled, the Association
had adopted DuBois's platform, which proposed three goals: first,
internationalization of the former German colonies looking toward partial self-government under the "guidance of organized
civilization"; second, creation of a program for these colonies
based on public opinion as represented by the chiefs and intelligent Negroes in German Africa, other educated African Negroes,
American Negroes, and educated Negroes in the West Indies and
South America, all of whom would speak through a proposed Pan-
African conference; third, the merging of modern cultural advantages—science, education, communications, philanthropy — with
the "curiously efficient African institutions of local self-government through the family and the tribe." Such a program, the platform concluded, would inspire a "last great crusade for humanity.
With Africa redeemed, Asia would be safe and Europe indeed
triumphant."[22]

When the Association sent DuBois to Europe on the press ship
"Orizaba," primarily to collect material for a Negro war history,
it also authorized his call for a "Pan-African Congress" to stimu-
late popular support for this program. DuBois's statement in the
Crisis that such a congress would "focus the attention of the peace
delegates and the civilized world on the just claims of the Negro
everywhere" suggested that the agitation of the African question
could cut two ways: it could help the natives, to be sure, but it
could also provide a forum for Negro propaganda.[23]

DuBois's Pan-African movement, however, did not aim at political or geographical unity. He specifically disavowed separatist
sentiment: Negro Americans were Americans, indeed few Americans were more indigenous. When Marcus Garvey built up mass

Negro support for a back-to-Africa movement in the early 1920's, DuBois, after two years of hot-and-cold appraisal of various aspects of the movement, totally rejected its "spiritual bankruptcy and futility."[24] He likened Pan-Africanism to Zionism, "the centralization of race effort and the recognition of a racial fount."[25]

The Pan-African movement that emerged in Paris[26] was a curious international revival of the Niagara Movement: a handful of self-appointed spokesmen challenged a staggering problem by passing resolutions. Even the principal techniques were similar: the periodic conferences to recodify the platform, refresh personal contacts, and exchange enthusiasm and information, and the manifestoes designed to rally colored support and to convert white opinion. In the end the congresses accomplished, if anything, less than Niagara.

Faced by European indifference tinged with hostility, the first congress met in Paris in February, 1919, through the influence of Blaise Diagne, a Senegalese member of the Chamber of Deputies who badgered Premier Georges Clemenceau for permission. Fifty-seven delegates—including sixteen Americans, twenty West Indians, and only twelve Africans—attended the meeting. *Le Temps* of Paris reported some of its resolutions, which on the whole endorsed DuBois's program for Africa, although they were somewhat less specific on the retention of tribal organization.

DuBois returned home exuberant. The congress, he said, had passed resolutions applauded by the press of the world despite the inclusion of a paragraph on racial equality; representatives of the conference had been heard by Clemenceau, by David Lloyd George, the British Prime Minister, by Colonel Edward M. House, Wilson's confidential adviser, and by ministers of Belgium and Portugal. He added that "if the Negroes of the world could have maintained in Paris during the entire sitting of the Peace Conference a central headquarters with experts, clerks, and helpers, they could have settled the future of Africa at a cost of less than $10,000."[27] As this statement suggests, the Pan-African congresses were to be for DuBois an exercise in self-deception.

DuBois continued to organize congresses all through the 1920's, but with no more success. At the 1921 sessions, when DuBois proposed the same program, he faced not only white indifference but

the opposition of a segment of those very native blacks whom he
wanted to redeem. The London meeting passed strong resolutions.
But when the congress reconvened in Brussels, DuBois's reading
of the London resolutions led to cries of "Bolshevik," and in Paris
Diagne, who put loyalty to France above allegiance to race, refused to join in condemnation of French colonial power. This
led DuBois to warn of the "crying danger" to black France—that
educated leaders of the blacks would take part in the industrial
robbery of Africa rather than lead the masses to education and
culture. Jessie Fauset's account of the congress in the *Crisis* condemned Diagne as guilty of "bad faith," and sometime after,
DuBois expressed regret that educated colored Frenchmen held
to the "ordinary European attitude of the classes toward the
masses."[28] The congress could, however, record one specific
achievement: it asked the League of Nations to include a section
on Negro labor in its International Bureau of Labor, and this
section was later set up.

The second congress brought DuBois some favorable European
press notices, but beyond that, very little. He listed three accomplishments of the congress,[29] but under examination they prove
to have little substance. First, he said, the congress brought into
personal contact educated Negroes "of the calibre that might lead
black men to emancipation in the modern world." This face-to-
face meeting was undoubtedly pleasant, and perhaps stimulating,
but the attitude of Diagne, certainly a prominent spokesman for
educated Negro opinion, gave little hope for a unified world race
movement. The high caliber of conversation simply gave heat to
disagreement. Second, DuBois went on, the congress uncovered
more points of agreement than of disagreement. Yet agreement
on general principles meant little if their application resulted in
violent and irreconcilable differences. Third, DuBois said, the
congress agreed on the need for further meetings and for a strengthened permanent organization. The alternatives to this agreement
were either an admission of total failure or a claim of total success.
Agreement to further meetings came cheap.

After the second congress, the Pan-African movement had little
besides DuBois's enthusiasm to sustain it. Even at the second
meeting, European newspapers spoke of DuBois as the "soul" of

the conference. The Association had already refused to under-write the expenses of congress meetings. By the time of the next conference, in 1923, three Americans—DuBois, Rayford W. Logan, and Ida Gibbs Hunt—made up the executive committee, and only thirteen countries, compared with thirty in 1921, were represented. As France gave further recognition to its black citizens, the French delegation became increasingly inactive. Ever hopeful, DuBois reported for the *New Republic* that the congresses had "weathered a natural crisis of growth in a time of universal industrial crisis."[30] The fourth congress, which met in New York in 1927 and which DuBois hoped would "settle for all time the question as to whether Negroes are to lead in the rise of Africa or whether they must always and everywhere follow the guidance of white folk," repeated the substance of previous platforms; it was somewhat more specific in opposing American intervention in Haiti. One new note was added: "We thank the Soviet Government of Russia for its liberal atittude toward the colored races and for the help which it has extended to them from time to time."[31] (DuBois, the general chairman, had visited Russia two years before.) The fifth congress, scheduled for 1929 or 1930, did not meet.

DuBois blamed the failure of Pan-Africa on the opposition of governments, the failure of philanthropy, a deliberate boycott by white men determined to act for Africa without consulting black men, and the lack of understanding by educated and think-ing Negroes. He also thought that the excesses of Garvey's Back-to-Africa drive muddied the waters of Pan-Africanism beyond re-covery.

Actually there was another cause as well. DuBois limited his vision in international politics to white exploitation of colored peoples. He assumed that the foreign policies of white nations were directed primarily toward imperial gains, and that colored peoples thought primarily in terms of anti-imperialism. Certain corollaries followed: Since "white" was the criterion of evil, "col-ored" (especially "black") became the criterion of good. Since colored peoples were oppressed, they could not be oppressors. Indeed, since imperialism was white exploitation of colored labor based on the assumption of racial superiority, colored nations could not be imperialistic. The trouble lay in DuBois's premise, for many forces other than imperialism motivated the foreign offices of white nations, and, even more important, the color line was not a monomania among all colored peoples. If this racial chauvinism had been the dominating force in world politics, DuBois might have headed an epic movement, and American Negroes would have had a billion new allies, perhaps even a billion followers. As it was, his captivity within his own racial philosophy blocked his recognition that a colored man could act from nationalistic or economic, as well as racial, motives.

This captivity may have been voluntary and tactical—the call to arms of a militant leader for whom clearly defined moral issues were more urgent than many-sided analysis. If so, it was scarcely a success, for few heard his call to action.

DuBois's chronicle of the expansion of Japanese power suggests the extent to which racial ideas colored his view of world events. After the Washington Conference in 1922, he wrote that the "Anglo-Saxon Entente" which had attempted to drive a wedge between Japan and China had failed, and that "the day is in sight when they will present an unbroken front to the aggression of the whites."[32] Five years later he noted regretfully that although Japan was the logical leader of Asia, she ranked among China's oppressors. He hoped that the current financial crisis would bring a change and align Japan with the colored races "where she belongs."[33] In 1929 he reported that the refusal by the League of Nations to endorse racial equality had helped Japan realize that its future lay in the development of the colored world. He assumed that as the national government of China grew in strength and the basis of democracy in Japan broadened, mutual understanding would increase because much of their antagonism had been fostered by Europe, especially by Great Britain.[34] After the Manchurian incident, he warned Japan and China against white arbitration: "Did you ever hear of the Spider who arbitrated between two flies on the basis of World Peace?"[35] His analysis of the invasion was typical: Japan was seizing the "dismembered parts of China nearest to her" before European nations could stop her. Japan knew that China could not have been saved from Europe and America unless Japan "made Manchuria Asiatic by force." England, France, and the United States, he said, cry shame on

Japan, whom they forced to choose between militarism and suicide.[36] When no other argument carried conviction, he fell back on the defense that what was right for England in the nineteenth century was right for Japan in the twentieth.[37] In 1933 he was "extremely pleased" by the report of an Ethiopian concession of sixteen million acres of land for Japanese exploitation. Here was a "rapprochement between Asia and Africa which foreshadows closer union between yellow and black people"; it was a thrust at the "impossible domination of one mad race."[38] DuBois could not escape this notion of the unity of the colored races. In a fantasy he wrote when Haile Selassie was crowned emperor of Ethiopia, Japan and Turkey were silent as Europe and America angled for financial control, but their eyes gleamed as Abyssinian horsemen, wild mountaineers with machine guns and modern rifles, rode past the emperor. DuBois was sure that he could perceive Japan's pleasure in seeing this armed strength in colored hands.[39]

DuBois's myopia toward Liberia was both more incorrigible and more understandable. Here were real kinfolk—not only were they black men, but the ruling class in Liberia was descended from American Negroes repatriated in the midnineteenth century. Like DuBois, whose family had been free since the Revolution, Liberia's rulers could look back to families of freemen for at least three generations. DuBois reported, with evident sympathy, that Liberians were bitter when "descendants of slaves who meekly submitted to their slavery presume to ladle out loads of obvious advice to people who for a hundred tremendous years have dared to be free."[40] DuBois had established personal contact with them. As envoy extraordinary and minister plenipotentiary, by designation of President Calvin Coolidge, to the inauguration of President C. D. B. King of Liberia, he said he was sure that President Coolidge would want him to hail the ability of Negroes to rule in Africa as a "great and encouraging reenforcement" in the great battle against color caste in America.[41] But when Liberia was guilty of practices that would have outraged his Negro sensibilities if performed by white nations, DuBois was tolerant and understanding. When an American-born Liberian was burned to death in a building as he was being arrested, DuBois excused the action as being merely the result of bad judgment. Several years later he acknowledged the existence of slavery in Liberia and urged its abolition, but for the time being he tolerated "pawning"—a form of compulsory labor little removed from slavery—as a way of raising the ignorant into an educated status; and anyway, he added, the British had only just released two hundred thousand slaves in Sierra Leone. When he continued to defend Liberia even after George S. Schuyler published *Slaves Today*, a vigorous attack on Liberian rulers, Schuyler commented that DuBois's "belligerent and commendable Negrophilism" warped his vision.[42]

The judgment contained a good deal of truth. DuBois had trapped himself in what Margaret Halsey has called the "myth of the Wonderful Oppressed"[43]—the notion that because a group suffers from persecution, it automatically encompasses all virtue and is purged of all faults. Blinded by this myth, DuBois had to explain away Japanese imperialism and Liberian pawning, or at least to excuse them as the products of white exploitation. This process gave DuBois a coherent point of view, but it led him some distance from the real world of the 1920's.

But not from the real world of the 1940's and after. Ironically, his vision of racial nationalism led nowhere after the first World War but was vividly prophetic of the world created by the second World War. His analysis of Japan's attack on China was way off the mark; but his view of Japan as the leader of the colored world in revolt against its white overlords was stunningly confirmed by Japan's success in interpreting the second World War to Asians as a campaign to win "Asia for the Asiatics." The postwar movements for independence in India, Indochina, and Indonesia—to mention only three of the revolts against three of the principal colonial powers—took place in a nationalistic atmosphere remarkably similar to the one DuBois sought to encourage. He was wrong about the time, but he was right about the locations and about the intensity of the revolutions. Diagne held aloof from DuBois's charges against French colonialism; would Diagne's constituency have elected him to the Chamber of Deputies forty years later? The cooperation between Ethiopia and Japan seemed anomalous in 1933; after the Asian-African conference at Bandung in 1955, who had the last laugh, DuBois or his critics? DuBois was a generation ahead of his time. The leaders of at least two of the new

African nations, Eastern Nigeria and Ghana, have publicly made explicit acknowledgment of their debt to DuBois's inspiration. DuBois never surrendered his interest in Pan-Africanism. There was always the hope that a turn in world events would provide the Negro with an ally from another part of the nonwhite world. In the meantime, the association of the American Negro with other rising colored peoples might help to impress white America with the urgency of racial justice. In any case, the existence of an American spokesman for the darker races was itself an indication of American Negro progress: the Negro had come far enough to supply leadership for the whole colored world. DuBois visualized himself at the apex of this double movement—in the United States and in the world—directing both campaigns from his editorial chair at the *Crisis*. If the Pan-African movement had caught fire, DuBois might have stepped from his position with the Association into the higher role of director of the Pan-African movement and editor of its proposed journal, the international *Black Review*. Jan Christian Smuts of the Union of South Africa apparently sensed a self-serving aspect in DuBois's Pan-African activities, for, challenged by DuBois to a joint debate in New York City in 1930, Smuts replied archly that he had not come to America "to advertise Dr. DuBois."[44]

The collapse of the planned fifth congress in 1929 before it met closed one door of Negro amelioration for the next decade and a half. As DuBois said, "We are not yet Pan-African-minded."[45] Thereafter he continued to follow the activities of the nonwhite world as an observer rather than as an organizer, as a propagandist looking for new clubs with which to bludgeon the white world— and white America—rather than as a prospective leader.

Rebuff From White Workers and Their Spokesmen

"The African Roots of the War" had pointed to a second possible ally, the great masses of labor excluded from the fruits of modern industry. "Democratic despotism" might ally some workers with their employers by sharing both political power and the economic spoils wrenched from backward nations and from colonies, but the employers were senior partners and kept labor in line with the carrot and the stick: the benefits of state socialism and public threats of black competition. Furthermore, not all workers shared in the spoils. Below the aristocracy of skilled labor, an ignorant unskilled mass, including the overwhelming majority of Negro workers, threatened to revolt from its oppressed position.

In the next decade DuBois added a new dimension to this analysis. In an essay significantly entitled "The Negro Mind Reaches Out," he warned that the color problem and the labor problem were two sides of the same tangle. White labor, ignorant, and captivated by its share of the profits of exploitation, served the capitalists' purposes by discriminating against black workers; white capitalists used the antipathy between the two races to control the entire world labor supply. Colored labor knew this; white workers were only beginning to see it dimly. As colored men grew in organization and intelligence—he pointed hopefully to a quickened India, the South African and West African congresses, the Pan-African Movement, the Association, a rising China, a risen Japan—they would counter the ceaseless propaganda of inferiority with a "gradual but inevitable spread of knowledge."[46]

Because DuBois saw socialism as the voice of these depressed masses, black and white, he welcomed the spread of Socialist power in the postwar world. Just after the war he was delighted because he thought he saw Socialists ruling in Russia, Germany, Czechoslovakia, Italy, France, and Belgium; Socialists were strong, he said, in every other leading nation except Japan and the United States. Even in America their strength was growing rapidly, he said, despite the attempt to "fasten on Socialism every crazy scheme that any radical ever advocated."[47] The English general strike of 1926 was a "second step behind Russia for realizing industrial democracy in the world."[48] DuBois's definition of socialism—"the assertion by the community of its right to control business and industry; the denial of the old assumption that public business can ever be a private enterprise"[49]—was so broad that it was a meager month when he could not find some evidence of its advance somewhere.

Receptivity to socialism was not, of course, a new departure for DuBois. While still at Atlanta, he had endorsed many socialist

views in the *Horizon*, and in 1911 he had briefly joined New York
Local No. 1 of the Socialist party. What was new was his specific
attempt to link Negro advancement with the world-wide socialist
current.

The revolution in Russia in the name of socialism made Du-
Bois watch the Soviet Union. Though excited by the Bolsheviks,
he was not ready to jump too quickly. In the course of an Association membership drive in 1921, he mocked the "horde of scoun-
drels and bubble-blowers, ready to conquer Africa, join the Russian revolution, and vote in the Kingdom of God tomorrow."[50]
Two months later, in response to a sharp protest from Claude Mc-
Kay, a frequent contributor to the radical magazine, the *Liberator*,
DuBois refined his position. He denied that he had intentionally
sneered at the Russian revolution; it might be the greatest event
of two centuries and its leaders the "most unselfish prophets." But
the *Crisis* could not be sure, and despite DuBois's sympathy with
the Third International's statement on race, he saw that the immediate problem of the American Negro was in America. Two
questions concerned him: What form would socialism take? Du-
Bois held back from embracing either state socialism or the dictatorship of the proletariat. The larger question was more disturbing to him: Could the colored world trust the white working
classes, especially when history gave so little assurance that workers would welcome Negroes when Negroes accepted the workers'
program? American Socialists discriminated against Negroes, he
continued, and European Socialists against Asiatics; the AFL discriminated against black workers, and the "unlettered and suppressed masses of white workers" lacked the clearness of thought
and the sense of brotherhood necessary for joint action. Until
labor solidarity was accepted on both sides of the color line, he
said, Negroes should espouse the cause of white labor only when
it did not conflict with their own interests. Black men must have
bread. If white workers drove Negroes from their jobs, Negroes
had no choice but to accept indecent wages at the danger of being
branded scabs. Until this situation clarified, it was foolish, he
concluded, to give up the Association's program "to join a revolution which we do not at present understand."[51]

From this starting point—incidentally, one of his clearest

pieces of expository writing—DuBois debated the possibility of an alliance with world socialism as led by the new Communist government in Russia. Gradually all his doubts were resolved in favor of Russia. In 1922 he called it "the most amazing and most hopeful phenomenon" in the postwar period.[52] The following year he published two articles by McKay on "Soviet Russia and the Negro" which argued that while the growing influence of American capitalism in Europe increased anti-Negro propaganda, the American Negro's kinship to the rising proletariat in Russia became ever more apparent. After the tenth anniversary of the Bolshevik coup against the Kerensky government, he criticized the American press for not giving the "Russian experiment" a decent hearing; he hoped that the past ten years had been only the first decade of a Bolshevik century.[53] The previous year, 1926, two months in the land of the Soviets had impressed him deeply.

An anonymous American of Russian descent, whom he characterized in his autobiography as probably a "clandestine" agent of the "communist dictatorship," paid for the trip, accepting DuBois's condition that he obligate himself to no particular conclusion or course of action and that he be allowed to see the situation with his own eyes.* The Russian Foreign Bureau made no overt signs of directing his trip, and his interpreter, he told his *Crisis* readers, was known to him before he went to Russia. Like Lincoln Steffens, who reported that he had "seen the future; and it works," DuBois returned to the United States in awe. "I stand in astonishment and wonder at the revelation of Russia that has come to me. I may be partially deceived and half-informed. But if what I have seen with my own eyes and heard with my ears in Russia is Bolshevism, I am a Bolshevik."[54] The following year he explained further: if Bolshevik means people striving with partial success to organize industry for public service rather than for private profit, he was proud to fit the description. Russian education aimed at creating workingmen of skill and intelligence and at preparing future rulers; "this is what the Russian Dictatorship of the Proletariat means." Since the workers were not yet sufficiently skilled

* William A. Nolan suggests that paid trips to Russia may have been arranged for other Negroes as well. He mentions Claude McKay as an example. Nolan, *Communism versus the Negro* (Chicago, 1951), p. 27.

or intelligent to assume their responsibilities, he went on, the Communist party was "directing" them until they could assume power on their own. This, he commented, paralleled the United States where "we have elaborate and many-sided arrangements for ruling the rulers." The difference was that Russia was "really preparing future rulers"; the United States was not. He noted limitations: the hotels lacked the "*savoir-faire*" of London and Paris, some dissidents resented the regime, dishonest officials and inefficient politicians held back the revolution. As long as organized capital in America, England, France, and Germany used every weapon to crush Russia, he said, only a minimum of free discussion and democratic difference of opinion could be tolerated in the Soviet Union. But Russia was creating a "workingman's psychology," and the real question in Russia was: "Can you make the worker and not the millionaire the center of modern power and culture? If you can, the Russian Revolution will sweep the world."[55]

Like Pan-Africa, Russia seemed to offer a glimpse of the future, especially because of its "workingman's psychology" and its freedom from a color line. Negatively, Russia gained by the hatred of those white powers which bore the special brunt of DuBois's disapproval.

Yet the paragon existed only at a distance. However right Russia might be, the acid test of the Negro's alliance with world socialism would take place in America, more specifically among American workers. In America DuBois's hopes floundered, because white labor, skilled and unskilled, stayed in the vanguard of discrimination against the Negro, third parties remained equivocal, and even the American spokesmen for the Bolshevik dictatorship failed to convince DuBois that they would support the Negro worker if they had any chance of capturing the white.

In 1919, even as the Association reported that trade unions seemed to be relaxing their ban on Negroes, DuBois warned that they did so only because Negroes would underbid them if they did not. As if to give point to his words, Negroes played a major role in breaking the steel strike in the same year. His tolerance of white labor was wearing thin: in 1921 he wished defeat and smashed unions to the railroad workers, the "head and foot" of the "con-

temptible monopoly of labor" which openly excluded any disad-
vantaged group—including Jews and Italians as well as Negroes—
and built "their own high wages and exclusive privileges on the
starvation, unemployment, sickness and destitution of the common
laborer."[56] Only when unions surrendered "monopoly and aristocracy as methods of social uplift" could a unified labor movement achieve justice for all.[57] The fact that white laborers discriminated with less conscious intent than their imperialist masters, DuBois said, diminished their guilt; but no longer was he
willing to excuse them from responsibility.

In working for labor solidarity, DuBois opposed influential
spokesmen within the race. The Negro Press Association in 1924
vigorously condemned unionism at almost the same time that the
Association was making formal overtures to the AFL for a joint
interracial labor commission to propagandize against disunion and
prejudice. Kelly Miller, a perennial spokesman for moderation,
admitted that logic placed Negro labor more in line with white
labor than with capital, but insisted that Negro opportunities lay
outside the organized labor movement. The National Urban
League even engaged in strikebreaking.

For a while DuBois held stubbornly to his hopes, returning
always to the basic theme that unions had given workers whatever
they had. William Green's "reactionary" control was no excuse
for blanket condemnation. But continued rebuffs frayed his hopes.
A perfunctory reply from the AFL ended the Association's pro-
posal for a joint commission, and union walls seemed as impene-
trable as ever. In DuBois's mind the war between hope and
stubborn fact led him into a belief in miracles, almost an attitude
of *credo quia absurdum*. Negro and white workers, separated by
the "width of the world," hated and despised each other, lynched
and murdered body and soul, he said. "And yet—and yet, stranger
things have happened under the sun than understanding between
those who were born blind."[58] There the matter rested. For five
years the *Crisis* remained silent on organized labor except to support A. Philip Randolph's successful organization of the Pullman
car porters, to set the record straight on the Association's advances
to the AFL, and to cite William Doak, president of the Brother-

hood of Railway Trainmen, as a terse explanation of the Negro's hostility to organized labor. Then in May, 1930, a comment tucked in the letter column of the *Crisis* told of the end of the dream. After advocating the trade-union movement for years, DuBois announced that he was through with it "until the trade union movement stands heartily and unequivocally at the side of Negro workers."[59] It was a tragic moment—after ten years of trying to ally himself with the future, he was no further along than Kelly Miller and Booker T. Washington.

DuBois's hopes for a third party as a spokesman for socialism hit the same obstacle. Socialist fervor and a strong affection for trade unionism did not, to be sure, necessarily go hand in hand. Still, since any third party with a hope of success needed overwhelming labor support, the very attempt to appeal to organized labor—and to unorganized labor as well, in all probability—vetoed a forthright stand on the Negro question. But DuBois's despair of the two major parties forced him to try: "May God write us down as asses if ever again we are found putting our trust in either the Republican or the Democratic Parties."[60] In 1924 the Progressive party's platform put DuBois in a dilemma: as a Socialist he welcomed the most advanced proposals ever offered by a serious national party; as a "race man," how could he ignore the party's silence on Negro rights? Even Wilson had spoken brave words before the election. How could one be sure of Robert M. LaFollette, the Progressive's presidential candidate? There was no certainty, but before the election LaFollette condemned the Klan and promised to free Haiti. The gesture won DuBois's vote, especially since he apparently was permitted to write the statement on the Negro in the party's political handbook.

Four years later he urged a protest vote for *any* third-party candidate. He recognized that no third party had a chance. While the South cast a solid electoral bloc for the Democrats, a third party, in order to win, had to capture most of the North, and if it failed to do so, but succeeded in winning some electoral votes, it handed the election to the Democrats, the "least liberal of the two old parties." But he could not abandon his planning. The month after the 1928 election, following a campaign so abusive in its racist appeal that colored leaders of all persuasions joined to protest in an "Appeal to America,"* DuBois told his readers that the Negro must in the future throw his political weight to a single third party. The Negro's price was enforcement of the war amendments, federal supervision of federal elections, allotment of seats in the House of Representatives on the basis of votes cast rather than on population, socialization of wealth and income to protect the interests of the poor laborer against the political power of the rich investor. To this banner he hoped to rally other politically "homeless" groups—women, liberal white Southerners, organized labor, farmers, pacifists.[61] Bunching up unhappy minorities gave this program a deceptive plausibility, but it could not overcome two fatal obstacles: First, DuBois's pre-election analysis of the difficulties facing a third party shrewdly and accurately appraised the facts, and no third party could escape the same fatal political logic. Herbert Hoover's inroads into the South, DuBois admitted, offered no support for progressive hopes; it had occurred because of religious bigotry, fear of the Negro, hatred of the domination of the Democratic party by New York, and prohibition. The Southern electoral votes, he said himself, could always be counted on to "keep reaction and plutocracy in power." Second, within fifteen months of this analysis, DuBois's repudiation of the AFL, still the backbone of organized labor, left little substance to his hope for a rapprochement with labor inside a third party. Labor's influence had kept LaFollette from making a firm statement on the Negro. Organized labor had not become friendlier in the intervening years.

The answer forced upon DuBois was that national politics did

* The "Appeal" complained that the Negro had been slandered more in this campaign than in any since the Civil War, and, what was more alarming, the calumny had drawn no rebuke from the leading candidates and spokesmen for both parties, and from few religious leaders and social reformers. The Negro leaders asked for a public repudiation of the campaign by white America, especially by the candidates and the church. "Is there in truth any issue in this campaign, either religious tolerance, liquor, water power, tariff or farm relief, that touches in weight the transcendent and fundamental question of the open, loyal and unchallenged recognition of the essential humanity of twelve million Americans who happen to be dark skinned?"

not offer a way out for the Negro. His programs for national political action were as fruitless as his hopes for labor solidarity.

The self-appointed spokesmen for world socialism in the United States, the Communist party, inspired little more hope. As a friend of Russia, DuBois defended the right of American Communists to study and to sympathize with Russian and English socialism. He opened the pages of the *Crisis* to McKay and to Will Herberg, managing editor of the *Revolutionary Age*, a weekly Communist paper. He commented on the striking parallels—more apparent to him than to others—between the Association's program and that of the American Negro Labor Congress. But he choked on American Communists' ideology and tactics.

At the beginning of the decade DuBois warned that the ready-made Marxist analysis of the class struggle could not be indiscriminately applied to Negro America. Although Negroes were theoretically part of the world proletariat, the exploited class of cheap laborers, practically they were not recognized by the white proletariat. In fact, Negroes were victims of "physical oppression, social ostracism, economic exclusion and personal hatred on the part of the white proletariat." Furthermore, the small group of affluent Negroes—Negro capitalists—had achieved their wealth through manual toil and were "never physically or mentally separated from the toilers." He warned the Negro to look carefully at proletarian movements before joining them.[62]

The Communists' attack on the Association and on DuBois himself for the next fifteen years did little to endear them to him. One Communist writer dismissed the Association as "an organization resembling in its pattern the ancient abolition society and breathing the spirit of white philanthropists in benign collaboration with colored bishops and lawyers, and, of course, the white Republican politician[s] of the border states and other parts where Negroes can vote and where anti-lynching speeches can be made."[63] Rejecting reformist activities, the Communist party listed DuBois among the "betrayers of the Negro people" and included him in a list of faithful followers of Booker T. Washington who were attempting "to chain the Negro people to the chariot of American imperialism, to perpetuate and build further the distrust and antagonism toward white workers of the country."[64] In 1932 the *New Masses* published a cartoon of the "Scottsboro Legal Lynching" in which white bosses hid behind a mask of the Association while they lynched the nine Scottsboro boys.[65] Later the *Daily Worker* joined the chorus: "Negro bourgeois reformism" as represented by the Association was the "main social bulwark of imperialist Jim Crow reaction among the Negro masses."[66]

DuBois persistently rejected the Communist characterization of the Association as an upper-class minority opposed to the workers' stand. The charge, he said, was a criticism not of what had happened, but of "what might be expected to happen according to the formula of Marxian socialism." The Communists, he said, were captives of a rigid ideology created with little direct knowledge of the Negro problem in America; as a result, they were blinded to the facts of the Negro's true condition in America.[67] DuBois was not willing to attach himself to this blind ideology: while aligning himself with those who sought to correct the abuses of capitalism, he wanted to "preserve its tremendous possibilities for good," and he did not believe in violence as the method of reform.[68]

The Communists' bull-in-the-china-shop intervention in the Scottsboro case provoked DuBois into a long denunciation of them. In 1931 nine Negro youths were arrested in Alabama, charged with raping two white girls. The National Association went to their defense, but the accused turned their cases over to the International Labor Defense, a Communist group. The Communists then organized mass meetings all over the country to protest the indictment and trial and made the case an international issue. The nine were convicted. In the course of successive appeals, the Communists withdrew, and a committee headed by Allan Knight Chalmers and supported by the Association took charge. Defending the Association's orderly method of "hiring bourgeois lawyers and appealing to bourgeois judges," DuBois, in a *Crisis* editorial condemned the sensational tactics of the Communists: "If the Communists want these boys murdered, then their tactics of threatening judges and yelling for mass action on the part of white Southern workers is calculated to insure this."

He asserted—and in this opinion he was not alone*—that the Communists' ultimate object was to make the case a center of agitation to prove that nothing less than the Communist program could emancipate the Negro. To accomplish this, they were intensifying white prejudices, terrifying white capitalists, and leaving the Negro helpless. While white workers were in a lynching mood and capitalists were terrified of mob violence, he said, "the Communists, seizing leadership of the poorest and most ignorant blacks, head them toward inevitable slaughter and jail-slavery, while they [the Communists] hide safely in Chattanooga and Harlem. American Negroes do not propose to be the shock troops of the Communist Revolution, driven out in front to death, cruelty and humiliation in order to win victories for white workers. They are picking no chestnuts from the fire, neither for capital nor white labor."

Moving from this particular attack to the party's general onslaught against the Association, DuBois denounced as "fantastic" the Communist charge that Negro Americans had a petit bourgeoisie which dominated a helpless proletariat and then surrendered to white profiteers. That notion, he said, had died with Booker T. Washington. Actually, he went on, there were few Negro capitalists of any size, and while a full-fledged capitalist system might develop, no such tendency was then apparent, especially in the Association the leaders of which shared a "common cause" with the lowest members of the race. As a matter of fact, he continued, the foresight and sacrifice of educated Negro Americans, "and these alone," had saved the American freedman from annihilation and degradation. The "quintessence and final expression" of this leadership was the Association, which "deserves from Russia something better than a kick in the back from the young jackasses who are leading Communism in America today."

The attempt by Socialists and Communists to unite Negroes with white labor was a "red rag to a bull," he continued, for the Negro had had no honest advocate in the ranks of white labor

* A restrained statement of this view appears in Allan K. Chalmers, *They Shall Be Free* (New York, 1951), especially p. 202. Somewhat more heat is generated in Irving Stone, *Clarence Darrow for the Defense* (Garden City, 1943), p. 497.

since Terence Powderly. (DuBois's repudiation of the AFL had come sixteen months before.) The more intellectual white workers became and the higher they rose, the more determined they became to hold the Negro down: "Whatever ideals white labor today strives for in America, it would surrender nearly every one before it would recognize the Negro as a man." Norman Thomas became "vague and incoherent" only when he touched upon the black man; his attitude was that if the emancipation of white labor did not help the Negro, let him remain in slavery. The Communists, DuBois said, younger, largely of foreign extraction, bound by an alien ideology, ignored the "dead blank wall" of white prejudice and blamed Negroes for their failure to back white unionism, forgetting that not labor but American wealth had educated forty thousand Negro leaders and had opened up a million jobs to them in the previous ten years. Though white capital had done this for profit, the Negro would have been crazy to have refused the gift. DuBois said that the Negro still saw that the real interest of white and black labor was identical, but he declined to invite black labor to be the "sacrificial goat" when white labor did not share that recognition. "Negroes owe much to white labor," DuBois observed, "but it is not all, or mostly, on the credit side of the ledger." He pointed out grimly that it was white proletarians who were trying to lynch the Scottsboro boys.

After this analysis—by far the longest editorial which DuBois ever published in the *Crisis*—what was left of his alliance with world socialism? At the end of the editorial, DuBois picked up the pieces: the Negro—that is, DuBois—was sympathetic to Russia, "hopeful for its ultimate success in establishing a Socialist state"; sympathetic to the American workingman's attempt to secure democratic control of industry; certain that the Negro's interests were with labor. But he would accept no ground except equality with white labor, and the first steps had to come from white labor.[69]

As the depression deepened after 1929, prospects for unity dimmed. After black construction workers were forced off the job on the new British embassy in Washington by a direct appeal from white workers to Ramsey MacDonald, the former British Labourite Prime Minister, DuBois sneered: "Black brothers, how would you welcome a dictatorship of this proletariat?"[70] Little indeed remained of his alliance with the rising tide of socialism except his uninterrupted respect for the Soviet Union, and a fresh acquaintance—perhaps his initial first-hand acquaintance—with the writings of Karl Marx.* (He conducted a seminar, "Karl Marx and the Negro," on a visiting professorship at Atlanta in 1933.) White labor had rebuffed the Negro. National political action had yielded little and showed no prospect of yielding more: neither major party had adapted itself to the Negro vote, and no third party could wrest enough votes to make a dent in what he regarded as a jointly held monopoly. Socialists had nothing special to offer to the Negro; and, as DuBois said, with "American communism led by a group of pitiable mental equipment, who give no thought to the intricacies of the American situation, the vertical and horizontal divisions of the American working classes; and who plan simply to raise hell on any and all occasions, with Negroes as shock troops,—these offer in reality nothing to us ex-

* DuBois had not previously read Marx at any length. At Atlanta, a list of books he recommended to *Horizon* readers (*Horizon*, Vol. 1, No. 6, June 1907) suggests that he was drawing his socialist inspiration from American sources such as John Spargo, Jack London, Jane Addams, W. J. Ghent, Richard T. Ely, Henry George, and Jacob Riis. Though he mentioned Marx along with twenty or thirty other economists in a college essay (XYZ [pseud.], "A Constructive Critique of Wage Theory: An Essay on the Present State of Economic Theory in Regard to Wages," 1891, Harvard Archives), and though he made passing reference to him in an occasional essay or editorial, these references do not appear to have been based on firsthand knowledge. And, in all candor, it must be said that even his essay "Marxism and the Negro Problem" (*Crisis*, XL, 103-4, 118 [May 1933]) had the once-over-lightly form of an undigested summary of *Capital* and the *Communist Manifesto*.

Sterling D. Spero, in reviewing *Black Reconstruction*, seems to share this view: he speaks of the book as the "child of this strange intellectual marriage" between racial loyalty and Marx, and he implies that DuBois read Marx for the first time as an old man. (Sterling D. Spero, "The Negro's Role," *Nation*, CXL, 108-9 [July 24, 1935].) George Streator, who was managing editor of the *Crisis* under DuBois and was DuBois's candidate for editor of the *Crisis* after the break in 1934, wrote in 1941 that he doubted that "with all his talents DuBois ever did more than turn to those vivid pages where Marx hammered with telling effect against the English society that gained its wealth through the African slave trade. All the rest to DuBois was just so much Hegel, and I doubt that DuBois did much to Hegel when he was a student in Germany" (George Streator, "A Negro Scholar," *Commonweal*, XXXIV, 31-34 (May 2, 1941).

cept social equality in jail."[71] The depression made the Negro's position even more difficult, for in a traditional pattern of last hired, first fired, the Negro felt acutely the impact of unemployment, which rose from less than three million in 1929 to more than eleven million in 1932.

DuBois could not escape the conviction that American Negro policy had to take a new direction. An alliance with the colored races of the world had produced a few unheeded manifestoes; when the Pan-African Congress failed to meet in 1929, even the manifestoes stopped. And though the Russian revolution might point the way to a future industrial order based on justice for all workingmen, the color line gave it little immediate relevance in the United States.

His people facing disaster, DuBois turned to the only allies on whom he felt the Negro could count: his twelve million Negro fellow Americans.

NEGRO CHAUVINISM

Racial exclusiveness had tinted DuBois's thought since boyhood. Now in the late 1920's and the 1930's, after rebuffs from white liberals, colored people elsewhere, and the Socialist movement made him despair of alliances with outsiders, DuBois retreated. He drew back into the protective shell of his own race until he found himself accepting, even welcoming, a largely self-sufficient Negro culture stretching across state and class lines. The virus of racial nationalism appeared earliest in his comments on literature and the arts and then spread to politics, to education, and, most important, to business and industry.

The "Jim Crow" editorial in 1919[1] had shown him at the crossroads: since a separate Negro America inside America was impractical, the relations between the races had to be based on knowledge and on the sympathy of long contact; on the other hand, if Negroes were to develop their own gifts and powers not only to fight prejudice successfully but to unite "for ideals higher than the world has realized in art and industry and social life," then they must work together to build a "new and great Negro ethos." By 1934 the quest for a separate Negro ethos and culture dominated his thought.

The new spirit appeared almost everywhere in DuBois's work: in asserting that the work of the Association was "our work and we must do it";[2] in demanding Negro aid for black men accused of crimes; even in accepting the word "Negro," not only as "etymologically and phonetically good," but as the symbol of "all those spiritual ideals, those inner bonds, those group ideals and forward strivings of this mighty army of 12 million. . . . They are our most precious heritage."[3]

For DuBois, those "inner bonds" became ever stronger and more comprehensive.

An Autonomous Negro Community

At the dawn of the postwar Negro literary renaissance—the "New Negro" movement—DuBois warned that the white man's caricature of Negroes had sunk into their half-conscious thought so deeply that "we shun in print and paint that which we love in life." These "thought-chains and inchoate soul-shrinkings," blinding Negroes to the beauty of a black skin, he said, made them instinctively abhor portraits in darker shades.[4] What was worse, the Negro public shrank from the truth about itself; Negro writers deliberately passed over their own experience lest they draw criticism on the race and rebuke to themselves. When white writers, such as Eugene O'Neill in *The Emperor Jones*, caught the Negro temper, he said, they became "great benefactors" as forerunners of Negro artists yet unseen. But even O'Neill, Dubois reported, drew condemnation from educated Negroes; his soul "must be lame with the enthusiasm of the blows rained upon him."[5] This squeamishness, DuBois argued, was nonsense, for the Negro stood secure enough in accomplishment to "lend the whole stern human truth to the transforming hand of the artist." DuBois was sure that it was better in the long run to face the "Truth of Art" than to bend art to propaganda.[6]

Development of art and appreciation of beauty were, DuBois insisted, the peculiar mission of the modern Negro. Even as early as 1913 he had spoken of the Negro as "primarily an artist." The race which had held the tropics at bay had gained thereby a sensitivity to sound and color, he said; the Negro blood in the Pharaohs had accounted for much of Egyptian art, and Negroes had brought music to America. Economic stress and bitter persecution still consumed the "leisure and poise for which literature calls," yet DuBois was sure that Negroes had an abundance of material and that they were developing the technical skill to use it.[7]

By the 1920's they were ready, and DuBois set aside modest claims for recognition in order to claim a monopoly: "We are the only American artists." Even in the "dull brain of America," he added later, the Negro was clearly becoming the "most virile future force in this land, certainly in art, probably in economics, and

possibly in science." Even the age of Pericles and the fifteenth
century, he believed, could not compete with the fertility of the
Negroes' material—"tragedy such as the modern world has seldom
surpassed, comedy of exquisite depth and appeal, new and unusual
beauty in contrast, color and tone."[8]

More than a critic, DuBois contributed directly to this creative
renaissance. He published the *Brownies' Book,* a monthly magazine for children which lasted two years. A short story on a cross-
racial theme had appeared in *The Souls of Black Folk;* the *Horizon* had published several of his short stories and poems; he occasionally used the Christmas or Easter issue of the *Crisis* for parables toying with traditional Christian stories, which he adapted to
the color line. He produced a pageant, "The Star of Ethiopia," in
1913, and revived it successfully with a cast of three hundred and
fifty actors in 1925. Delighted and encouraged, he hailed this new
art form in which education and race pride could deck themselves.
Race pride was certainly served, for this tale of the "eldest and
strongest races of mankind" made quite a list of the Negro's gifts
to the world: the gifts of iron, of freedom and laughter, of hope
and faith and humility. Together with the Semite, the Negro had
made Egypt the first nation of the world, DuBois asserted, and the
Negro by himself had spread Mohammedanism over half the world.
After such glories, George Washington's recognition, in a later
pageant, of Phyllis Wheatley, Benjamin Bannecker, and Crispus
Attucks—Negroes from the period of the Revolution—seemed tame
indeed. But the pageant as an art form, unable to compete with
the mounting popularity of the movies, did not flourish.

All DuBois's fiction dealt with the Negro problem, and for
the most part it appeared in publications he controlled rather than
in magazines of general circulation. In the potpourri published
as *Darkwater* in 1921, he reprinted some selections from his earlier
work along with some new fiction and poems. The quality of his
work varies, but never achieves distinction. "The Litany at Atlanta" undoubtedly packs a wallop, but much of its strength comes
from the shock of sacrilege—"Surely Thou, too, art not white, O
Lord, a pale, bloodless, heartless thing"—rather than from any
striking or new association of words or ideas. Indeed the same

may be said of his parables, one of which comes close to a burlesque of Christ's life. The plot of his stories can usually create suspense: when a Negro man and a white woman think themselves the sole survivors of a collision of the earth with a comet, the reader is impelled to read further. (As it turned out, they were wrong.) But his people rarely move, they are pushed. With predictable monotony, the actions of his characters depend on social position: the white bishop is pompous and worldly, the young Southerner urbane and haughty, the poor white Southern woman merciful but unheeded; and the mysterious dark-hued stranger usually turns out to be some variant on the "Jesus Christ in Texas" who appears in one of his short stories.

DuBois's first novel, *The Quest of the Silver Fleece*, published in 1911, however, had received less critical attention than it deserved. In form a love story, it traces the courtship of Blessed Alwyn and Zora, the daughter of a Negro conjurer. The story begins in an Alabama school run by a Wellesley graduate, but before the wedding day, it works its way through white high society, colored political machinations in Republican Washington, and a lynching party back in Alabama. The schoolmarm's Northern industrialist family makes an alliance with Southern crop-lien landlords, both groups depending on starved, ignorant Negro labor forced into competition with poor white farmers. The tension becomes even greater when the industrialist's factory is transferred to the South; the competition between black and white workers leads to the lynching. But by the last page the tension is eased, the Bourbon patriarch endows the school for Negroes, and Bles and Zora are married.

As even this brief outline suggests, *The Quest of the Silver Fleece*, gave DuBois a chance to work over a wide variety of Negro problems. In his autobiography he characterized the book as "really an economic study of some merit," but actually its range made it much more. Its economic theme was certainly important —the image of Northern capital and Southern planters plotting for profit wrung from a peasantry enslaved by the crop-lien system. However, other themes, related to economics yet important in themselves, appeared: the thirst for knowledge among young Negroes; the persistent slave mentality among older ones; the reactionary ignorance of Negro preachers; the Southerners' picture of the Negroes as the "lowest-down, orneriest . . . good-for-nothing loafers" who had to be cared for like children; and the Negroes' reciprocal picture of the Southerners as cruel fools duped by cunning black men who "fly right through them." The easy seduction of Negro women by white men provided the motive for moving the story to Washington. The presence of the school for Negroes allowed DuBois to retell his analysis of the Negro industrial schools supported by white men desperate to keep a tractable labor supply. The trip to Washington opened the door for criticism of the alliance between white industry and politics. Even more revealing was the picture of Negro politicians serving the Republicans in exchange for governmental jobs and of Negro newspapers yielding to Republican domination at the bidding of an influential—unnamed—Negro.

William S. Braithwaite's review compared the *Quest* favorably with Frank Norris's trilogy on wheat. The comparison was not without merit, and the book also suggested the documentary range of Theodore Dreiser's trilogy, in scope if not in technique, for by the end of the book, most of the "radical" Negro's picture of America had been forced into its pages. At the same time, however, Blessed, Zora, and the schoolmarm were shuttled back and forth to Washington like river ferries, and accidental meetings and a death-bed conversion borrowed the dramatic license of melodrama. Much of the conversation was stilted—"Bles, almost thou persuadest me to be a fool"—and white society matrons talked in caricature. But one character at least, Zora, developed within the book, changing from an elflike girl into a mature, self-possessed woman. If not enough to justify the novel as a work of art, she at least raised it steps above an economic tract.

Not so much could be said for DuBois's second novel, *Dark Princess*, which appeared in 1928 after almost a decade of the Negro literary renaissance. Published as a "romance," presumably to license its diffuseness, it won DuBois's enduring affection—"my favorite book," he calls it—without evoking any comparable enthusiasm elsewhere.

Matthew Towns, a Negro barred from an obstetrics course es-

sential to complete his medical degree at a New York City university, goes to Europe to finish his work. There, having fallen
in with an international conspiracy of the colored elite seeking to
replace the dominant world-wide white aristocracy, he accepts a
commission to survey the American Negro's competence to join in
such a project. As part of his research, he becomes a Pullman
porter, but soon goes to jail for his share in an attempt to dynamite
a special Ku Klux Klan train on its way to a Chicago convention.
When paroled through political influence, he enters politics himself. Seduced by political ambition, he is about to sell out to the
local machine when Kautilya, Maharanee of Bwodpur and a leader
of the world colored group, appears, converts him to an honest
career as a laborer, and finally marries him, thus giving Bwodpur
its heir.

Towns's varied career—medical student, traveler, Pullman porter, secret diplomat for the colored races, politician, and finally
laborer—gave DuBois a chance to cover two continents; and his
reports to the colored conspirators gave a plausible excuse for
including what Alain Locke called "rich deposits of sociology."[9]
DuBois's handling of the material ranged from photographic real-
ism so precise that a reviewer for the Chicago Defender obligingly
identified one character,[10] to personal fantasy so obtuse as to be
meaningful only to the author. For example, he dedicated the
novel "To Her High Loveliness, TITANIA XXVII, by her own grace
Queen of Fairie, Commander of the Bath; Grand Medallion of
Merit; Litterarum Humanarum Doctor, Fidei Extensor, etc. etc.,
of whose faith and fond affection this romance was surely born."
He constantly paraded his cultural breadth by irrelevant references to Croce, Proust, Picasso. For the most part, his characters
were static spokesmen for particular points of view. Towns was
an exception: he was so volatile that he could move from the
idealism of pan-colored revolution to the cynicism of Chicago
machine politics and back again with scarcely a ruffle to his psyche.
Kautilya herself changed from maharanee to waitress and later to
union organizer with equal aplomb. Here again, however, a
woman almost came to life: Sara Andrews, the secretary to a
Negro politician and for a while Towns's wife, who bears some re-
semblance to Sadie Burke in Robert Penn Warren's All the King's

Men. But a single character, a minor one at that, was hardly enough to redeem the novel. Except for DuBois's surprisingly sensitive treatment of the Negro common laborer, the same material was handled in a more satisfactory way in the pages of the *Crisis.*

In his poetry and novels, DuBois's style fell between sociological prose and vague grandiloquence. In the field of *belles lettres,* he strained so hard for effect that, at its extreme, he ended up with the exalted nonsense of his dedication in *Dark Princess,* or with labored, obtuse metaphors—"the panting blindness of our ears." His characters talked in set speeches, and his plots went beyond even the limits of fantasy. The tone of his writing changed constantly as the sociologist interrupted the novelist.

DuBois's real strength was in the emotional prose of propaganda. For example, he concluded *The Gift of Black Folk,* a hastily written survey of the Negro's contribution to America, published in 1924, with this passage:

> Listen to the Winds, O God the Reader, that wail across the whipcords stretched taut on broken human hearts; listen to the Bones, the bare bleached bones of slaves, that line the lanes of Seven Seas and beat eternal tom-toms on the forests of the laboring deep; listen to the Blood, the cold thick blood that spills its filth across the fields and flowers of the Free; listen to the Souls that wing and thrill and weep and scream and sob and sing above it all. What shall these things mean, O God the Reader? You know. You know.[11]

The reference to the "laboring deep" remains cloudy, but the remainder of the passage has unmistakable strength: its metaphors stand up to a second reading, its oblique historical references draw skillfully on the material of the previous pages, and the appeal to the readers' emotions makes the volume a useful servant of propaganda as well as a handbook of analysis. This passage could be matched by "Of the Passing of the First Born" in *The Souls of Black Folk* in which the pathos inherent in the loss of DuBois's only son carries emotional intensity without an overlay of highly charged words. Most of his best writing appeared in his monthly editorials in which he clothed his facts with wit, paradox, indignation, and a call to arms. His editorials, with their brevity, luster, and punch, are his lasting literary monument.

It was in commentary on Negro artists rather than in his own creative output that DuBois found his true role in the Negro renaissance. He was proud of the achievement of Florence Talbert, Marian Anderson, and Roland Hayes, who, he said, had better voices than the Metropolitan Opera could buy, but were kept out by racial prejudice. He greeted Richard Harrison's portrayal of De Lawd in Marc Connelly's *Green Pastures* as a triumph of interpretation, and praised Nathaniel Dett's "epoch-making" choir at Hampton. In 1926 and 1927 he worked hard to get the Krigwa Players' Little Negro Theater on the boards as a going concern. He organized the *Crisis* book club, awarded the annual DuBois literary prizes, and goaded his readers into helping Negro poets. He pledged the support of the *Crisis* to Negro writers, prudently adding some time later that this did not commit him to "cheap flattery and misspent kindliness"[12]—never for DuBois a real danger. By 1926 he reported in the *Encyclopædia Britannica* that the extent of the Negro renaissance was apparent in the fifteen volumes of the *Crisis*, a "compendium of occurrences, thoughts and expression among American Negroes," in which, he said with some exaggeration, most of the newer Negro writers had first published their work.

As he watched the Negro renaissance—both what Negro writers were turning out and what white authors were saying about life behind the Veil—his pride in the race turned him away from the "Truth of Art"; he finally announced bluntly: "I do not care a damn for any art that is not used for propaganda."[13] Month after month he reviewed books which portrayed the dregs of Negro society, and the total picture affronted his image of the race. Carl Van Vechten's *Nigger Heaven* he condemned as an insult to "the hospitality of black folk," for both the title and the novel's sordid material amounted to caricature, even though every event described might have happened.[14] The atmosphere of Julia Peterkin's *Black April*, a "veritable cesspool of incest, adultery, fighting and poverty," he said, illustrated a fact about white Americans: they thrill to read "gleefully and with sparkling eyes" about "some poor devils" with whom they had no sympathy, all the while affirming a stand for freedom of art.[15] Even DuBose Heyward's *Porgy*, which, DuBois acknowledged, portrayed the black man with unusual sympathy and understanding, could not escape damning criticism because it limited its vision to the lowest level of Negro society. When Heyward followed with *Mamba's Daughters*, the roots of DuBois's complaint became clearer: the book was excellent, artistically successful, he said, but he did not like it— partly because he recoiled at feeling the hands of strangers on the heart of his problem, partly because he resented the portrayal of the "debauched tenth" as characteristic of the whole race. Catfish Alley and the "trite old tale" of the white Charleston aristocracy did not meet DuBois's demand for a picture of "real, ordinary people."[16]

This discomfort in alien hands extended even to McKay, a West Indian. *Home to Harlem* was dismissed as a resourceful attempt "to paint drunkenness, fighting, lascivious sexual promiscuity and utter absence of restraint" with bright color and without a "well-conceived plot." Only its variations on the theme of the loveliness of the colored skin gave it a glimpse of beauty.[17] *Banjo* three years later, DuBois said, was better; but "with the characteristic reaction of the West Indian who does not thoroughly know his America," McKay failed to understand the upper-class Negro and pictured Negro "society" as a cheap imitation of its white counterpart.[18]

As the hardest blow of all, even American Negro writers gave themselves over to what Redding calls "brooding pessimism." Of Rudolph Fisher's *Walls of Jericho*, DuBois could only say that it was a step up from Van Vechten and McKay. Taylor Gordon's *Born To Be* was the "dregs," its rambling, anecdotal style unworthy of the name of literature. Gordon was simply "cutting up for white folks," even criticizing Dett's choir as a "sop to his [Gordon's] literary gods."[19] When Arna Bontemps published *God Sends Sunday*, DuBois dismissed it as a mate to *Home To Harlem*, and then turned criticism into sentimentality: "Somehow, I cannot fail to see the open, fine, brown face of Bontemps himself. I know of his comely wife and I can imagine a mother and father for each of these, who were at least striving and ambitious. I read with ever recurring wonder Bontemps' noble 'Nocturne at Bethesda' ";[20] but here in this novel, nothing of that other side is hinted.* Occasionally guarded praise broke into the chorus of condemnation. He greeted George Schuyler's *Black No More* as rollicking good fun (an astonishing judgment, incidentally, since the book is a vicious caricature of Negro leadership—"the humor scalds like burning tar," Redding says[21]—and the portrait of Du-Bois as Dr. Agamemnon Shakespeare Beard was hardly meant as flattery). Walter White's *Fire in the Flint* won approval for its narrative and for the strength of its propaganda against white Klansmen and black "pussyfooters," even though its characters were "labelled figures on a chess board."[22] Though DuBois said he did not understand some of Jean Toomer's *Cane* and complained of its "objective" emotion, he praised the book's "strange flashes of power, their numerous messages and numberless reasons for being."[23] Among the poets, Langston Hughes and Countee Cullen won approval. Hughes's "Song for a Banjo" had "the exquisite abandon of a new day," DuBois said, and in the "Ballad of the Brown Girl," Cullen "achieves eight lyric lines that are as true as life itself."[24] But the occasional snippets of praise merely highlighted DuBois's disapproval of the direction which the Negro renaissance was taking. As he drew more into his own race, he became insistent that the Negro artist serve not art, but morale. A doctrine was emerging in his analysis: the white world wanted to hear only about the dregs of Negro society. White writers like Van Vechten and Heyward played up to this taste, and by 1931 DuBois was ready to imply that Connelly intended *Green Pastures* as slapstick. Negro writers followed suit because white publishers would accept nothing else.† If American magazines devoted an issue to the American Negro, DuBois noted in 1925, *Harper's* and *Scribner's* would turn it into a minstrel show, the *Atlantic* and *Century* would make a "timid adventure in spiritual swamps,"

---

* More than twenty years later Bontemps gave a striking indication of the impact of DuBois's reviews: "I know by heart that review of *God Sends Sunday*, and I have forgiven it completely because the motive was pure." Bontemps to author, April 28, 1953.

† James Weldon Johnson promptly rejected this contention as "not in consonance with the facts," pointing out, to the contrary, what had been published in the preceding years. Johnson, "Negro Authors and White Publishers," *Crisis*, XXXVI, 229 (July 1929).

and most of the rest would undertake a "statistical study in rape."[25]
What was worse, Negro artists were themselves reproducing the
white man's picture of the Negro, not just to attract a publisher,
but because their own vision was still blurred by the lenses of
white America. The Negro artist, he told the 1926 Association
convention, must turn his art into conscious propaganda, because
for the Negro, though not for white America, art and propaganda
were unified by their common devotion to truth, beauty, and
right.[26] When Locke argued in *The New Negro* for beauty, not
propaganda, as the goal, DuBois twitted him by saying that his
own book disproved his point: *The New Negro* was full of propaganda. Locke's thesis pushed too far would turn the renaissance
into decadence, DuBois warned, because if the Negro ignored
the fight and tried to do pretty things, he would kill the beauty in
his art. DuBois's prescription for short stories in the *Crisis* showed
the gulf between him and Locke: he demanded fiction "clear,
realistic and frank, and yet fiction which shows the possible if not
the actual triumph of good and true and beautiful things. We do
not want stories which picture Negro blood as a crime calling for
lynching and suicide. We are quite fed up with filth and de-
featism."[27]

In short, DuBois was calling for a literature of uplift in the
genteel tradition. The date of this last statement, 1931, was itself
significant: as DuBois moved toward the ideal of a closed Negro
civilization, he expected all Negro artists to serve as its heralds,
vibrant and hopeful. They had to serve the race, and he would
judge them on a racial, not on an artistic, standard. The review
which rejected *Mamba's Daughters* endorsed the pretty innocuous-
ness of Jessie Fauset's *Plum Bun*. Such standards were racial, not
literary, and all DuBois's platitudes about truth, beauty, and right
could not conceal his insistence that Negro artists refuse to submit
to the "passing fancy of the really unimportant critics and publishers"[28] and that they use their talent in the direct service of the race.
Down that road lay cultural separatism.

By its nature, political activity did not lend itself to the same
type of separatism. Long habit, nurtured by decades of emotional

struggle for the ballot as a symbol of deliverance, made it difficult
to abandon hope in national politics, and, as a matter of fact,
DuBois did support Warren G. Harding in 1920, LaFollette in
1924, and any third-party candidate in 1928. Though he supported no candidate in 1932, he vigorously repudiated Herbert C.
Hoover because of an "unanswerable" list of charges against his
administration: lily whitism, race hatred in the 1928 campaign,
the failure to make any significant Negro appointments, policy in
Haiti and Liberia, a forgotten Negro general. Yet as early as 1920,
DuBois had urged Negroes to concentrate on Congress and state
legislatures, on aldermen rather than on presidential hopefuls.
They must work not through parties, but through individual
politicians and through friendly local political machines. Long-
range campaigns for Negro *advancement* through politics no
longer had relevance, he told an Association convention in 1928;
in the face of the postwar reaction, the rule of an oligarchy, the
Negro had to struggle to consolidate what he had already won.

The two political devices which DuBois endorsed indicated
the distance he had traveled since the days of *The Philadelphia
Negro*. For the South, where the white primary effectively ruled
out the Negro's vote on candidates, he approved the action of the
Atlanta branch of the Association in solidly voting down munici-
pal bond issues for new schools until it received assurances of an
equitable share for colored children. After pursuing this campaign for three years, Atlanta Negroes were rewarded with the
Booker T. Washington High School and four elementary schools.

In the North, DuBois frankly accepted a Negro alliance with
corrupt political machines. Faced with a choice between corruption and segregation, was the Negro to blame, DuBois asked, "if
he votes for the worst, when it is only in this sort of alliance that
he can receive the semblance of decent treatment?"[29] In coupling
the Negro with Tammany Hall in New York City and with the
Thompson machine in Chicago, DuBois was sacrificing the uncertain friendship of white liberals for concrete political gains.
The exchange did not please one's ethical sense, but it paid off.
The twenty or more Negro policemen on New York City's force
in 1922 gave visible evidence of racial gains won by support of the

local Democratic party; could the American intelligentsia outbid Tammany? Even after Charles F. Murphy no longer headed Tammany, the alliance continued, gradually admitting Negroes into the inner circle of leadership in accordance with the traditional pattern of assimilating immigrant and minority groups into full political partnership. In 1925, DuBois did an article for the *Crisis* on Frederick Q. Morton, Exeter- and Harvard-trained Democratic boss of Harlem and a Civil Service commissioner. Morton, DuBois reported, "is neither demi-god nor demagogue. He is just a strong, skillful, courageous man, cynical surely, but honest and sound; and he deserves respect."[30] When Mayor James J. Walker faced a tough campaign for reelection in 1929, DuBois rewarded Tammany for its recognition of Negroes by supporting Walker even though DuBois regarded Norman Thomas as the better candidate. Walker had paid off; Thomas would not commit himself.

When Chicago's singularly unsavory Republican machine sent Oscar DePriest to Congress in 1928—the first Negro Representative from the North and the first Negro in Congress in almost a generation—DuBois refused to stand on high moral ground. DePriest stood for Negro causes: the War Amendments, the Dyer antilynching bill, the abolition of Jim Crow in interstate commerce. DuBois wished that DePriest also stood for the destruction of a political alliance with big business, bootleggers, and criminals, but he "acknowledges with bowed head" that if DePriest had stood for virtue, he would never have been elected, for the only organized interests which would support a Negro for Congress were allied with the rule of crime and wealth. For the Negro, DePriest's racial platform was more vital than prohibition, crime, and privilege.

By 1932, politics thus offered concessions, not solutions. Gone were the whole issues of the *Horizon* devoted to careful appraisals of presidential candidates—an alderman meant more to New York's Negroes than a President: a President might denounce lynching, as Harding did, but an alderman could logroll for new schools, better street lighting, more appointments in the school system and on the police force. Teaspoons of patronage to an increasingly isolated Negro community in payment for political support represented the practical limit of white largesse.

A field as important as education could not safely be left outside the racial community. Despite the long tradition of white philanthropy, of which DuBois had repeatedly been a beneficiary, he determined that only Negro support and control of their own universities could make them effective servants of the new Negro life.

Just after the war, DuBois devoted an editorial to the decrease of "White Charity" to Negro colleges. Part of the loss, he said, was unavoidable, since the older fortunes were declining, and the new rich were ignorant of charity. But some white men were withholding contributions because they had exaggerated notions of Negro wealth or, even worse, because they resented insistent Negro demands. DuBois warned this latter group that nothing bound poor Negroes to the rich and powerful except strings of charity; could the rich afford to break that leash? "Is it wise for white folk to forget that no amount of almsgiving on their part will half repay the 300 years of unpaid toil and the fifty years of serfdom by which the black man has piled up wealth and comfort for white America?" On the other hand, he added, the sooner the Negro rose above charity, the sooner he would be free.[31] Shortly thereafter, DuBois applauded Moton at Tuskegee for standing up to a white mob which tried to keep Negro doctors and nurses off the staff of a new veterans' hospital at Tuskegee. When the endowments at Tuskegee and Hampton were sharply increased, DuBois told their principals to stop running their schools for the benefit of Southern whites: "Your new wealth is New Freedom."[32]

His plea fell on the deaf ears of college presidents. At Fisk, Lincoln, and Howard universities, he reported anxious timidity in administrators more concerned with not offending white contributors than with educating Negro students. Lincoln, he said, was run only to suit its "rich Presbyterian donors." Fisk, his own university, he assailed in 1924 for curbing Negro vision, humiliating its students to attract white support, hiring white teachers to replace Negroes, restricting student self-expression, and governing them by a reign of terror.

But the students seem to have heard him. When three quarters of the students left Fisk shortly after DuBois's attack, he was ecstatic:

I am uplifted by the student martyrs at Fisk. At last we have real radicalism of the young—radicalism that costs, that is not mere words and foam. . . . Here is the real radical, the man who hits power in high places, white power, backed by unlimited wealth; hits it and hates it openly and between the eyes; talks face to face and not down "at the big gate"! God speed the breed! Suppose we do lose Fisk; suppose we lose every cent that entrenched millionaires have set aside to buy our freedom and stifle our complaints. They have the power, they have the wealth, but glory to God we still own our own souls and led by young men like these, let us neither flinch nor falter but fight and fight and fight again. Let us never forget that the arch enemy of the Negro race is the false philanthropist who kicks us in the mouth when we cry out in honest and justifiable protest.[33]

Within two years the virus of student revolt spread to Howard and Lincoln as well, and when it hit Hampton, DuBois said that the limit of Negro endurance of the "insult of impudent Almsgiving" had surely been reached.

The revolts appeared to fail when parents for the most part sent their children back to largely unchastened schools. Yet the spirit of the revolt seeped into faculties, administrations, and trustees, and DuBois's "pilgrimage" around Negro colleges two years later, in 1929, satisfied him that the students' uprisings, though quelled, had eventually led to enough reform to prepare the offending institutions for his next demand: after a thorough reconstruction, Negro colleges were to serve as planning headquarters for a new Negro economy.

Addressing the Howard commencement in 1930, DuBois made a fresh appraisal of his half-forgotten educational feud with Booker Washington. Washington, in stressing the primacy of making a living, had the right goal but the wrong method, DuBois said, for his handicraft industries had been already out of date when he built his Institute on them. The colleges, on the other hand, had the correct general method—setting no limits to the educational and cultural horizons of its students—but they lacked a definite objective, for in turning their students away from economic problems, they failed to equip them for the modern world.

The colleges had produced leaders empty of real culture and ignorant of the impact of organized industrial power on government,
religion, and social philosophy. Now as the two extremes were
converging, as Negro colleges were introducing vocational training
and industrial institutes were adding work of college caliber, he
said, the new united college–vocational school had to train industrial technicians *and* men aware of the world's problems, for "Ours
is the double and dynamic function of timing in with a machine
in action so as neither to wreck the machine nor be crushed or
maimed by it." If the task were impossible, so was the Negro's
future economic survival. But DuBois would not face that possibility; instead he looked to the colleges for unselfish planners for
a group in whose hands lay the economic and social destiny of the
darker peoples of the world, and by that token, of the world itself.[34]
A "General Staff of Negro Economic Guidance," stationed in a
large university, he said, could in a generation find opportunities
which, by dovetailing with American industry, could transform
the economic outlook of Negroes throughout the world.

DuBois was gradually drawing the Negro college into his orbit
of Negro self-sufficiency. Its graduates were to be race men wedded
to poverty, eager for work, thirsty for knowledge, thriving on sacrifice. Three years of the depression made clearer that his program
of "education and work" led to the acceptance of segregation. In
1933 he told his *Crisis* readers that no college for Negroes could
fail to be a "Negro college," a "center of applied knowledge and
guide of action," inspired by "unhampered spiritual expression in
art and literature." Facing enforced segregation for "centuries to
come," the Negro college had to deal with the reality of 1933 and
not fall into the older pitfall of broad cultural training which erred
in starting from where the Negro wanted to be rather than where
he was. If this was a change from his own former ideas, DuBois
said, the American public's step backward in caste intolerance,
mob law, and racial hatred had made it necessary.[35]

In no other field was the revolution in DuBois's public statements as marked. From almost the beginning of his public career,
certainly for thirty years, his defense of college training paralleling
the curricula of white universities had been the hallmark of his
thinking. It had been the focal point of his struggle with Wash-

ington. On it he had based his hopes for Negro advancement under the leadership of the Talented Tenth. Now, when the industrial schools were acknowledging the importance of college work, DuBois scoffed at the "growing mass of stupidity and indifference" being turned out by the colleges and defended technical training as essential for the economic security of the race.[36] In so doing, he bowed to a condition which he did not shrink from calling "segregation." "Either we do this or we die," he said. "There is no alternative."[37]

The depression of 1929 provided the fillip required to make cultural separation explicit in economic terms. Already intensely critical of American capitalism for its racial overtones and its class exploitation, DuBois regarded the stock market crash as a more revealing condemnation than anything Socialists could say or do. More important, he expected the crash to undermine America's faith in all private capitalistic enterprise. As the depression deepened, he scoffed at Hoover's confidence in the fundamental soundness of business. The whole system, DuBois said, rested on the basic fallacy that private profit would produce the best social result automatically. DuBois looked hopefully for production controlled through wider industrial democracy and for distribution based on social ethics.

Yet socialism alone was not enough, he thought, for color discrimination took on new forms in the poverty of the depression. When bank failures brought on by the crash of 1929 came to include two Negro banks in Chicago, DuBois blamed not the crisis in credit, but the determination of white men to frustrate Negro advancement. One bank closed, he said, because its president, Jesse Binga, was an aggressive Negro, resented by the whites; the other, the Douglass National Bank, was allowed to stay open a year longer only to keep Negroes out of the Loop.

Yet, however depressing the failure of Negro banks may have been for Negro morale, the Negro was primarily a workingman, and the Negro problem primarily the problem of the Negro workingman. The depression made urgent a solution to the problem of Negro unemployment, of economic insecurity in a discriminatory America.

Even before the depression DuBois had been exploring the possibility of Negro progress through manufacturing and consumers' cooperatives. In industry, he said in 1928, Negroes almost never rose above unskilled jobs where, underpaid, they ousted white competitors and deepened racial hatred. In small shops, they courted economic suicide by competing against chain stores. In personal service, they received wages inadequate to support either themselves or the professional men who depended upon their patronage. In agriculture, thirty years of Tuskegee and Hampton had failed to increase the proportion of farmers in the Negro population, and the general failure of farming in America was unrelieved for Negroes, for farm credit and farm relief never found their way to Negro pockets. Only the careful reorganization of manufacturers' and consumers' cooperatives could offer economic salvation. Starting slowly and growing on a careful plan, cooperatives could win prosperity for the whole race. Raw materials drawn from Negro farmers, transported by Negro trucks and turned into finished products in Negro factories, would eventually find their way to intelligent and loyal Negro customers who patronized Negro cooperative stores. Such an organization, "beyond race prejudice and trust competition," would, he said, insure the Negro's economic independence for all time, and would, through credit systems, even bring the Negro into cooperation with the West Indies, South America, and West and South Africa.

The depression gave urgency to DuBois's hopes. In a "Pre-Script, 1932," he promised that the *Crisis* would study Negro unemployment as its "paramount" problem. Though Negroes felt helpless because the Machine had fallen apart, he said, all was not lost. The prevalent economic philosophy in the United States began with the problem of production, he said, but actually the economic cycle began with consumption, and twelve million Negroes spending seven hundred and fifty million dollars a year were not helpless. This was the economic resource on which the Negro could build: let bed sheets be ordered from Tuskegee, and let amusement be provided in Negro theaters, and the wealth of the Negro would serve his own community.

DuBois also suggested a second gambit: pressure to force concessions from white entrepreneurs. In 1929 and 1930, the Chicago

Whip led a vigorous threat of boycott to compel firms catering to
Negro trade to hire Negro clerks. Here was a new weapon, Du-
Bois said, a weapon of great initial importance because of the ease
with which it could be put into operation. If the *Whip* could
make it succeed at Woolworth's, he said, it could work elsewhere
and would prove to be "one of the paths leading out of our economic wilderness."[38]

Yet a handful of jobs in white stores was like the piddling gains
of politics—attractive morale-builders but irrelevant to the long-
range problem. When these small gnawings at the wilderness of
poverty did little to clear the road to economic security, DuBois
went back to the ideal of an internal Negro economy. He turned
to his history books to recall Robert Owen and Fourier; he roamed
geographically to draw confirmation from Denmark and Russia.
And always the logic of cooperatives seemed even more applicable
to the American Negro—not only economic common sense but
racial pride dictated an escape from insult and "social death."
Caught up by his own vision of the Negro's future, DuBois was
prepared to advocate even social ostracism against individual
Negroes who refused to adhere to the racial goal.

More than ostracism was necessary for the new ideal. DuBois
called for a revolutionary change in Negro attitudes—not merely
a reconstruction in economics, but a revolution in ideas: a "spiritual" disclaimer of the profit motive and a new concept of service.
He was inviting Negroes to a crusade. The path of Negro advancement in the past twenty-five years, he said, indicated that it would
be a crusade in isolation, for the only Negro progress in that
period had been in segregated efforts and institutions and not in
effective entry into American life. The Negro had to do it alone,
DuBois said, for "there seems no hope that America in our day
will yield in its color or race hatred any substantial ground and
we have no physical nor economic power, nor any alliance with
other social or economic classes that will force compliance with
decent civilized ideals in Church, State, industry or art."[39] This
statement effectively wrote off all plans for Negro amelioration
which DuBois had been pursuing since the World War.

The racist undercurrent now became the main stream. Now
when the depression made his hopes for integration seemed uto-

pian, he turned easily to the secondary program which had always lurked just below the surface of his thought.

By his acceptance of segregation, DuBois completed the walls of Negro separatism. Without hope in white America, despairing of allies, he turned to his own people to challenge their capacity for self-sacrifice. Ennobled by his artists and guided by his colleges, the Negro would withdraw into secure autonomy with only petty gains from white politics to remind him that he was an American.

The Break with the Association

DuBois worked out his plan for Negro self-sufficiency independently of the Association. When in 1934 he defended his program as nondiscriminatory segregation, his use of the word "segregation" put the flame to the Association's combustible internal tension—an open secret in the Negro world for years—and set off the blaze which led to DuBois's resignation and ended his second career.[40]

DuBois's difficulty with the Association was partly semantic. The word "segregation" meant to him primarily the development of a separate Negro culture within white America. This program might incidentally involve residential separation, for the Negro community could function most efficiently if it was united physically. But residential segregation was a by-product of DuBois's program, not its conscious end. The Association, on the other hand, had fought for years against segregation enforced by legal and administrative agencies and by nongovernmental groups like churches and trade unions. DuBois used the word "segregation" in connection with his total program. When the officers of the Association saw it in the *Crisis*, they could interpret it only as a direct attack on the Association's primary reason for existence.

The segregation issue filled the *Crisis* editorial page for the six months beginning in January 1934. In that month DuBois warned colored people against being stampeded by a word; Negroes had never opposed segregation as such—living and working among their own people—but merely the discrimination which was its partner in America. Segregation without discrimination, that is, voluntary segregation, should, he said, evoke no opposition. The next month, after pointing out that his editorials, appearing over his own signature in a "free forum," were not the responsibility of the Association, he argued that the Association had never explicitly denounced segregation, but, facing facts and not a theory, had accepted it when other roads to Negro advancement had been blocked. The acceptance of Negro officers' training camps during the World War had been an example.

In March the officers of the Association responded in the *Crisis*. Spingarn, then chairman of the board, said that the Association's position "squarely opposed to segregation" had always been so clear that no explicit statement had ever been necessary; the officers of the Association had individually stated this for years without rebuke. Though occasionally segregation had been accepted as a necessary evil, that was a far cry from regarding it as a positive good. Walter White, the executive secretary, reported that DuBois's editorial was being used to delay Negro admission to governmental relief projects. The fight for full integration, White said, was longer, but was essential both for the Negro's welfare and for America. DuBois's January editorial, therefore, represented only his own view. DuBois's rebuttal came the following month. He said White's Caucasian appearance disqualified him from really understanding the Negro problem. And he told Spingarn that if the Association had, as Spingarn thought, opposed segregation for a quarter of a century, its net gain had been "a little less than nothing." The Negro people "can not base their salvation upon the empty reiteration of a slogan."

While DuBois kept up his barrage in the *Crisis*, the battle moved to the room of the board of directors. At the April meeting, the board affirmed its opposition to the principle and practice of enforced segregation. In May, after DuBois reported this resolution in a critical manner in the *Crisis*, the board filled a loophole in its statement: its opposition to "enforced segregation" did not imply acceptance of other forms, for all forms of segregation, in origin if not in their essential nature, were enforced. The board opposed them all. Furthermore, it rebuked DuBois for violating the strict confidence of board meetings and made it a matter of record that the *Crisis* was the organ of the Association and that no salaried officer was permitted to criticize the work, policy, and officers of the Association in the pages of the *Crisis*. DuBois replied to the board that he refused to be limited in his expression and therefore was unwilling to comply with the resolution. The *Crisis*, he insisted, "never was and never was intended to be an organ of the Association in the sense of simply reflecting its official position." Therefore, he resigned. The July issue of the *Crisis* still listed him as editor, but when a committee on reconciliation failed to reach an agreement with DuBois, the August issue reported his final resignation.

DuBois's second and final letter of resignation, released to the press eight days before the board to which it was addressed met, made public the depth of the rift which separated him from his long-time colleagues. He discounted the segregation issue as a minor point of difference open to amicable negotiation. But he would not yield when the board "peremptorily" forbade criticism, for, he said, the organization in 1934 found itself in a time of crisis without a program, without effective organization, and without executive officers able or disposed to guide the Association in a right direction. A program which had been imperative and effective in 1910 was no longer adequate, he went on; the Association needed a new "positive program of construction and inspiration." His own efforts toward revivifying the organization had been "absolutely unsuccessful," his program for readjustment "totally ignored." His demands for a change in personnel were labeled petty jealousy, his protests against blunders were seen as disloyalty, his criticism went unheeded. If he remained, he shared responsibility by quiet consent. Hence, he had to make the "supreme sacrifice" of withdrawing, hoping that the shock would rekindle the Association's initial fervor. He would applaud the Association when it rescued itself from "its present impossible position" and reorganized itself to meet the "demands of the present crisis."

The board released for publication its acceptance, with regret, of his resignation. It paid tribute to his leadership: he had been useful because of his independent judgment, fearless expression, and acute intelligence. But in the privacy of the minutes of the board, it rejected his "excuses" for leaving. For years, the board asserted, the *Crisis* committee had supervised what appeared in the pages of the magazine, and even DuBois had accepted as "self-evident" that his editorial utterances were subject to the board's approval. Furthermore, the board scoffed at his charge that his program had fallen on deaf ears. As a matter of fact, DuBois had attended only two board meetings in the previous eighteen months, and none in the previous ten.

After his departure, even his old friend, Miss Ovington, was relieved; she wrote to Villard: "Now [that] we are rid of our octopus, for of late he has been draining our strength, I hope we shall do better work."[41]

DuBois's resignation climaxed a long struggle with the Association on two issues: a program for Negro advancement, and control of the *Crisis*. However much DuBois's departure shocked the Negro world, it was less remarkable than the longevity of the partnership, because the Association had turned its back on every new direction DuBois's program had taken after the World War. It withdrew its financial support from the Pan-African movement even before the second congress. After the failure of the Association's overture to the AFL in 1924, its conference of executives reported to the board that the matter of Negroes and labor unions "does not come exactly within the scope of the Association's activities."[42] (The National Urban League took over this responsibility.) When DuBois supported LaFollette in the pages of the *Crisis* in 1924, despite the gamut of party loyalties among the Association's officers and directors, one Republican director resigned in protest against what he called the Association's endeavor "to lead the Negro into the meshes of the democratic and so-called progressive or socialist parties."[43] The Association had indeed, as DuBois charged, ignored his drift toward Negro self-sufficiency during the 1920's and 1930's and when his acceptance of voluntary segregation finally provoked them into explicit disagreement, it was merely the end of a long trail of cross-purposes. DuBois had criticized the Association publicly. In 1932 he even used the forum of an Association conference to criticize the centralization of power in the national office and to demand a positive program to replace the "mere negative attempt" to avoid segregation and

discrimination.* The next year he asked in the *Crisis* what the
Association had published on the present problems of the Negro,
especially of recent college graduates, and replied, "Nothing."

The conflict affected DuBois more intimately when it touched
on the control and finances of the *Crisis*. In 1924 the board affirmed that the *Crisis*, as the property of the Association, was assumed to be its spokesman. The directors, although leaving the
editor "all reasonable freedom" to defend his principles, set up
techniques of control, the most significant of which required that
editorials and other material which might lead to criticism be sent
to members of the *Crisis* subcommittee at least five days before the
magazine went to press. Even at this early date, the board complained of the treatment of Association news. Four years later,
the president of the District of Columbia branch made the criticism more explicit: when the Washington branch sought more
publicity for its fight against segregation, DuBois had used about
four full pages of pictures and text in one issue to report his
daughter's marriage to Countee Cullen. Charles E. Russell, a
member of the *Crisis* committee, was already on record as wanting
the magazine "less obviously" devoted to propaganda.

The independence which the *Crisis*' financial success had
brought in its earlier years dwindled as the approach of the depression made the magazine a financial liability. (Its circulation was
down to 21,000 in 1932.) At a special meeting of the board held
in 1929 to consider the magazine's finances, DuBois broached the
possibility that the *Crisis* might need an annual subvention of
$5,000 "indefinitely." Later the same year, he asked for $10,000
to adjust to "post-war conditions." In 1930, the board recognized
the necessity for a regular subsidy and added that because of the
"new financial conditions," full power over editorial and business

---

* Ralph J. Bunche echoed this criticism eight years later: "The escape that
the Negro mass seeks is one from economic deprivation, from destitution and
imminent starvation. To these people, appealing for livelihood, the N.A.A.C.P.
answers: give them educational facilities, let them sit next to whites in street-
cars, restaurants, and theaters. They cry for bread and are offered political
cake." "Extended Memorandum on the Programs, Ideologies, Tactics and
Achievements of Negro Betterment and Interracial Organizations" (typescript,
1940), p. 144. This memorandum, prepared for Myrdal's *An American Dilemma*, is in the Schomburg Collection.

policy was to be exercised by a committee of four including Du-
Bois and two paid executive officers of the Association. DuBois
accepted this arrangement, not without distaste. The matter, however, was never really settled. When the board urged DuBois to
give more time to his job and less to independent lecturing, the
resolution created the necessity for a new committee to explore
the whole question of DuBois's relation to the Association. The
next year, 1933, DuBois recommended that publication of the
Crisis be suspended.

The strain within the Association crystallized into a personal
feud between DuBois and the executive secretary, Walter White.
In 1929, the board approved a motion by Spingarn that the secretary was the executive officer of the Association and that all officers
and salaried employees "shall be subject to his authority." After
White replaced Johnson as secretary, DuBois, in a private letter
to Spingarn, threatened to resign unless the *Crisis* editorial board
was changed—he made no secret of the fact that White was his
target. Two months later, the offending minute passed in 1929
was repealed. In 1931, DuBois used a directors' meeting as an occasion to question the disbursement of funds in the national office,
a direct affront to White. The two engaged in a periodic tug of
war over prospective appointees to the staff of the Association and
of the *Crisis*. When DuBois was making his plans for a visiting
professorship at Atlanta, he told Spingarn that he would not work
under any editorial board of which White was a member if that
board had more than advisory authority. His departure for Atlanta left the *Crisis* in the hands of two managing editors, one his
appointee, one from White's camp, though DuBois was to make
whatever contributions he felt were appropriate. By that time,
DuBois's independent editorship had become only a memory.

DuBois's absence from New York cushioned his resignation.
Urged by John Hope, then president of Atlanta, to accept a permanent academic appointment in a familiar and well-loved place,
DuBois could look back on New York without enthusiasm. Despite numerous "Save the *Crisis*" campaigns, the magazine faced a
bleak economic future, and its loss of solvency insured increasing
control by the unfriendly officers of the Association. At Atlanta,
in a Negro university headed by a Negro president, he had the

setting in which to implement his project for a Negro general staff exercising its leadership from a university milieu. In New York his program was unheeded, and the organization of which he had been a part for twenty-five years was, in his view, moribund. In Atlanta he was respected, even revered. He stayed.

A Leader Without Followers

The road back to Atlanta was a lonely one. Twenty-four years before, DuBois had come North to win the Negro from Washington's patient gradualism, and by 1920, he had stood as a prophet preaching a successful gospel. But by 1934, the times had passed him by, and the "deaf ears" on which his new program fell belonged to many outside the Association's executive offices. When he defiantly returned to Atlanta, a prophet still breathing fire, few followed in his train.

DuBois had, in a sense, outlived his usefulness. He would be remembered as the pioneer who won his battle to commit Negro America to an uncompromising struggle for full equality. Even Washington before his death had come part way. When in 1932, Moton's book, *What the Negro Thinks*, won him the Spingarn medal, awarded annually by the Association for outstanding Negro achievement, the victory of the older Negro "radicals" needed little further documentation. For DuBois, this victory was a tremendous personal success. Few would have questioned Walter White's assertion in 1932 that DuBois was "beyond all doubt" one of the "chief molders of modern thought regarding the Negro," the individual chiefly responsible for the militant school of Negro thought.[44]

This achievement, however, was the prelude to battle rather than the battle itself. It did not guarantee DuBois a role of continuing importance. New proposals had to win in a market crowded with leaders who, though ready to canonize DuBois, were unwilling to surrender to him their independent power in specific areas of Negro life.

DuBois never really grasped this new situation. Coming to full maturity in the era of Booker T. Washington, DuBois inherited an image of the all-embracing leader, the universal pundit creating total solutions for the Negro problems. He thought that his victory over Washington made him lead dog in a pack, when actually it made him one caravan leader on a very broad frontier. Such an attitude led him into two errors fatal to his continuing leadership: First, it teased him into explorations of universal movements like Pan-Africanism and world socialism so remote from the Negro's humdrum day-to-day struggle for existence that they commanded neither attention nor support. Second, it forbade deviation from DuBois's views under pain of anathema. Robert Vann of the Pittsburgh *Courier*, for years an influential fighter for Negro rights, was abused by DuBois on more than one occasion for his allegiance to the Republican party. DuBois said that the *Courier*—one of the best Negro newspapers then and now —had had "mental and physical dyspepsia" ever since Coolidge failed to reward Vann. The *Courier* and other newspapers were dismissed as croaking toads.[45] When a Negro Non-Partisan Conference met in Washington in 1932, DuBois gave thin praise to its platform and then pounced upon its plank on economics (his own resolution had been rejected) as "economic flap-doodle" which should have seemed unnecessary "even to the jaded digestive system of Kelly Miller."[46] Even Schuyler, so often praised in the *Crisis* for his work with cooperatives, was opposed as not the right type for an Association job—after he had been recommended by White. DuBois's difficulty was neatly summarized by his obituary of Trotter, who had been a prominent "radical" back in the days when DuBois was still equivocating with Washington: Trotter had been a free lance at a time when the mailed fist of the twelve million Negroes had to be clenched. DuBois felt that the arm of that fist must be his. But that was no longer possible, not on any conceivable program. As Schuyler said in the *Nation* in 1935, thousands of intelligent Negroes agreed with neither the Washington nor the DuBois school; in a race with hundreds of leaders, one or two men could not speak for the entire group.

Yet DuBois had to try, for he felt that the persistence, perhaps even the growth, of anti-Negro discrimination reflected on his own leadership. From 1928 to 1930, his frustration, created by fear of failure, showed through in the snobbisms which appeared in the

Crisis with unusual offensiveness and frequency. Annoyed by un-announced visitors, he excused his brusqueness by saying: "I often discount human facts in comparison with divine thoughts."[47] His column in the *Crisis*, "As the Crow Flies," was for sophisticated people, he said, not for fools and illiterates. Presumably it was these sophisticates who would find useful his formula for enter-taining: "Good food well cooked and a lot of it, served on excellent china, with good linen and good silver."[48] The *Crisis*, written for the "Seldom Sort," was not adapted to morons and idiots; DuBois was speaking to the "aristocracy." Impatient with failure, he ap-peared to be petulantly narrowing the already thin vector of his influence.

The comprehensive plan for Negro self-sufficiency changed all this. Again the prophet of a new gospel, he lost his irritation in impatient fervor. He found anew the Negro workingman, and dedicated the *Crisis* to a restudy of all principal areas of Negro activity. From defense he turned to a striking offense through which the race, like the communitarian colonies of the nineteenth century, would try to gain security for itself and to show the way to the rest of the world. If gradual gains were impossible, he would jump directly to the millennium. But, as his friend of many years, Francis J. Grimke, said, if DuBois thought he could lead Negroes back into segregation, his leadership was at an end. The Negro had followed too long the old DuBois, uncompromising fighter for full equality, to turn to a new DuBois who sounded like Booker T. Washington.

Yet the conditioning of a lifetime would allow DuBois nothing less than a final effort at an over-all solution for the Negro. Failure in other directions had left Negro self-sufficiency as the only ap-parent possibility. With a neat rational unity, it provided a role for every Negro American, drew on the reservoir of racial pride and talent, and left ample room for the exercise of leadership. The size of the venture, its complexity, and even its implausibility only made it the more challenging. If it doubled back on the path of Negro progress to the point at which Washington had left the race, DuBois felt that the Negro would have to face that retreat with courage, confident that Negro gains thereafter would be perma-nent because they were based on Negro unity. DuBois's new program, like the Program of a Hundred Years, was the characteristic product of the man: impatient with small projects, he sought salvation for the Negro in a grandiose scheme which would be magnificent even if it failed.

Failure was almost inevitable. Like Pan-Africa, Negro self-sufficiency built on a racial chauvinism which the race would not sustain. It called for unselfish, dedicated leaders, but in 1933, DuBois himself was mourning that even then educated leaders were trying to sidestep Negro problems by aloofness and by escape into the white community. Negro autonomy required its artists to act like heralds, but DuBois's *Crisis* reviews of the Negro renaissance indicated how little they would meet his demand. Langston Hughes had spoken for many in his race when he said, in what Locke has called the "young Negro's spiritual declaration of independence":

> We younger Negro artists who create now intend to express our individual dark-skinned selves without fear or shame. If white people are pleased, we are glad. If they are not, it does not matter. We know that we are beautiful. And ugly too. The tomtom cries and the tomtom laughs. If colored people are pleased we are glad. If they are not, their displeasure doesn't matter either. We build our temples for tomorrow, strong as we know how, and we stand on top of the mountain, free within ourselves.[49]

The colleges were to produce young Negro radicals, yet, in 1929, of the 127 Negro students at Lincoln University 81 opposed having a colored professor, a poll which DuBois characterized as the "most astonishing blow" which Negro education had sustained in years. Negro self-sufficiency called for businessmen willing to be racial servants unmoved by personal profit. Yet studies of class structure and capitalists in the Negro world by E. Franklin Frazier and Abram L. Harris were leaving little doubt that Negro capitalists behaved like capitalists and not like Negroes. Even as DuBois called for all-Negro trade unions, the National Urban League and younger Negro leaders were making new approaches to the white labor movement. Harris's article on the Negro worker, which urged renewed efforts toward joint Negro-white cooperation, had appeared in the *Crisis* almost simultaneously with DuBois's final rejection of organized labor. The rising current of Negro thought on labor was running against DuBois, and the formation of the Committee on Industrial Organization the year after he left the Association confirmed hopes for a better deal from organized labor.

Just as three conferences of Negro leaders during the decade of the first World War testified to DuBois's prominence, three more in 1932 and 1933, by rejecting his program, chronicled the eclipse of his influence. The Non-Partisan Conference in 1932 and the Rosenwald Fund Conference in 1933 gave respectful hearing to his economic plans, but passed over them. At the second Amenia conference—the first, in 1916, had practically established DuBois's right of succession to Washington—the young Negro intellectuals present only thinly masked their impatience with some of their elders for having ignored the economic roots of the Negro problem, and with others like DuBois, for having "completely failed in facing a necessary adjustment between black and white labor."[50] Unlike the NAACP, DuBois had explored the economics of discrimination; as Bunche points out, DuBois was well aware of the deficiencies of the Association's program. But his solution went down the road of reaction. Young Negroes looked forward to integration.

His old programs frustrated, his new plan rejected, DuBois retired to Atlanta virtually alone. He knew in his soul, he said, that the time had come for a clean break with the Association. It was hard—dissolving the bonds of twenty-five years. Yet there was really no choice.[51]

The Chicago *Defender* published his epitaph. Over a picture of Booker T. Washington, it asked mournfully: "WAS HE RIGHT AFTER ALL?"; over a picture of W. E. B. DuBois: "IS HE A QUITTER?"[52]

VII

THE TIME OF HESITATION

Atlanta offered not a pasture for declining years, but a base for new activity. New York and the tensions of the Association's home office were finished chapters, and, except in autobiographical pieces, DuBois rarely wrote about either during the next decade.

He had left Atlanta with his reputation in eclipse; he returned with his great years behind him, his program no longer commanding organizational or popular support. But he returned with dignity and with prestige. Atlanta, now headed by John Hope—an old friend, perhaps DuBois's closest friend in a long life—welcomed him as an elder statesman well qualified to direct its sociology department and to undertake new scholarly projects. No longer a controversial figure at the center of Negro agitation, DuBois won new honors: a ceremonial homage on his seventieth birthday; honorary degrees from Atlanta, Fisk, and Wilberforce; membership in the National Institute of Arts and Letters. In these ten years he wrote two books and contributed to a third, made progress on the preparatory volume for a Negro encyclopedia, wrote a weekly newspaper column, organized a regional conference on Negro land-grant colleges, appeared as guest lecturer at some leading Northern universities, and founded *Phylon*, a quarterly "Review of Race and Culture." When his contract at Atlanta was abruptly ended in 1944, he still had enough vigor for another new career, one so controversial that it invited criminal prosecution in the United States courts.

A decade so busy points to a diffusion of DuBois's talents: the classroom teacher trained a new generation for leadership, the historian built up the race's past and investigated its present, the journalist picked his way through the swift changes of the New Deal and puzzled over the world-wide significance of the color line as the second World War approached. His annual lecture tour continued, and in 1936–1937, he added a trip around the world. The schedule was crowded, the obligations many, and as a result the quality of DuBois's work suffered. Yet, buoyant with self-confidence which the years never sapped, he took on many tasks with energy best hoarded for one.

In referring to the ambiguities of the early Roosevelt era, DuBois called these years a "Time of Hesitation." The phrase also describes his own withdrawal during the long moment between his fall from power in 1934 and his reemergence in 1944.

A Second Round of Scholarship

In his academic work DuBois picked up familiar threads laid down years before. *Black Reconstruction*, the scholarly book for which he will probably be remembered longest, spun out a point which he had suggested to the American Historical Association in 1909; *Black Folk Then and Now* expanded his thin older work, *The Negro*; and even the preparatory work for the ambitious *Encyclopedia of the Negro* recalled an earlier notion for a multinational *Encyclopedia Africana*. In launching *Phylon*, he made the identification with his younger days even more explicit by speaking of the new quarterly as "in a sense" a revival of the Atlanta University *Publications*. When he hailed the "First Phylon Institute" as the twenty-fifth Atlanta University conference and started again a familiar refrain, the duty of the Talented Tenth, his older readers must have felt themselves moving through deeply grooved roads. In 1941 and 1942, the echoes of *The Philadelphia Negro* and of DuBois's early statements on sociological technique rang all through his lectures and reports on the conferences of Negro land-grant colleges: he analyzed the distinct social classes among Negroes; he looked for leaders trained to sacrifice and equipped to bring forward a whole people; he promised to search for truth through the scientific method and for laws, based on regularities and change, which would serve as hypotheses for future investigation. When he reported to the General Education Board in 1943 on his progress in planning a continually refreshed "total study of a complete situation as a contribution to the Negro race, America, the world, and social science,"[1] he might just as well have called it a Program of a Hundred Years.

Retiring from the arena, DuBois felt that his return to sociological research would open decades of useful work which would
guarantee the solvency of his claim to leadership. The support
of President Hope made his plans plausible, and his own self-
confidence, strengthened by thirty years of repute as the scholarly
Dr. DuBois, gave them an air of inevitability.

Black Reconstruction (1935) mocked these hopes. A major
work, supported by grants from the Rosenwald Fund and the Carnegie Foundation, it was a model of DuBois's strengths and weak-
nesses as a scholar. At the core of the book were his defense of
Reconstruction governments and his economic interpretation of
the North's desertion of the Negro. He covered a wider period
as well, at every point emphasizing the special significance of the
Negro. The "black worker" was the "underlying cause" of the
conflict, he said, and Negroes played the crucial role in the North's
victory, both by providing willing fighters for freedom to replace
reluctant Northern soldiers and by abandoning their Southern
masters in a widespread cessation of work which DuBois called a
"general strike." As novices in freedom, the Negroes extended
American democracy by supporting the carpetbag constitutions,
which spread the franchise, instituted a system of public education, and explored the use of the taxing power to redress social
inequities. DuBois discounted the traditional picture of carpetbag corruption either by pointing to parallel excesses in Northern
states—the Tweed ring in New York—or by minimizing the Negro's
actual role in Reconstruction capitals or by showing that the loot
went mainly to white men. The overthrow of Reconstruction governments he blamed on a "new feudalism based on monopoly"
which suppressed labor governments in both North and South and
made the national government its servant.

Stated thus simply, DuBois's theme had plausibility. His vigorous defense of Reconstruction governments, though based on
existing monographic studies, brought together in one place an
impressive case and gave the book its enduring value. His economic interpretation of the North's desertion of the Negro was
strikingly argued. But the faults of the book could be listed more
readily: its bulk passing for scholarly weight; its reliance on secondary works, and a relatively small number at that; its argu-

mentativeness and special pleading; its fragments of unrelated information. Sprouts of useful material had to struggle for survival among dreary weeds of racial apologetics, emotional outbursts more suited to a revival meeting than to a historical survey, and Marxist terminology bordering on burlesque. At one point, his half-assimilated and misapplied Marxist terminology produced the fantastic dictum that "the record of the Negro worker during Reconstruction presents an opportunity to study inductively the Marxian theory of the state."*

His account could not be sustained historically, for all modern history was brought to focus on the Negro. Black labor was the foundation stone not only of the Southern social structure, but of Northern and English manufacturing and of European and world-wide commerce. The problems of white workers everywhere in 1935 were "directly traceable to Negro slavery in America." In the Civil War the Negro's support of the North and defection from the South "decided the war." When "labor" government failed in the South and carried the Negro back toward slavery, triumphant capital was prepared for its world-wide "exploitation of white, yellow, brown and black labor, in lesser lands and 'breeds without the law.'" Furthermore, Negroes were good men. A white man bribing or bribed was corrupt; a Negro "convicted of technical bribery" was just "not a strong man," but his voice was "sincere." In general, Negroes were bribed and misled because they were poor and ignorant; they were poor and ignorant because of slavery. In any case, they never accepted bribes against their beliefs: on measures affecting land and education, they were pure; only on "things connected with government and its technical details" did they succumb. All this was a far cry from DuBois's preface where the Negro was assumed to be an average and ordinary human being subject to his environment.

DuBois's eccentric notions of Marxian phraseology blockaded clarity. Negro plantation workers emerged as a black proletariat. Reconstruction governments, sustained by the military force of

* Howard K. Beale's summary gives a fair picture: the book presents "a mass of material, formerly ignored, that every future historian must reckon with," but it is also "wordy" and "distorted." "On Rewriting Reconstruction History," *American Historical Review*, XLV, 809 (July 1940).

the United States, were held up as "one of the most extraordinary experiments of Marxism" that the world, before the Russian revolution, had seen. He backed off from calling the Reconstruction government of South Carolina "the dictatorship of the proletariat" only because someone had warned him that universal suffrage did not lead to real dictatorship "until workers use their votes consciously to rid themselves of the dominion of private capital"— confusion twice compounded. Negro desertions from plantations during the war, which Villard in reviewing DuBois's book characterized quite reasonably as "the natural, unconscious, unorganized drift of embattled and endangered masses in the direction of freedom and safety," were, in DuBois's lexicon, part of a "general strike against slavery." He assumed that leaders such as Charles Sumner and Thaddeus Stevens looked toward a government which, without their knowing it, would lead "necessarily" to a dictatorship of labor over capital and industry in the South. The West followed the abolitionists, he said, until it was "seduced by the *kulak* psychology of land ownership" and emerged as a "petty bourgeoisie." When Reconstruction governments were overthrown in the "counter-revolution of property," the old agrarian feudalism was replaced by a new "monarchical dictatorship that displaced democracy in the United States in 1876." Though Marxian thought can suggest sharp insights into the Reconstruction period, DuBois's unsure hold on Marx's ideas and his misuse of Marx's vocabulary led him into slippery distortions. As Sterling D. Spero said in the *Nation,* when DuBois equated Negro and proletarian, his racial consciousness distorted his Marxism, producing more confusion than light.

The book was a long morality tale based on historical material: good men triumphed for a while but were crushed by bad men. Yet the good men would succeed in the end because they had to in order that the world should achieve peace. In such a tale, it was legitimate for the storyteller to be on the side of the angels and to report periodically that God wept or laughed. His list of references became not a critical bibliography, but a division between goats (anti-Negro historians) and sheep (fair and sympathetic writers). A devil—Andrew Johnson—was an asset. Flames in time for the last curtain supplied the appropriate dramatic touch: DuBois pictured Professor John W. Burgess of Columbia telling his students that Republican administrations would never again work for the political equality of man. "Immediately in Africa, a black back runs red with the blood of the lash; in India, a brown girl is raped; in China, a coolie starves; in Alabama, seven darkies are more than lynched; while in London, the white limbs of a prostitute are hung with jewels and silk. Flames of jealous murder sweep the earth, while brains of little children smear the hills."

Though passable as polemic or melodrama, this was not history. The preface of DuBois's next book, *Black Folk Then and Now* (1939), pointed up his dilemma. He liked to affirm that "the truth of history lies not in the mouth of partisans but rather in the calm Science that sits between. Her cause I seek to serve," he said, "and wherever I fail, I am at least paying the Truth the respect of earnest effort." He recognized the shortcomings in this volume—especially his pro-Negro bias. Though the kernel of the book was a "body of fairly well-ascertained truth," he said, it also contained areas "of conjecture and even of guesswork" which he would hesitate to publish under other circumstances. But fearful lest the rising American curiosity about the Negro be satisfied by the "champions of white folks" who have long left the Negro "the clown of history; the football of anthropology; and the slave of industry," he wrote a rebuttal in anticipation of misrepresentations on the other side. This candor isolated his difficulty: he paid lip service to truth, but the times needed his talent for argumentation. History, like art, had to serve in a larger cause.

The same pressure was at work in his editing of *Phylon*. In the first issue he restated his familiar goal, a factual study of one racial group; he said he would lay a special emphasis on economics. By the beginning of the fifth volume, however, the tone had changed: the Negro migration to America had been the "greatest social event of modern history," for it had founded modern capitalism in industry, and it had tested modern democracy, forcing it to new heights. Although Negro development was "the greatest controlled laboratory test of the science of human action in the world," he said, it had been neglected, smeared, forgotten. If balancing this distortion was propaganda, "we're propagandists."[2]

(Two issues later, he was gone, the editorship passing into the able hands of Ira DeA. Reid, trained in a different generation of scholarship.)

Characteristically for DuBois, autobiography became an integral part of his sketches of the Negro's past. Each new venture invited public reminiscence; and a newspaper column could be filled with memories without research. The celebration of his seventieth birthday at Atlanta provided the occasion for a protracted review of his life decade by decade, and, much revised and expanded, this appeared in 1940 as *Dusk of Dawn,* a pretentious volume which identified the Negro race problem with his own development. Four years later this identification became even more explicit. When Rayford W. Logan assembled a wartime anthology of fourteen statements by leading Negroes on the subject *What the Negro Wants,* DuBois blandly contributed more autobiography, entitled "My Evolving Program for Negro Freedom." The *Negro Digest* asked for an article; DuBois rearranged some memories—"Reading, Writing and Real Estate." If he sought truth, he looked within, for, as he said in the week of his seventy-fifth birthday, "I think I have felt particularly in the last twenty-five years a certainty of judgment and depth of knowledge concerning the world which is new, inspiring and astonishing. I began to realize what an omniscient God who has lived a million years must have accumulated in the shape of knowledge, and how near that knowledge may make him omniscient."[3]

A propagandist so long, DuBois could not be anything else. His clipped monologues might make his classes inspirational; but he was too far along in his career for small research projects to satisfy him; and for the larger projects, he had neither time nor temperament.

A Voice Not Silent but Unheard

The momentum of the controversy with the Association carried DuBois's notion of Negro separatism into his weekly newspaper columns, first in the Pittsburgh *Courier* and then in the New York *Amsterdam News.* Even as the New Deal renewed his expectations from the white community, he never repudiated this notion. But as the reforming years moved toward the war years, he continually shaded the meaning of Negro autonomy until it became sufficiently equivocal to lose significance as part of his general plan for Negro advancement.

An article for the *Journal of Negro Education* the year following his departure from the *Crisis* argued the need for separate colored schools. White schools discriminated against Negroes and covered up the Negro's past by the "legerdemain and metaphysics of nomenclature," he said. There was only one solution: distinct schools which could offer Negro history, Negro sociology, and "even physical science taught by men who understand their audience and are not afraid of the truth."[4] During his first month on the *Courier* staff, he spoke hopefully of a "closed economic circle" planned by a Negro "brain trust," and shortly thereafter he said that long centuries of race segregation and compulsory degradation had given birth to a new loyalty welding Negroes into a nation within a nation. Cooperatives still seemed the tool of economic emancipation. They promised more than "idiotic" complaints or civil suits, he said, for the Negro was now in the position of the pig who climbed the tree because he had to. And if wholesalers sabotaged consumers' cooperatives, then Negroes would move into manufacturing. Even when the Congress of Industrial Organizations disavowed the color line, he warned that race prejudice was still too strong for the realization of the Marxian dogma of labor's class consciousness. At the summit of this plan, his perennial capstone, the Talented Tenth, had to "subject" Negro labor to its guidance, just as Russia's economic salvation "involves vast regimentation, unquestioning obedience until the cumbersome super-human economic machine can run in rhythmic order."[5] As late as 1941, *Phylon*, in its report on the "twenty-fifth Atlanta University Conference," still carried the same old pack of ideas.

DuBois never formally repudiated this program: it appeared again in summary form in his autobiography in 1940. In a sense he could not repudiate it. On it he had staked his reputation; because of it he had broken with attachments of twenty-five years; from it he drew the psychic warmth of courage and independence. Yet his columns during the decade hinted that it no longer commanded his full allegiance. Behind the Veil, he found that groups essential to the program's success avoided their responsibilities. Too many cooperatives turned to frankly capitalistic plans for investment and profit; Negro enterprises, such as the successful Mme. C. J. Walker Manufacturing Company, which with a "little broader knowledge and far-seeing advice" could have moved toward cooperation as part of a socialist mass movement, continued to behave like businesses run for profit. Though few Negroes were bourgeois, he found "bourgeois thinking" all too widely spread among the race, and Negroes, unaware of the "new economic morality," aped the business ethics of the worst whites. Negroes as a whole were, like his own grandfather, guilty of "racial provincialism," but, even more fatal to DuBois's now traditional hopes, the upper classes, the talented and educated tenth, scorned racial nationalism and tried to escape into the white world, while the clear pattern of social strata in Negro colleges betrayed heresy even in the seminaries of racial leadership.

Meanwhile white America gave cause for hope. After two and a half years of the New Deal, DuBois told a convention of Negro Baptists that the administration had given Negro labor a due share of recognition; it had implanted the idea of the general welfare as the object of industry, and it regarded a decent living for the masses as a more important goal than the protection of land and property. He insisted upon the government's right to tax (preferably by a graduated income tax) and spend to the limit for the job which needed to be done. If Franklin D. Roosevelt, his Haitian adventure overlooked, found it necessary to employ a "dictatorship which did not depend upon democratic control" to achieve ends variously defined by DuBois as fascism and socialism, he must be defended. If his reforms failed, there would follow a "Counsel of Despair," a Communist revolution.[6] At the beginning of Roosevelt's second term, DuBois affirmed his faith in the "slow and even discouraging method of reform without revolution," even though sometimes this method "seems utterly to fail."[7] In 1940 DuBois scorned the Republican possibilities and rejected Norman Thomas; Roosevelt, now engaged in foreign maneuvers of which DuBois disapproved, apparently won DuBois's half-hearted vote on the Democrats' domestic record.

Outside the government, the *Courier* column noted tentatively, the new industrial unions (CIO) were welcoming Negroes, but a union card could not prevent discrimination in wages, treatment, or promotion, nor could it guarantee jobs. Therefore, DuBois thought, Negroes still had to form their own unions and through competition to induce white workers to adopt a genuinely non-racial membership policy.* Yet the CIO's official stand was encouraging. In the South he found more reason for hope, for the "slow but undoubted advance toward democracy" there was obvious.

The long night of hostility, running from the late 1920's into the middle 1930's, seemed to be ending. In 1940, at the "dusk of dawn," DuBois recalled that his two earlier autobiographical essays had been written in tears and blood; a new one he set down "determinedly but yet with wider hope in some more benign fluid."[8] As the second World War galvanized America, Negro advances both in industry and in the armed forces overcame his initial misgivings as the war broke out. Even the horror of race riots was pared somewhat for him by "almost invariably decent" newspaper and periodical comment, white and black, North and South.

The uncertainty of the evidence—hope for the white world, faltering in the colored—led DuBois to equivocate on his own position. Almost two years after his reference to a Negro "closed economic circle," he rejected autarchy as a description of his plans, for Negroes, he said, could not build a complete economic nation within a nation. Some time before, he was urging Negroes to move with dignity and caution into the surrounding civilization. The confusion percolated into *Dusk of Dawn*: on some pages he argued that Negro enterprise could cover only the "smaller part" of Negro economic activity, in the "interstices" of a collapsing industrial machine, but as his enthusiasm warmed further to the topic, wholesale and manufacturing cooperatives reappeared.

* The path to labor solidarity could only come, he said, through "a perfect Hegelian category: the thesis of Negro race consciousness; the antithesis, the union of all labor across racial, national, and color lines; and the synthesis, a universal labor solidarity arising through the expansion of race consciousness in the most exploited class to all labor."

Actually the confusion did not matter. Few were listening, for his ideas failed to mesh with his era. He had broken with the fighters for integration and with his own great past just as the struggle for integration was about to register real gains. Galloping after a chimera of Negro separatism, he found himself far from the battlefield when his side started winning, and that part of his make-up which may be called either tenacity or stubbornness prevented his easy return. As he returned unsurely, he made peace with his old foes. In the early months of the war, he acknowledged that different areas required different attitudes toward Negro problems, that a man who stood straight and suffered in Mississippi deserved as much credit as a Harlem gesturer. Shortly thereafter he praised Tuskegee for several reasons, the most striking being that its industrial training anticipated available opportunities for work, such as service in dining cars and hotels. Two years before, he had spoken of Booker Washington as the "greatest Negro leader of his day"—without all the usual reservations and amendments. But the truce was taking place on the wrong plain; the war had moved. In his reconciliations DuBois had made his peace with the past. But he still had not come to terms with the present. A younger generation was indifferent to him. When Benjamin Stolberg attacked DuBois's racial chauvinism and lumped Washington's and DuBois's ideas together as two aspects of the same program — "Today [1935] DuBois winds up pretty much where Booker T. Washington started"[9] — four of the brightest young Negro intellectuals commended Stolberg's "brilliant and sound analysis of the tragic predicament of the American Negro today."*

DuBois felt a part of this isolation. In an early column in the *Courier,* he was defensive about his role as leader, and five years later (1941) he commented sardonically on his isolation: if you want to lose friends and jobs, then oppose wars, defend strikes, and say that even Communists have rights. In the fall of 1943 he complained that national Negro organizations were not democratic and never really discussed anything. That winter he denounced a joint program issued by twenty of these groups. Seven

* Letter to the Editor, *Nation,* CXLI, 17 (July 3, 1935). The four were Sterling A. Brown, Ralph J. Bunche, Emmett E. Dorsey, and E. Franklin Frazier.

of the eight points, he said, were the old stuff of two generations, and the vagueness of the eighth made it meaningless.

Out of touch, out of sympathy with current Negro planning on domestic matters, DuBois turned more and more to the world picture.

The World Crisis and a New Function

DuBois's analysis of the foreign policy of his own and other nations started with two questions: Had the nation moved toward a socialistic organization of society? Was it nonimperialistic, that is, was it a white nation free of the taint of extending political or economic control over a darker people? Russia, answering "yes" to both questions, was highly favored; England, and the United States as well, answering "no," felt the brunt of his attack. Of the two principles, the requirement of nonimperialism was the more important. The Japanese, as advance agents of the rising colored races, received favored treatment because the color of their skin saved them from the charge of imperialism even when they were taking over as much of China as their armies could capture. On occasion there was a strain in fitting events into his principles. The Soviet-German pact of 1939 created embarrassment; but at other times his preconceptions could guide him into striking prophecy. At the beginning of 1944 he predicted that after the war China would call out to Russia for help. (He expected India to do the same.)

In the Ethiopian crisis of 1935–1936, the facts were ready-made for his interpretation—a white nation invading a backward black kingdom, relatively defenseless. The rest of the white world raised no hand in opposition, DuBois said, for "economic exploitation based on the excuse of race prejudice is the program of the white world."[10] Benito Mussolini "killed the faith of all black folk in white men."[11] DuBois expected the impact of the war to ramify among colored peoples: If Italy won, the colored world would agree with Japan that force was the only way to freedom and equality. Then China and Japan would agree to resist white aggression in Asia, and India would no longer postpone open rebellion. If Italy lost, the spell of Europe would be broken by a blow to white prestige comparable to the Russo-Japanese war. China would have to follow Japan or fall into chaos. The black world saw this crisis as the last European effort to subjugate black men, DuBois said; if Haile Selassie were anything but brown, the white world would have fought in his defense.

He expected that the British, as unrepentant imperialists, and, to a lesser extent, the French would repeat the errors which led to the first World War. England, he said, nearly always had a "powerful group of selfish interests, working silently and correctly, with decorum and respectability" to hold "her profoundly selfish grasping course." The British government and people, he thought, genuinely wanted to help the black kingdom, but investors and aristocrats forced the government to sacrifice it.[12] As Germany rose to power, he predicted that England would offer the labor of black Africa in return for security in white Europe. France's traditional policy of recognition to its colored citizens won it gentler treatment: France was not a champion of the Negro race, he said, but she was friendly and fair; realistically she could not risk her national life for Ethiopia.

A round-the-world tour in 1936–1937, with special attention to Germany, Russia, and Japan, reinforced DuBois's authority to comment on world affairs as the war years approached. Of Nazi Germany he had a mixed view. He deeply admired the efficient totalitarian planning of German industry—"a splendid accomplishment"—and the national control of German capital, and he welcomed the new German state as the greatest exemplar of Marxian socialism outside Russia, a characterization which might have surprised his German hosts. A visit with a German bureaucrat with the eyes and deep earnestness of the German idealist moved him deeply, and the following week he referred nostalgically to the sense of fellowship there. On the other hand, the Nazis' treatment of the Jews reminded him of the American treatment of the Negro, and he charged that German persecutions set civilization back a hundred years. Adolf Hitler, whose rise to power he blamed on the confusion in Germany caused by American, British, and French capitalists, he labeled a "paranoic." After the war started in 1939, he warned Negroes that Nazi racism struck at yellow, brown, and black races. A German victory, he said, would force colored people to ally themselves with conquered white nations against the new white master of the world; a stalemate would help darker nations to reach freedom. So far as Hitler stood for a denial of a people's voice in its own government, in conditions of work, in the distribution of wealth and for a racial theory with no basis in science, philanthropy, or common decency, DuBois hoped for his defeat.

Russia and Japan—the fountain of socialism and the first-born of budding "colored" world powers—were generally given the benefit of every doubt. During the Ethiopian crisis DuBois noted Russia's "frank and open arraignment of colonial exploitation," though he recognized that it was "nullified" because she had no colonies and because she had to align herself with imperialist powers.[13] As Russia's world-wide Communist parties adopted the tactic of the Popular Front, he restated his confidence in the Russian experiment; and on the occasion of his visit to Russia, he said that Russia would deserve the gratitude of the world if it could substitute public welfare for private profit as the motive for industry. He loved the victim Karl Radek more than the tyrant Josef Stalin, and he deplored the murder of Leon Trotsky, but he insisted that the Communists had accomplished more than they had destroyed. After the Soviet-German pact stunned the Western powers in August 1939, he clearly felt himself on the defensive. The pact was no more inexplicable, he told himself, than was the alignment of Japan, Russia, and France against Germany, Great Britain, Italy, and the United States in their respective attitudes toward the color line. As for Finland, Latvia, Estonia, and Lithuania—which Russia had just invaded—they had been stolen from Russia after the first World War and were ready to gang up with England, France, and Germany against the new Russia. And anyway, the West had stolen too. The following year Russia still seemed to him the "greatest single hope for future industrial democracy" despite its pact with Hitler, and he justified Russian neutrality as the best assurance for that hope.[14] When Hitler obligingly attacked Russia in the summer of 1941, it cleared DuBois's thinking considerably: he had seen the war as "inevitable" in 1936 and had been amazed by the Soviet-German pact.

Good and evil were sorted out: Germany, having laid aside its camouflage, was now leading Europe against communism, trying to halt the spread of the idea that the state must control capital to achieve the well-being of the working masses. Though England and France recognized the fact only dimly, Russia's "industrial democracy" held the hopes of the modern world; if this idea were crushed, modern culture must fail. Since the great democracies had forced Stalin into the arms of Hitler, not magnanimity but "expiation for sins" required them to give full aid to their new Russian ally.

Japan, in its expansion in Asia, could always count on sympathetic understanding, and even defense. In 1936 DuBois observed that Europe and America screamed when Japan stole Western techniques of imperialism because the West felt that only its own imperialism could be benevolent. He was confident that the common race consciousness of China and Japan *vis-à-vis* the British Empire would keep Japan from extending its holdings in China; in any case, Japan offered "infinitely greater" chances for economic reform than any European power except Russia. During his world tour he took special notice that in Manchuria Japan imposed less of a caste system than any other occupying power. Though he was appalled by the Chinese hatred of Japan, he continued to regard Japan as the savior of the East against white domination and to blame England for Japanese action against the mainland: English colonialism stimulated Japanese fears, and only expansion could allay them. His visit to the island empire, where he was much feted, created some doubts in his mind on Japanese enlightenment, for he reported that Japan was thinking in terms of capitalist culture, a formula causing acute hostility to Russia. Yet when the Sino-Japanese war broke out again in 1937, DuBois had a pat explanation: Japan was fighting Europe by attacking China; Japan was forced to annex northern China because of the availability there of raw materials which Europe refused to sell to Japan. When China truckled to England, when it refused to organize itself against Europe, he said, Japan "undertook this duty herself." Four years later he noted that "to Japan alone is due the fact that the whole continent of Asia is not today in hopeless serfdom to Europe."[15] Even ten months after the attack on Pearl

Harbor he still hoped for a miracle to overthrow Japan's governing imperialist elements which, wincing under imputations of inferiority, had learned too much from nineteenth-century European standards. Perhaps he could recall the assurance of Yosuke Matsuoka at the time of DuBois's visit to Japan that "within and essentially" Japan was communistic, the only possible leader of a democratic movement without a color line.

DuBois was profoundly suspicious of American policy. In 1936 he wondered whom Americans feared when they passed their greatest peace-time budget for war equipment. When the war started in 1939, he gave his readers little direction. Where, he asked, was the Negro's stake when he was allied to colonial peoples? Did it depend on the victory or defeat of the controlling empires? Imperial England had never given the world democracy, neither would imperial Germany—"So what?" In January 1941, he formally identified himself with nonintervention. The United States should defend itself against attack, but no one was attacking. England had in the past, Germany might in the future, but her hands were fairly full at the moment. Were we afraid of Hitler's racial theories? he asked. We practiced them in the United States, he replied, and we applied them to Asians and Africans. If the United States were preparing for self-defense, why did it have a fleet in Asia, where it owned nothing not stolen? Were we protecting China from Japan, or hoarding China as our private preserve for exploitation? Already he had scoffed at Henry L. Stimson's appeal for a strong policy in China: Asia had good reason to fear Americans bearing gifts, he said, and he did not recall Stimson's public protests against Italy's attack on Ethiopia. Stimson, Cordell Hull, and Roosevelt had driven Japan into an alliance with Hitler. Joseph C. Grew had been ordered back to Japan to stir up a Japanese-American war. The Atlantic Charter seemed hollow to DuBois because it avoided mention of colonial peoples; while we put pressure on Russia to change its religious policy as the price of "dribbles of aid," he said, billions could not make England promise to give up India. Americans could justify English and Russian seizure of Persia as self-protection, but when Japan took Indochina, they condemned it as aggression. The root of all this seemed quite clear: Americans could agree on war against Japan because she was colored. "For Japan to seize Borneo oil when we refuse to sell her this life blood of the nations, is cause for a white crusade against yellow presumption."[16] In 1943, when Congress was considering a bill to eliminate discrimination against the Chinese in immigration policy, DuBois commented that its passage would show that "the war with Japan was unnecessary, since a similar yielding to Japan would have avoided the chief cause of the war."[17]

DuBois was judging world powers by two criteria: their sympathy for colored colonial peoples and their aversion to capitalism. Of the two, the first was the more important. Russia, rated high on both counts, was forgiven its tyranny and murders. Japan's role in fighting Western imperial powers made up for its affection for capitalism and for its expansion in Asia. Germany's rationalization of industry won praise, but its racial doctrines and its attack on Russia damned it. England was the ancient sanctimonious imperialist; when the Luftwaffe buffeted the English homeland, DuBois scoffed at the notion of Britain as a "suffering saint" and said that what it received was no worse than what it had imposed: the British Empire had caused more human misery than Hitler could in a hundred years. France was only slightly better. And the United States tagged behind British policy in Europe and exported racial discrimination to Asia.

Yet when war came to the United States, DuBois recalled his loyal slogan of 1918, "Close Ranks," and said that Negroes would fight, now as then, for "democracy not only for white folks but for yellow, brown and black."[18] Here was the hint for DuBois's later thought: he would test the Allies' performance in rebuilding the world after the war by the fidelity to democratic principles. Would the United States and Great Britain guarantee self-determination and democracy to Asia and Africa?

Freedom for colonial peoples was the crucial issue. When President Roosevelt sought a name for the war, DuBois suggested "War for Racial Equality." In reviewing Jawaharlal Nehru's autobiography, DuBois made a single package of the world's racial problems: all were primarily matters of economic exploitation, racial arrogance, and utter failure to recognize the essential humanity of people of different appearance. As the war years ad-

vanced, he found little in British or American policy to approve.*
He charged that the silence on Africa was "determined and deliberate," and that the mission of Leo T. Crowley, Foreign Economic Administrator of the United States, to Ethiopia in 1944 was
more concerned with investments for America than with the re-
covery of Ethiopia. An article in *Foreign Affairs* defined the crux
of the African question: "European profit—or Negro development?" He feared that Europe would snatch Africa's resources to
help pay the cost of the war and to reestablish prosperity. As early
as 1943 he saw signs that after the war England and the United
States would continue to oppose communism in Russia and to
keep Africa down.

Just as DuBois's decade at Atlanta was coming to a close, he
summarized the "Prospects of a World Without Race Conflict" in
the *American Journal of Sociology.* By that time he expected the
doctrine of biological differences to persist after the war, for there
was little evidence of willingness to change: India was not eman-
cipated, Asia and Africa were not treated as equals. The Allied
attitude (except for Russia) toward postwar problems, he thought,
provided for Europe and America without a thought of the darker
races. Russia, which was showing sympathy for the Chinese coolie
but no sympathy for Chiang Kai-shek, he said, might challenge the
Allies' plans. But the colored peoples themselves offered little
hope, for their economic inexperience and their false leaders—
"willing instruments of European economic oppression"—made
it essential that someone act for them. DuBois suggested a solution: "A union of economic liberals across the race line, with the
object of driving exploiting investors from their hideout behind
race discrimination, by freeing thought and action in colonial
areas is the only realistic path to permanent peace today."[19]

Shortly thereafter, DuBois's contract at Atlanta was abruptly
terminated. The cause of this rupture has not been discussed publicly, but internal evidence in *Phylon* suggests that DuBois's public
criticism of Atlanta's educational policy, together with the university's alarm that *Phylon* was becoming too much an instrument
of propaganda, contributed to the decision. With magnanimity

* The similar fears felt by white liberals are discussed in Eric F. Goldman,
Rendezvous with Destiny (New York, 1952), pp. 385-98.

unwarranted by DuBois's persistent discourtesy a decade before, Walter White recalled DuBois's contribution to "straight thinking by the Negro" and immediately initiated a move among the Association's directors to bring DuBois back to the Association to direct work on a Committee to Present the Cause of the Negro at the Next Peace Conference. On the understanding that his connection with the Association would continue for the rest of his working days, DuBois accepted the post and returned to New York.

In August 1944 his column in the *Amsterdam News* closed out his decade at Atlanta and opened the new—and probably final—era. The greatest question before the world, he said, was whether democracy in Europe and America could survive as long as the majority of the people of the world was kept in colonial status, poor, ignorant, and diseased, for the profit of the civilized nations of the world. "This is the problem to which I propose to devote the remaining years of my active life."[20]

The time of hesitation had passed.

THE ECLIPSE OF RACE

.ibn

The calm interlude at Atlanta left DuBois out of practice for the rigors of his next eight years, 1944–1952. Back at the Association's offices where once he had thundered, he found his influence narrowed to postwar colonial policy and "special research," while other hands—to DuBois, cold hands—wove the fibers of policy. For four years, tensions about organization, administration, and policy taxed the patience of both sides. By the end of 1948 the Association decided on a clean break and discharged DuBois with a pension. The Council on African Affairs, of which Paul Robeson was chairman, quickly welcomed him as a nonsalaried vice-chairman; his office there was a headquarters for his travels, lectures, and writing. In the spring of 1950 he became chairman of the Peace Information Center, organized to spread sentiment for peace and to secure American signatures to the "Stockholm Appeal"; and in the fall, he ran for the United States Senate against Herbert H. Lehman and Joe R. Hanley. The following year, in time for his eighty-third birthday, he and four associates at the Peace Center were indicted by a federal grand jury for failing to register the Peace Information Center as the American agent of a foreign principal.

The troubled postwar world which landed DuBois in a criminal court changed basically the direction of his thought. The struggle for power between the United States and Russia made DuBois increasingly critical of American foreign policy, which he conceived to be directed by American imperialists, and ever more cordial to the "peace" movements spurred by the Soviet Union and, as he thought, by the masses of people everywhere. Against this background, the trauma of his trial led him in 1952 to cast off race action as a guiding philosophy and to turn to "a World conception of human uplift . . . one centering about the work and income of the working class."[1]

The Fight Against "American Imperialism"

Shortly after his return to the Association in 1944, DuBois told a radio audience that unless colonial peoples received a share of power, their masters were inviting future wars among themselves and against subject peoples in revolt. He regretted that the preliminary conferences of the United Nations Organization at Dumbarton Oaks had provided no direct representation for the billion people in colored colonial areas. Did the slight mean that colonial powers would recoup their wartime losses by more vigorous exploitation of backward areas? Workers, he feared, would be bribed by government aid at home into supporting imperialism—"democracy in Europe will continue to impede and nullify democracy in Asia and Africa."[2]

As long as the outline of the peace remained unclear, DuBois balanced a modicum of hope against his fears. In a timely book, *Color and Democracy: Colonies and Peace,* published in 1945, he heralded the dawn of a new day.* But the evidence in his own book did not sustain his optimism. He noted that the discussion on international organization at Bretton Woods turned on the stabilization of currencies and on loans for reconstruction, ignoring investments in colonial cheap labor and raw materials. China, on hand at Dumbarton Oaks to represent colored peoples everywhere, was hardly consulted on plans for the UNO, he said, and in any case, China's status was suspect. Was China being built up as one of the five great powers, with a permanent seat on the Security Council, as the Asian cat's paw for European and American dominance? The Netherlands had made some tentative gestures toward greater freedom in Indonesia, he reported, but "much depends on how far the poverty and destruction in Holland will allow political freedom and industrial planning for the Natives to proceed in East Asia at the expense of Dutch investors." England's rule in India was still "totalitarian," he said; he wondered if pressure from the Labour party could break down Winston

---

* "The day has dawned when above a wounded tired earth unselfish sacrifice, without sin and hell, may join thorough technique, shorn of ruthless greed, and make a new religion, one with new knowledge, to shout from the old hills of heaven: Go down, Moses!"

Churchill's stubborn determination to maintain the power of the privileged British aristocracy. The United States was a constant puzzle, he went on, because the provincialism of the Senate and the Negro problem predisposed the Americans to empire and to disfranchisement for a majority of the people in the world. Even Russia's future was uncertain, for although its record on colonialism and race prejudice gave grounds for hope, plans were already apparent for establishing spheres of influence in the Balkans.

The San Francisco Conference in 1945 left him without hope. As an associate consultant to the American delegation, DuBois drafted a "first statute of international law" which forbade every nation to deprive any group of a voice in its own government. It was rejected, and the United Nations Charter left the international organization without power to interfere in "domestic" matters like colonies. As a result, DuBois said in an interview, 750,000,000 people were unrepresented in the new world order. The wordy promise to recognize the interests of colonials as paramount over investors and civil servants, he added later, was inadequate without machinery to compel dilatory powers to keep their word. He hoped that he was wrong, but he feared that American expansion in the Pacific strategic area had cost the United States its chance to vote with Russia and China in a great-power majority against colonialism. He feared that Americans would take on the task of holding Asia and Africa in subjugation while voting with the two powers bitterly opposed to Russia's economic program. Organized business in England, France, and the United States, he said, was ready to fight Russia. This was the meaning of the "continual pinpricks" of Russia during the conference. DuBois felt sure that the third World War was taking shape around the suppression of Asia and the strangulation of Russia.

Disappointed at San Francisco, DuBois returned to familiar ideas: England and the United States were imperialist and discriminatory, Russia was neither. The simple clarity of this balance gave order in a complex world.

The Labour victory in England in 1945 led to a few months of renewed optimism, for DuBois felt that it put England in the procession of socialism behind Russia, leaving the United States as the only reactionary power. (Chiang's China was only "partially progressive.") But a visit to London the same year suggested that the Socialist movement, carrying on with imperialism "from sheer momentum," had not yet learned that Asia, Africa, and the Balkans needed democratic socialism as much as Great Britain. On his return he condemned Labour's colonial policy as even worse than that of the Tories. The following year he doubted that the Labourites would ever learn. If Clement Attlee swallowed Churchill's domestic policy as he had accepted his imperialism, and if Americans were "beguiled by this siren song of the British aristocracy," civilization would hopelessly plunge into war after war and "go down to hell to the beat of drums and display of military pageantry."[3] When Burma and India gained their independence, England won no credit, for both dependent nations, DuBois said, had forced the issue. The continued British control in Kenya as late at 1948 and the spectacle of Smuts speaking in favor of the United Nations Charter of Human Rights while he maintained white supremacy in South Africa seemed to DuBois visible evidence of "the hypocrisy, double-dealing and coldly-calculated cruelty of the modern world."[4]

By DuBois's standards the United States was worse: conciliation having died with Roosevelt, the American government had aligned itself with the forces of reaction determined to hold Russia in check and to maintain colonialism. DuBois claimed that business interests controlled American policy. Fearful that peacetime use of atomic energy would make its investments obsolete, he said, business hid behind the Baruch plan while Russia sought effective control of atomic energy; the Truman Doctrine was a device to arm Greece against Russia for the benefit of Great Britain; the Marshall Plan promised large profits to American investors and aimed at reestablishing European wealth at the expense of the colonies. At the United Nations John Foster Dulles, an American delegate, was conspicuously silent as Nehru's sister, Mrs. Vijaya Lakshmi Pandit, spoke against the exploitation of native labor. For DuBois, America's sins were retroactive: captains of industry had seduced the government into sympathy toward Germany and Italy until the unreasonableness of the fascist demands and popular pressure forced the government to enter the war in self-defense. Elsewhere he declared that Japan, in attacking America, had "furnished the one reason, based on race prejudice, which brought America immediately into the war."[5] The war itself had been "due . . . principally to American greed," the attempt to make money out of the distress of the world.[6] Since this same concentration of economic and industrial power ruled the United States in 1947, he said, any other nation which did not fear America's imperial power lacked common sense.

While the British and Americans were viewed as plotting for war, DuBois could see no evil in the Soviet Union. Russia was right in keeping the Poles behind the Curzon line, he said, for the Poles had to learn to govern themselves before they ruled over an alien people. He reported in his column in the Chicago *Defender* that Molotov was the "one statesman at San Francisco who stood up for human rights and the emancipation of colonies."[7] DuBois liked Stalin's "straight talk" in listing the second World War as the "inevitable result" of the economic and political expansion of monopoly capitalism. While the American press whitewashed the British Empire, DuBois said, the Soviet delegation negotiated for the withdrawal of Western troops from Greece and the Middle East, for Indonesian independence, and for immediate trustee-ships. DuBois admired Russia's accomplishment in abolishing race hatred. Russian atomic proposals were more realistic than the Baruch plan. He praised the Soviet delegation for favoring a hear-ing for the Association's petition before the U.N. Subcommission on the Prevention of Discrimination and Protection of Minor-ities—any assertion that Russian support was politically motivated, he said, was "wholly gratuitous." Always looming behind DuBois's cordiality to Russia was his conviction—held now for more than twenty-five years—that communism embraced the goals of every unselfish thinker of the previous century: abolition of poverty and illiteracy, production for consumption not profit, social control of nature's riches, and abolition of unemployment. Against this statement of the ideal, mortal men in capitalist nations were hard pressed to compete.

As always with DuBois, analysis led to a program. He took up again the mantle of universal pundit, and his advice to this group and to that seemed at times a review of his career. In a speech to a national Negro fraternity, the Talented Tenth re-emerged, decked with twentieth-century garlands, as a "Guiding Hundredth"; less than a month before his dismissal from the Association, he urged onward its legal fight against discrimination; he demanded that Negroes pay for and control their own universities; and he revived his insistence on consumer's cooperatives. To a Southern Negro youth conference he recommended that young Negroes stay in the South and fight their battle for justice in the section of the world which, he said, was matched only by South Africa in reactionary discrimination. Most important of all, he suggested two new courses of action: first, working through the United Nations where friendly voices, like Russia and India, could take up the Negro's plea, and, second, supporting forces favoring peace and friendship for Russia.

The San Francisco Conference had barely adjourned when DuBois revived old notions for a Pan-African movement. Premature in 1919, the idea now had more plausibility, for the second World War had stirred every continent, and colored peoples indifferent to Sarajevo felt the impact of the fall of Singapore. Major colonial powers like Great Britain and France were sufficiently drained by the war to give hopes to a determined colonial people, and Russia was always willing to applaud any disintegration of its Allies' empires. Airplanes and cheap cables replacing slow ships and uncertain mail had created one world. And finally, the charter of the United Nations lent the prestige of world sentiment to the improvement of colonial conditions. Ebullient as ever, DuBois issued a call for a Pan-African Conference in London for October 1945. Frantically organizing the conference by mail and cablegram, DuBois felt confident that the meeting, if properly guided, could become "the real movement for the emancipation of Africa." The meeting was a great triumph, attended by representatives from sixty nations and colonies, among them Kwame Nkrumah, later the first premier of Ghana. Returning from the conference, DuBois reported jubilantly that the mood of colored peoples had changed and that Britain would have to extend self-government in Africa and the West Indies "or face open revolt." The future of the world and of democracy, he stated early the next year, now depended principally on Asia and Africa; the twentieth century spelled the end of European domination of the world. Small loss, according to his next book, *The World and Africa*, because the science of our civilization had come from Africa, the religion from Asia, and nothing constructive from Britain and America. (DuBois characteristically said it with less reserve: "Africa saw the stars of God; Asia saw the soul of man; Europe saw and sees only man's body, which it feeds and polishes until it is fat, gross, and cruel.")

The next step was to mobilize American Negro opinion behind a direct protest to the United Nations. At DuBois's behest, representatives of twenty organizations met in October 1946 at the Schomburg Collection, a branch of the New York Public Library, but the responsibility for the petition fell finally to the NAACP, more specifically to DuBois. His strategy became clear in an unscheduled appearance before the Association's convention in Washington in 1947. Since socialism and the United Nations offered the principal hopes for backward races, American Negroes, who by their economic position were closely allied to these colonial groups, should look to the United Nations and to social reformers everywhere. After all, was not the American Negro in "quasi-colonial status"?

The petition to the United Nations, "An Appeal to the World" (1947), invoked world power against American discrimination. It took the form of six essays by separate authors: DuBois's introduction, two essays by Earl B. Dickerson and Milton R. Konvitz reviewing the history of the Negro's legal rights since 1787, two by William R. Ming, Jr., and Leslie S. Perry commenting on present discriminatory patterns, and one by Rayford W. Logan, examing the legal basis for U.N. action in protecting a minority. In his essay DuBois argued that the United States, as part of an imperialist bloc of private investors defying the wishes of their peoples, had withdrawn its sympathy from colored peoples and from small nations. At home it had been deaf to Negro appeals for equal rights; Mississippi offered more of a threat to America than Russia. Though the Negro question was "without doubt primarily an internal and national question," DuBois argued that as nations drew closer together, it would became a matter of international concern. Already United Nations delegates were suffering affronts when they were mistaken for Negroes. Further-more, thirteen million Negroes were by numbers "one of the con-siderable nations of the world," as populous as Scandinavia, and larger than Canada. If smaller nations had a direct voice in the United Nations, then American Negroes had at least the right to be heard.

A hearing on the appeal was favored by the Soviet Union and successfully opposed by the United States. This reinforced Du-Bois's estimate of the Negro's friends and foes. Despite the rebuff, DuBois continued to support the United Nations because its char-ter provided cogent authority for individual as well as colonial rights.

Yet, however useful as polemical reinforcement, the United Nations Charter—like Christianity and American democracy—was not self-enforcing. DuBois was again in the position he had oc-cupied at Atlanta from 1905 to 1910: an argumentative brief made the Negro's intellectual position stronger, but in action it seemed curiously irrelevant and had to be backed up by organization and agitation. After 1946, and especially after the failure of the pe-tition to the United Nations, DuBois directed his support to those groups in the United States which campaigned in the name of peace and of friendship for Russia.

Politically this carried DuBois into the new Progressive party. As the elections of 1946 approached, DuBois argued that the two major parties gave no opportunity to vote on six essential ques-tions: labor unions, imperialist control of colonial areas, Great Britain or Russia as an ally, rotten boroughs in the South, lynch-ing, and job discrimination. While Secretary of State Byrnes told Germany and Russia about American democracy, DuBois said, both Democrats and Republicans agreed on private greed, graft, and theft. In such a dilemma DuBois fully endorsed the "excel-lent" platform of the newly formed Progressive Citizens of Amer-ica (and incidentally condemned a "parallel movement," presum-ably the Americans for Democratic Action, for placing its first emphasis on fighting Communists). At the beginning of 1948, he called upon his newspaper readers to urge Henry Wallace to run for President even though his chances for winning were negligible: better to throw away votes on a great man than to allow other nations to think that all America could be deceived by the lies of reactionary Republicans and Southern-supported Democrats. DuBois supported Wallace in part because of his uncompromising stand on Negro questions, but even more because of his advocacy of peace and his friendship for Russia. DuBois refused to be diverted by the charge that communists, socialists, and New Dealers—groups indiscriminately regarded by some as subversive—would support Wallace. On the contrary, DuBois saw that support as an omen encouraging hope, not suspicion. Certainly it was no more suspicious than support by reaction and militarism.[8] DuBois carried his campaigning even into meetings of the Association. In June 1948 he told a gathering in Philadelphia that Wallace deserved its support because of his courage and because his attitude toward Negro problems was "satisfactory in every respect." Wallace's defeat in November ended this gambit. A year and a half later, when Wallace approved America's armed support of the Republic of Korea, DuBois wrote off Wallace the crusader as "Wallace the Weasel."[9] (As vice-chairman of the Council on African Affairs, DuBois denounced American aid as "foreign intervention.")

Two months before the election, DuBois had been dismissed from his post at the Association. The break came after the press secured a copy of a memorandum in which DuBois stated that the Association was abandoning its efforts to ease the world plight of the Negro in order to serve the interests of the Truman administration. DuBois attacked Walter White's appointment as a consultant to the American delegation to the United Nations General Assembly in Paris as a political act; White's acceptance of such a position without making a clear, open public declaration of his position on Truman's foreign policy, DuBois said, would "in the long run, align the association with the reactionary, war-mongering colonial imperialism of the present Administration."[10] No matter who was at fault in allowing this memorandum to slip out to the newspapers, White would not tolerate this public attack from a member of his own organization. He asked the Association's board of directors to dismiss DuBois, and the board did. Almost immediately DuBois found refuge with the Council on African Affairs, which gave him an office and a secretary and left him alone.

Beginning in March 1949, DuBois took an active part in the series of international meetings known as the "peace crusade." Operating outside the usual diplomatic channels, these meetings were designed to alert world opinion to the dangers of a third World War and to enroll millions as active "partisans for peace." Its supporters regarded the crusade as a spontaneous demonstration by millions of people all over the world for whom peace was the overriding issue of the day; its critics saw it as an oblique Communist-inspired attack on American foreign policy. Favoring peace and believing that the United States offered the greatest threat to it, DuBois had no hesitation in attaching himself to the movement. Once again an announced pacifist, he hoped that an international chorus for peace would exorcise the war clouds present since the defeat of Japan. His peace pilgrimages took him from a New York meeting in March 1949 to Paris in April and to Moscow in August. Then in August of the following year he journeyed to Prague as the guest of the Bureau of the World Congress of the Defenders of Peace. At all the meetings he was invariably given a place of honor.

The New York meeting, called the Cultural and Scientific Conference for World Peace, brought together an international galaxy including two major Russian figures, Dimitri Shostakovich and Alexander A. Fadeyev. DuBois said later that the conference "marked an era in the cultural history of the United States." In a formal address at the conference, DuBois delivered a short but freshly thought-out statement, "The Nature of Intellectual Freedom," in which, without accusation or partisanship, he warned against encroachments on the "gray borderland" between the necessities of natural law and the legitimate area of fantasy. At the closing rally at Madison Square Garden, however, he caught the spirit of the occasion and denounced the United States for systematic distortion of the purposes of the conference, for lies about Russia and communism, and for failure to enact civil-rights legislation. Russia, on the other hand, alone of all modern nations, he said, wrote a prohibition of race and color discrimination into its fundamental law and then enforced it.

At the Paris meeting of the World Congress of the Defenders of Peace, which he described as "the greatest meeting of men ever

assembled in modern times to advance the progress of all men,"
he denounced colonialism as one of the chief causes of war and
as the arch-opponent of the spread of socialism. Of the United
States, he said: "Drunk with power we are leading the world to
hell in a new colonialism with the same old human slavery which
once ruined us, and to a third World War which will ruin the
world."[11] At the All-Russian Peace Congress in Moscow, where
DuBois was the only American present, he summarized his lifetime's reading in a brief history of the Negro's relation to industry in the United States. The summary was, on the whole, an
optimistic one, for he closed by stressing the gradual advance of
social planning in the United States and the intensity of the desire for peace among millions of Americans.

By the time of the Prague meeting of 1950, however, the Korean War had started, and DuBois showed no forebearance. Not
in the fifty years of his experience, DuBois said, had "organized
reaction" in the United States wielded comparable power. By
control of the press and radio, by curtailment of free speech, and
by imprisonment of liberal thinkers, the controlling interests were
inducing Americans to believe in an "imminent danger of aggression from communism, socialism and liberalism" cloaked by the
peace movement. The overwhelming majority of Americans still
hated murder as a means of progress, he said, but it would take
"guts and the willingness to jeopardize jobs and respectability" in
order to "win the peace in America."[12]

As a result of these activities for peace DuBois had, by the time
of the Prague conference, already accepted the chairmanship of
the Peace Information Center with headquarters in New York
City. The Center concentrated on two projects: publishing a
periodic "peacegram" telling Americans what other nations were
doing and thinking about war and peace, and collecting signatures for the "Stockholm Appeal," an eighty-word petition that
demanded the absolute banning of atomic weapons and strict con-
trols for enforcement of the ban. The statement had been origi-
nally adopted at a meeting of the World Partisans for Peace in
Stockholm on March 15, 1950. After circulation of the petition
was well under way in the United States, Dean Acheson, then
Secretary of State, denounced it in a public statement as a "propa-

ganda trick in the spurious 'peace offensive' of the Soviet Union."
He labeled the Partisans of Peace as a Communist organization,
and he said that the American campaign was being actively promoted by the Communist party. DuBois replied immediately by
announcing that 1,000,000 Americans in forty states had signed
the petition, 400,000 since the outbreak of the Korean War. The
following day the House Un-American Activities Committee called
the petition "Communist chicanery." Three days later DuBois
released a full statement in rebuttal. The Secretary's statement,
DuBois wrote, invited the impression that Americans would use
the atomic bomb in Korea and that the American government felt
no desire for peace. He asked pointedly if a Russian policy of
peace made necessary American insistence on war. He interpreted
the Secretary's statement as meaning that "there is no possibility
of mediating our differences with Russia."[13] Meanwhile the Center's director, Abbott Simon, told the New York *Times* that since
the Center was not affiliated with the World Congress of the Defenders of Peace, which was circulating the petition elsewhere in
the world, it had no obligation to register with the Attorney-
General. The Center continued its activities until October 12,
and then, probably because of pressure from the Department of
Justice, started to disband.

Meanwhile DuBois had agreed to run for the Senate from New
York on the American Labor party ticket. Despite his eighty-two
years, he welcomed the chance to pursue his campaign for peace
and to help strengthen the ticket on which Vito Marcantonio was
running for the House of Representatives. DuBois ran his campaign on two rails: peace and civil rights.* He criticized both
major parties for their unwillingness to enact civil-rights legislation, but spent most of his ten campaign speeches hammering on a
now familiar theme: Hanley and Lehman were both fronts for big
business, which was driving the United States to war. At home,
he said, Americans were bidden to hate Russia when they should
hate war; they were denounced as subversives when they thought
for themselves and as traitors when they attacked segregation in
the Army. Abroad, while the Korean War shook our resources,

* The *Times* covered DuBois's speeches faithfully—rather better, in fact,
than did the *Daily Worker*.

the conspiracy of Big Business and Big Brass looked for ways of conquering China, Russia, India, and the Balkans; American aid programs had already opened the door to exploitation of the wage earners of Greece, Korea, and other nations. Big Business, DuBois said in perhaps his most violent thrust, "would rather have your sons dying in Korea than studying in America and asking advanced questions."[14] The American spokesman at the United Nations, former Senator Warren Austin, was "a neurotic, hysterical man, without self-control or logic"; it was a "disaster" to have him at that post. The *Daily Worker,* the Communists' New York newspaper, gave DuBois full support in what it called his campaign against Winthrop W. Aldrich, the chairman of the Chase National Bank. Even with this backing, DuBois polled less than 4 per cent of the Senatorial vote; he even fell behind the American Labor party's candidate for governor.

Always a fighter, DuBois enjoyed the campaign. A resilient octogenarian, he had lost little of the passion for controversy which had become a Negro legend. But the focus of his ideas had by now narrowed. If he was anything, he was a "functional" leader in foreign policy—a leader, be it said, whose peace crusades and sharp words for America brought him relatively few Negro adherents.

The Extreme "Left" Woos DuBois

DuBois's postwar views drew a curtain over his old feud with American Communists. In the early 1930's, tempers had been hot. DuBois's view of American Communist "jackasses" was warmly reciprocated. A writer in the *New Masses* noted DuBois's valuable early scholarly work, but roasted him as a "typical careerist—full of vacillations, hatreds, and pettyfogging," whose accomplishments were outweighed by his "high-hat demeanor, his disdain for the mass, his stewardship of the elite, his reformist-nationalist darker-race program and his latter-day segregationism."[15] Later the same year, moderation set in, for the Communists moved into the era of the Popular Front. Prominent Negro leaders ceased being lickspittles of capitalism and Judases to their race and were welcomed as allies in the "progressive" fight. In any case, DuBois's seclusion in Atlanta absented him from public notice, and there was no occasion to abuse him. A tardy observer of *Black Reconstruction* even noted in *Science and Society* that DuBois had been the first to break through the traditional interpretation of Reconstruction, though J. S. Allen's Marxist volume on the period was preferred.

DuBois's attitude remained firm. He approved of the Russian revolution as he always had, but he continued to view cautiously the tactics and program of the American Communists. In 1936 he welcomed the Popular Front, and the following year he praised the National Negro Congress as a good outfit lined up with labor and not with capital. He hoped it would eventually fill a role comparable to the Indian National Congress. In 1940, when the Popular Front lost Communist support because of the Nazi-Soviet Pact, however, the Communists' program seemed "fundamentally wrong" to DuBois, its suggestions for a Negro party "arrant nonsense." Yet when Earl Browder, the Communist leader, was indicted for making false statements in connection with a passport, DuBois condoned Browder's offense as harmless and charged that Browder was being sent to jail not for lying but for being a Communist. One might disagree with Browder's beliefs, DuBois said, but it was "cowardly evasion" to call them a crime. The issue was not communism, he insisted, it was the right to free speech and to free belief, even in communism. The next year DuBois joined a Citizens' Committee to Free Earl Browder.

The second thoughts on both sides paved the way for postwar amity as Marxist and Communist groups started to woo DuBois. First, in 1945, the *New Masses* published DuBois's tribute to Roosevelt's "superb" accomplishments. Then Benjamin J. Davis, Jr., reviewed *Color and Democracy*. He regretted DuBois's "somewhat careless and abstract comparison" of the German and Soviet dictatorships, but he approved as "on the whole correct" DuBois's central thesis—that peace and security were inseparable from colonial rights. The book, Davis said, was the best on the colonial question to come out of the war. The next year, in 1946, the pace was stepped up. In January DuBois was honored at the *New Masses* Annual Awards Dinner; in May the magazine appointed him as a contributing editor; in September it resurrected his twenty-year-old article on Georgia and headed it with an introduction by Herbert Aptheker, who said that future historians would refer to the recent period of Negro history as "The Age of DuBois." The Southern Negro Youth Congress followed in October by preparing a "book of reverence" signed by all its delegates and presenting it to DuBois, the "senior statesman of the American Negro's liberation struggle," in a ceremony almost religious in tone. During the next year the *New Masses* continued to publish articles by DuBois: "Behold the Land," his talk to the Southern Negro Youth Congress; an attack on Smuts; and a critique of England's policy in Egypt and the Sudan.

After DuBois's break with the Association in September 1948, the political left was indignant.* The National Council of the Arts, Sciences, and Professions denounced the dismissal as "persecution." Shirley Graham (who later married DuBois) asked indignantly in *Masses and Mainstream* how the Association dared to insult the Negro's "most eminent statesman for half a century," and the *Daily Worker,* terming his dismissal a "reprisal" for having opposed White, asked editorially if the dismissal meant that the Association's leaders were turning their backs on the fight for freedom. Abner W. Perry, a regular columnist for the *Worker,* hinted at some "striking [though unspecified] indications" that the leak to the press of DuBois's memorandum had been engineered by his enemies.

DuBois's later career led to new levels of praise. In an article in 1949 in the *National Guardian,* a "progressive" weekly, Aptheker reviewed DuBois's "half century of distinguished service to humanity" in which "the promises of youth are the records of history." Aptheker noted that the unity of theory and practice in the life of DuBois had led him to praise Marx as the "greatest of modern philosophers."[16] The *Guardian* praised DuBois's candidacy for the Senate in 1950, and the *Worker* saluted him as the leader of the "Negro people's movement in this nation" and noted

* According to Wilson Record, the Communist party was anxious to have a "valuable and safe" man in the Association's national office. "Whether or not he would have lent himself completely to its purposes inside the NAACP is a matter for conjecture." *The Negro and the Communist Party* (Chapel Hill, 1951), p. 265 n.

that his candidacy had created a "nationwide stir" despite the slurs in the New York newspapers, the "reactionary spokesmen of Wall Street's political stooges."[17] In time for the election the *Worker* observed that this "Giant of a Man" gave the voters a chance to register a strong vote against war parties and for peace and civil rights—a handy condensation of DuBois's campaign speeches. After DuBois was indicted for his role in the Peace Center, Davis thundered that the arrest was an attempt to terrorize the Negro, to take malicious revenge for DuBois's American Labor party candidacy, and (somewhat anticlimatically) to break up his eighty-third birthday party. This birthday dinner had been conceived by DuBois's associates at the Council on African Affairs as a fund-raising device to maintain the Council and DuBois's connection with it, and also to set up a publication fund for DuBois's collected works. In time for the dinner Aptheker praised DuBois as the "greatest living American scholar." Meanwhile, in the *National Guardian,* Marcantonio called the forthcoming arraignment of DuBois the "last outrage against freedom," and Albert E. Kahn was shocked by the "shameful" treatment of "one of the greatest living Americans." The final accolade came from Doxey A. Wilkerson the next year: DuBois was the "recognized 'Dean of American Letters.' "

The rapport between DuBois and the extreme left clearly served the purposes of both. For "Progressives" and Communists, DuBois's international reputation lent prestige to unpopular programs and gave the impression of support from underprivileged groups.* In return they gave him responsive audiences, enthusiastic about his ideas. At a time when the Negro movement in the United States seemed to have passed far out of his hands, when even the Negro press was closing its columns, the fine clean print of well-edited magazines and the applause of approving audiences revivified a career that had appeared to be at an end. In

---

* Aptheker, for example, caught on to DuBois's incidental reference to American Negroes as "one of the considerable nations of the world" (see p. 206, above) and used it to demonstrate a "high point in national consciousness among American Negroes." American Communists, Aptheker said, regarded this expression as support for their argument that the Negro question was essentially a question of a minority "nation."

1946, for example, he wrote in his *Defender* column: "Nothing I have experienced in past years has touched me more deeply" than the "fire and homage" of the Southern Negro Youth Congress.[18] By the time of his dismissal from the Association in 1948, and in part because of it, DuBois had lost contact with the audiences which had once listened. Even before his dismissal, his column in the *Defender* had been discontinued with ill feeling on both sides. His dismissal from the Association closed the pages of the *Crisis* and ruled him off the platform at Association conventions. Journals of general circulation turned to him infrequently. His showing in the 1950 Senatorial race, especially his showing in Harlem, betrayed his weakness; indeed, the fact that he ran behind his ticket lent color to the guess that he was the beneficiary of a hard core of ALP votes in New York City and that he added few votes on his own. To this fading career his new friends offered new life.

DuBois, however, appears to have remained master of his own thoughts; the Party did not set them for him. The alliance continued, at least until 1951, on DuBois's own terms. On major issues—control of atomic energy, civil rights, the Korean War, the Marshall Plan—DuBois's voice sounded like an echo of the party's. Yet in all probability, DuBois cooperated with Communists because on major issues they agreed with his independent views. As he said at the four-hour "welcome-home" rally for Paul Robeson on June 19, 1949, he would be a "fellow-traveler with Communist or capitalist, with white man or black," as long as "he walks toward the truth."[19] After all, DuBois had been wary of white imperialism before the Russian revolution of 1917; he had been thinking favorably about socialism at least as early as 1907; he had gone on record as a pacifist many times.

DuBois made his deviations quite explicit. At the *New Masses* Annual Awards Dinner in 1946 he defended the Negro's concern for the color line in preference to common problems of labor and poverty: "Our problems are so fundamentally human that they often underlie the broader but more abstract social problems."[20] His speech at the Moscow peace parley attacked American policy, but in relatively moderate phrases which actually concluded with an optimistic forecast. Though he joined Paul Robeson and others in denouncing the "hysteria-breeding" arrest of the top leaders of the Communist party, he stubbornly rebuffed Communist efforts to induce him to testify at their trial.* Even at the burial service for Ethel and Julius Rosenberg, the convicted atomic spies, DuBois limited his participation to a reading of the Twenty-third Psalm. On the crucial theoretical definition of socialism, DuBois never approached Marxist orthodoxy. He told the Association's convention in 1947 that the New Deal was just another name for socialism, and when DuBois's definition in his latest book, *In Battle for Peace,* remained similarly clouded, the reviewer for *Masses and Mainstream* objected on Marxist grounds. Following current Communist doctrine, he also took exception to some of DuBois's remarks about the Negro middle class.

Ententes were an old habit with DuBois; they were temporary attachments, not permanent commitments. As he said in 1948, "With my particular type of thinking and impulse to action, it was impossible for me to be a party man."[21] He could be as irascible with radicals as with liberals—at the offices of the Council on African Affairs, personal contact was about as formal, tension almost as acute, DuBois equally aloof as at the Association. A kind fate had always made tenacity to conviction possible for DuBois. At the age of eighty he was not likely to change.

Turning His Back on Race

DuBois's trial gave him an exciting nine months.[22] The indictment was handed down by a Washington grand jury on February 9, 1951. The Peace Information Center was charged with failure to register as an "agent of a foreign principal" as required by the Foreign Agents Registration Act of 1938, as amended in 1942; DuBois and four others were indicted for "failing to cause the organization" to register. The "foreign principal" involved was the Committee of the World Congress of the Defenders of Peace and its successor, the World Peace Council; the bill of particulars

* According to a person close to DuBois, two emissaries from the party spent most of a day soliciting DuBois's aid as a witness. He refused.

made clear that the circulation of the "Stockholm Peace Appeal" was the main offense.

The indictment stunned the eighty-three-year-old man, whose only previous brush with the law had been a speeding ticket. As the news broke, DuBois was planning his marriage to Shirley Graham—his first wife had died the previous year—and completing arrangements for the elaborate birthday dinner planned by the Council on African Affairs for February 23. Yet though stunned, he could not have been surprised. For the previous six months the Justice Department had been urging the Center to register in order to comply with the law; the Department explicitly avowed that registration was "in no way intended to interfere with the operation of the Peace Information Center in its present program." But DuBois and his associates took the position that the Center was an American group conceived and operated by American citizens "apprehensive lest the growing tension among the governments of the world burst into a terrible conflagration which might well snuff out civilization as we know it." The fact that people elsewhere in the world expressed similar ideas, the Center held, merely demonstrated that "the minds and desires of men have always transcended national barriers." A statement issued by Attorney-General J. Howard McGrath on the day of the indictment indicated that the Justice Department took a different view. The Stockholm Appeal was said to serve a two-fold purpose: to promote the "unenforceable" Soviet proposals concerning atomic energy and to divert attention from Communist "aggression in other forms" by centering attention on the use of atomic weapons. When the Center's officers persisted in their refusal to register, the Justice Department turned to the courts. If convicted, each of the defendants faced a maximum penalty of a $10,000 fine and five years' imprisonment.

The arraignment took place on February 16. The trial date was set for April 2, but at the request of the defense was repeatedly deferred. A delay was particularly important to allow both government and defense attorneys to take a deposition from Jean Laffitte, secretary of the World Congress of the Defenders of Peace, the alleged foreign principal. (Though this testimony was never introduced at the trial, Laffitte denied any connection with the Peace Center: it was not an agent, his organization was not the principal.)

Meanwhile, DuBois and his new wife made a cross-country tour to raise funds for the defense. Unintimidated by the government's charges, DuBois continued to preach his familiar gospel: big business was paralyzing democracy by creating a military dictatorship; only some form of socialism could preserve the ideals of a democratic America; nothing could stop communism but something better than communism; and if disliking the present state of affairs in America was communism, "then by the living God, no force of arms, nor power of wealth, nor smartness of intellect will ever stop it." Deliberately DuBois avoided softening his line—no compromises, no equivocation, for "I wanted to dispel in the minds of the government and of the public any lingering doubt as to my determination to think and speak freely on the economic foundations of the wars and frustrations of the twentieth century."

The trial began on November 8, with Federal Judge Matthew F. McGuire presiding and with eight Negroes and four whites in the jury box. Vito Marcantonio served without fee as chief defense counsel. After five days in court, Judge McGuire entered a verdict of acquittal for all five defendants and for the Center. The prosecution disclaimed any intention of showing that the Soviet Union was operating behind the Paris committee, but it succeeded in establishing the parallels between the Center's activities and those of the World Council for Peace in Paris. Marcantonio insisted that parallelism did not establish agency, and on this crucial point Judge McGuire agreed. The court told the prosecution that it had to establish a "nexus" beyond a reasonable doubt. When it failed to establish a direct link between the Peace Center and the Paris committee, McGuire made his ruling without hearing any of the defense. DuBois was free. Poorer, but free.

It is difficult to generalize on the public response to DuBois's indictment. He could find some support in the Negro press, but he complained that the Talented Tenth of business and professional men was "either silent or actually antagonistic." An attempt to secure the signatures of prominent Negroes to a fairly mild statement of support did not attract enough signers to warrant its publication.* The directors of the Association avoided passing on the merits of the indictment, but noted that it "lends color to the charge that efforts are being made to silence spokesmen for full equality of Negroes."† The annual convention spun this theme out at greater length, but took no more definite stand. Essentially DuBois's support came from American peace groups, from self-styled "progressive" spokesmen such as the *Daily Worker,* the New York *Daily Compass,* and the *National Guardian,* and from "progressive" organizations such as the National Council of the Arts, Sciences, and Professions. A few labor unions, such as the Fur and Leather Workers and some locals of the United Electrical Workers, helped. The greater response came from abroad: from African and Asian organizations and from European spokesmen most likely to support the peace crusades. DuBois's own analysis shows the predominance of leftist sympathy: "clearly my support . . . came from Eastern European Communists, from western European Socialists, from Communist Asia, from Progressives, Socialists and Communists in the United States, and from the Left in India and South America. To this would be appended the colored peoples of Africa, the Caribbean and the United States, many of whom are conservative."

Almost as soon as the decision was announced, the DuBoises were at work on a new essay in autobiography, *In Battle for Peace,* published in book form nine months later by *Masses and Mainstream.* The trial had obviously affected DuBois very deeply. Mulling over the postwar years and his own trial, sorting out friends and enemies, sifting forces of progress and reaction, he cut himself loose from the struggle for Negro equality. In the

* In one appeal for signatures P. L. Prattis, editor of the Pittsburgh *Courier,* is quoted as saying: "The handcuffs on DuBois are meant to serve as a GAG on any Negro leadership that is disposed to 'shoot the works' for freedom." Copies of the appeals issued by the "Friends of Dr. W. E. B. DuBois" are in the Howard University Library.

† The full resolution read: "Without passing on the merits of the recent indictment of Dr. W. E. B. DuBois, the board of directors of the N.A.A.C.P. expresses the opinion that this action against one of the great champions of civil rights lends color to the charge that efforts are being made to silence spokesmen for full equality of Negroes. The board also reaffirms its determination to continue its aggressive fight for full citizenship rights for all Americans."

man's career it was an epochal moment. The last of the great triumvirate of Negro leaders, the heir to Douglass and successor to Washington, he abandoned race and aligned his hopes with the world forces that he saw to be fighting for peace and for the working classes. In DuBois's view these world forces were best represented by Russia.

Since DuBois has not assembled the reasons for this change in a consecutive account, it is necessary to piece them together from developments of the previous five years. In all probability nothing contributed as much as DuBois's view that colored leaders, in America and elsewhere, had abandoned the Negro's cause. In India poverty and religion were two major barriers to progress; the third was Indian capitalists "representing the tuition and the capital of Europe."[23] Liberians were subjected to the "overlordship of a small educated and well-to-do portion of the population," and Liberia, he said, was "part of American foreign policy, completely silenced."[24] England shut Ethiopia's mouth, and Haiti feared the enmity of the United States. DuBois felt that the majority of the American Negro intelligentsia, along with much of the West Indian and West African leadership, showed "symptoms of following in the footsteps of western acquisitive society, with its exploitation of labor, monopoly of land and its resources, and with private profit for the smart and unscrupulous in a world of poverty, disease and ignorance, as the natural end of human culture."[25] Four years before, he had publicly begged Jewish forgiveness for the "apparent apostasy" of Ralph J. Bunche (who won the Nobel Peace Prize for achieving a truce between Israel and the Arab states) for making the Negro an unwitting partner to the betrayal of democracy in Israel. Bunche should have "stood firm against vacillation, compromise, and betrayal by our Department of State."[26]

The more immediate catalyst which produced DuBois's new view came from the attitude of Negro leaders to his trial. He quoted with obvious approval the public comment of another Negro that "the important Negroes of this country, the headliners, the highly positioned, the degreed Negroes . . . Negroes who claim to be race champions and crusaders and fighters and leaders and uncompromisers to the last ditch actually deserted Dr. DuBois in the hour of his greatest trial."[27] The trial, DuBois thought, made clear the "distinct cleavage" in Negro opinion between the masses and the Talented Tenth: the latter had become fully American in defending exploitation, imitating "conspicuous expenditure," and hating communism and socialism. The relaxation of discriminatory pressures had left the Negro free to move in the wrong direction. More freedom had not led Negroes into a cemented cultural group helping to create a new haven in America, he said; it had freed them to ape the worst chauvinism and "social climbing" of the Anglo-Saxons. Therefore the hope for the future of the race "lies far more among its workers than among its college graduates, until the time that our higher training is rescued from its sycophantic and cowardly leadership of today, almost wholly dependent as it is on Big Business either in politics or philanthropy."[28]

DuBois's reference to the relaxation of discriminatory pressures suggests a second reason for his new view. In his own lifetime Negroes had made such tremendous advances in America that it now seemed a matter of time, not of principle, which separated them from full equality. Even in this last book, so hostile to America, he acknowledged what the United States had done "to contradict and atone for its sins against Negroes," and he expressed the belief that this nation would become a democracy without a color line. Over the previous few years he had expressed the same notion to a wide variety of audiences. On the question "Can the Negro Expect Freedom by 1965?" he predicted in the *Negro Digest* that although discrimination would persist in jobs, Negroes by that time would be well on their way to economic emancipation.* In a speech delivered just before his dismissal from the Association in 1948, he reviewed Negro improvement over the past forty years and praised the Association's share in it. Later that year much of the same material went into a "progress report" for the New York *Times Magazine,* in which DuBois argued that if the pace of Negro advancement for the past thirty years could be maintained for another generation, the goal of

---

* On the other hand, he came to a gloomier conclusion about the same time in *Phylon.* The old seesaw: seeing how far the Negro had come, or seeing how much remained to be done.

democracy in America would be in sight. In short, the road to Negro equality was so well laid that it no longer required the aggressive supervision which had been DuBois's habit for more than forty years.

In all these statements, however, there was one reservation—a young Negro could look forward to equality in his lifetime if, and only if, the United States averted war and moved forward in the direction of social justice set by the New Deal. These conditions, DuBois asserted, America was not meeting. The catalog of charges against a business-dominated government adamant against social progress and anxious for an anti-Communist war was familiar to anyone who had followed DuBois through his peace crusades and his campaign for Senator. Yet in a lucid and relatively temperate manner, DuBois drew them all together again for his book, *In Battle for Peace*. He thought that the boast of equitable distribution of wealth collapsed in the face of the "paradox" that most laborers got less than was necessary for a decent life, while capitalists received more than they needed, more than they could spend. Science and education, two special objects of American pride, were, he said, being channeled to serve business interests: history was becoming propaganda, economics was hiding in higher mathematics, social study was limited by military objectives, while science was encouraged mainly for private profit, "thus killing future scholarship." In short, "The nation was ruled by the National Association of Manufacturers, the United States Chamber of Commerce, and like affiliated organizations."

DuBois saw these same conspirators at work in his indictment and trial. The State Department, he believed, started the prosecution in order to quell Communists and retard the peace movement, which was bothering the Pentagon. The "Military" welcomed a chance to give a "needed warning to complaining Negroes." Actually his belief that the indictment sought to silence those who spoke for peace (as represented by the Stockholm Appeal) had plausibility. Though the judge did not even have to hear the defense in order to dismiss the indictment, the case had kept DuBois and associates occupied for the better part of a year, and their indictment served as a warning to others who might take up the same cause. To the extent that the United States government, or the Truman administration, used the machinery of law either to implement cold-war foreign policy or to harass individuals whose unpopular opinions could not be silenced in any other way, this was a politically motivated indictment.

DuBois's account of the trial itself, however, strains the credulity of those whose minds are not similarly grooved. He and his associates had been duly arraigned after indictment by a grand jury. They had been released on bail. They had received a delay to allow essential testimony to be taken in Paris. The case was heard by a jury of eight Negroes and four whites before a judge who rigorously excluded testimony about Russia's foreign policy and decided the case on the narrow grounds of the law concerning agency. Yet DuBois was amazed to have Negroes on the jury and "puzzled by the fairness of the judge" who "held the scales of justice absolutely level." His final "considered opinion" was that Judge McGuire at the last minute freed himself from political pressures of the moment when he and the State Department realized that the eyes of the world centered on this case. Continuous appeals to President Truman and to the Attorney-General by private citizens here and abroad were "ignored at the insistence of the State Department," DuBois said, until the volume of protest compelled attention, centered emphasis on the Negro question, and frightened the Catholic Church. Catholics were frightened, DuBois argued, because their proselyting among Negroes might have suffered since the Attorney-General was a Catholic and since Marcantonio, the chief defense counsel, had a large Catholic constituency.

One looks in vain for direct evidence of this epic in which all the elements of the reactionary ruling class coordinated their efforts in order to persecute DuBois. By 1952 DuBois did not need proof. Indeed he even spurned proof, for his beliefs had hardened into dogmas. The sense of personal outrage created by the trial gave dogma an emotional intensity impervious to the rules of evidence. As DuBois said while his trial was pending: "Perhaps you do not realize just the kind of reign of terror under which anyone who dares to speak for peace or who does not hate Russia is placed."[29] In such a state of mind, fears appeared everywhere: DuBois was convinced that he had risked prison by running on the American Labor party ticket. So had the thousands who had voted for him. The corruption of American life by a conspiracy of American capitalists had become DuBois's consuming theme. He was their victim, and he gave them a victim's hatred.

The blocks for his new program are now almost all in place. Negro "leaders" no longer lead; they ape the white man's worst traits. Class structure among Negroes will increase in rigidity as discrimination decreases. No hope for future progress there. The course upward is, however, well set. If the line of progress of the previous fifty years were projected into the future undisturbed, the Negro would see equality. But that projection *is* being disturbed—by American capitalist-imperialists hell-bent on curbing social welfare and destroying Russia. They are the new enemy. They have to be fought in an open battle for socialism and for peace.

In this final development of DuBois's ideas, the trial played a crucial role, for it made the evil of American "imperialists" very personal to him. At the same time, the indictment set off an international reaction—a very limited reaction in fact, but a worldwide "crusade" in DuBois's view. "Without the help of trade unionists, white and black, without the Progressives and radicals, without Socialists and Communists and lovers of peace all over the world, my voice would now be stilled forever." These groups, he thought, were fighting for the future, because socialism was the "one great road to progress," and the first step toward settling the world's problems was "Peace on Earth."

DuBois knew that people who spoke for peace and socialism were thought to be friendlier to Russia, the principal enemy of American foreign policy, than to the United States. No matter: "I utterly refuse to be stampeded into opposition to my own program by intimations of dire and hidden motives among those who offer me support." He was and expected to remain a loyal citizen of the United States, he said, but he respected and admired the Soviet Union. He denied that it was traitorous to follow the peace movement which arose in Russia and found there its chief support; "by the same token," he fought the "war movement in the United States which is transforming this traditionally peaceful nation into the greatest warmonger of all history." He singled out for special praise the Russian educational system which in a generation, he said, had "raised hundreds of millions of debased serfs out of illiteracy, superstition and poverty to self-respecting, hard-working manhood." He did not believe the evidence offered to show that Russia was a nation of slavery, an imperialist exploiting unwilling peoples, a nation faithless to its international commitments. On essential points—peace, socialism, education, race prejudice—Russia, in DuBois's view had no peer. The United States could expect his loyalty, but Russia won his hopes.

In the years after the trial, however, his hopes for Russia were entertained fairly privately, for the old man sank into the anonymity of retirement. So far he has enjoyed eight more birthdays without disturbance. The *Journal of Negro History* reported that he was searching in Haiti for evidences of his ancestors, and the public press has occasionally noted his activities. He delivered the eulogy, a fiery message reminiscent of forty years before, at the funeral of Vito Marcantonio. He was mentioned in the New York *Times* when the Council on African Affairs disbanded. He tried without success to speak on desegregation at Leavittown, New York, and invited (also without success) William Faulkner to debate desegregation with him. He had his say in the *Nation* on Democrats and Republicans in the 1956 election: a plague on both your imperialist houses. He was one of the sponsors of the American Forum for Socialist Education. When the Schomburg Collection unveiled a bust of DuBois in the spring of 1957, Kwame Nkrumah, the first premier of Ghana, gave him a most generous tribute. Recalling that for over fifty years DuBois had been in the front rank of those who fought against imperialism and against notions of white supremacy, Nkrumah called attention to the debt which Africans and their descendants owed their American friend.[30] On the occasion of Ghana's independence celebration in May 1957, Nkrumah invited DuBois as an official guest, but DuBois could not attend because the State Department denied him a passport when he refused to sign a non-Communist affidavit. Recently, in his ninetieth year he published the first volume of a trilogy, *The Black Flame*, an extended fictional work interpreting Negro history from Reconstruction times to the present. In his late eighties he appeared to have discovered the elixir of life.

The celebration of his ninetieth birthday was the occasion for a testimonial dinner in New York and for lecture engagements elsewhere. The venerable old fighter went through this demanding program with the vigor of a man thirty years younger. The clipped speech, the carefully prepared manuscript, and the deadly invective, long his trademarks, were still much in evidence, and he was careful not to take back a word of what he had been preaching for over a decade. If anything, he sharpened his barbs and spoke with new vigor, confident that history would vindicate him. His audiences paid him the deference due to a distinguished pioneer, but showed little disposition to follow his lead. The old spirit is there, but not a shadow of the old influence.

THE MAN BEHIND THE MYTH

In his own lifetime DuBois has become an almost mythical figure, and no one has contributed to this myth more sedulously than DuBois himself. In one autobiographical essay after another, he has reconstructed the heroic figure of an austere man of principle fighting a universal battle for the right against an ignorant or hostile world. *Darkwater* lists a parade of triumphs culminating in his appointment to the editorial chair at the *Crisis*. *Dusk of Dawn* sets DuBois's life in a setting of world history: "Crucified on the vast wheel of time," he "flew round and round with the Zeitgeist." His review of his career on his seventieth birthday pays tribute to the clarity of his own thought: he was "proud of a straightforward clearness of reason, in part the gift of the gods, but also to no little degree due to scientific training and inner discipline."[1] One of his columns in the *Defender* refers to his program in 1900 as "an absolutely correct scientific procedure, foolproof."[2] In his angry book, *In Battle for Peace*, no less than a regiment of influential Americans attempt to destroy him. All battles become titanic struggles, all disagreements monstrous conspiracies, all successes epochal contributions. His flimsiest work—*John Brown* and *Dark Princess*—must be especially defended lest the master appear to have moments of failure. Myth heroes are not permitted to know failure. If they meet defeat, it must be a cosmic defeat, a twilight of the gods.

DuBois's own view of himself reappears in the accounts by others. For those to whom his name has any meaning he is the great Negro scholar and writer, the uncompromising lonely pioneer for Negro rights who inexplicably deserted the fight in 1934, the race's great spokesman after the death of Booker T. Washington and perhaps for twelve years before. The political left has exalted his position for its own purposes: Aptheker referring to "The Age of DuBois" and commenting: "How few are those of whom one may say, after sixty years, that the promises of youth

are the records of history!";[3] Shirley Graham speaking of the
DuBois of 1912 as a voice "crying in the wilderness";[4] Wilkerson
promoting him to "Dean of American Letters."[5] But even writers
without an ax to grind have served the myth. Van Wyck Brooks
passes along DuBois's account of himself as James's favorite pupil;[6]
the first edition of John Gunther's *Inside U.S.A.* compares Du-
Bois's position—"the most venerable and distinguished of leaders in his field"—to that of Albert Einstein and George Bernard
Shaw.[7] (This was deleted from the revised edition.) Edwin R.
Embree's sketch in *13 Against the Odds* draws heavily on DuBois's
own view of himself in *Darkwater* and *Dusk of Dawn*. Even Henry
Steele Commager in 1948 states that DuBois "today perhaps best
represents the aspirations of the American Negro"[8]—this at a time
when DuBois was moving steadily away from the main stream of
Negro thought and action. Redding says that "only Carlyle stands
comparison" with DuBois's "combination of scholarship and emotional power woven into bolts of symbolism."[9] A young Negro
scholar, Youra Qualls, finds the universality of *A Pilgrim's Progress*
in *Dusk of Dawn*.[10] And William Stanley Braithwaite, the critic
and anthologist, predicts that "The career of W. E. Burghardt
DuBois will reflect a light across the memory of man as long as
man seeks and reveres the ideals of Justice and Liberty, of Intelligence and Beauty."[11]

These appraisals need revision. The *bulk* of DuBois's scholarly
articles and books commands attention, but no single work, except *The Philadelphia Negro,* is first-class. The diffusion of his
talents thereafter prevented DuBois from focusing his energy on a
single coherent work carried through to a successful conclusion.
Black Reconstruction will be remembered, but more because of
its eccentric racist-Marxist interpretations than because of its as-
semblage of new material. *The Negro, Black Folk Then and Now,
The World and Africa*—all possess some information, but nothing
which indicates the mind or hand of an original scholar. A judgment on DuBois's qualities as a writer moves into the difficult area
where judgment can not rise much above the level of taste, but it
seems unlikely that DuBois will be remembered as a literary artist.
Indeed when he is being most consciously literary—in his random

poems and short stories and in his two novels—he is least successful. He is at his best writing the language of analysis and of controversy, when trip-hammer sentences could be suddenly broken
by a graphic metaphor: The Negro's task in 1930 "is the double
and dynamic function of timing in with a machine in action so as
neither to wreck the machine nor be crushed or maimed by it."
As a writer DuBois never surpassed the month-to-month prose of
his editorials on social, political, and economic topics in the *Crisis*.
His reputation as a writer will rest more on the *Crisis* than on his
forays into *belles lettres*.

A review of DuBois's career also suggests that 1934 was less
surprising a turning point than is generally assumed. When
DuBois broke with the Association and recommended Negro
separatism, he was carrying to their logical conclusion racist tend-
encies apparent in his thought since his days in Great Barrington.
The depression, coming after DuBois's disaffection from white
liberals and his failure to locate colored and working-class allies,
provided the catalyst for an explicit acceptance of voluntary segregation, but the roots of separatism went deep, and racial nationalism was never far from the surface of his philosophy. If there was
a sharp break in DuBois's ideas, it came not in 1934, when he
separated from the Association, but in 1952, when he abandoned
the struggle for Negro rights to concentrate on world movements
for peace and socialism.

Finally, the nature of DuBois's leadership must be redefined
Longevity and productivity have given him a quantitative claim
hard to match. Because there is a written record, of substantial
size, of what he has thought, he has an advantage over other, less
prolix, Negro leaders who have left a less traceable trail. It is important to remember that DuBois's position was less that of a
pioneer than that of the first among equals: Trotter preceded him
in fighting Washington, as did Ida Wells-Barnett; the Association
brought Negroes and white men together in an entente in which
DuBois shared influence with others, first with Villard and Spingarn, later with Johnson and White. By the time of the second
Amenia conference in 1933, DuBois was being rejected, by-passed
by a new generation with ideas of its own. Furthermore, as

Bunche has pointed out, Negroes were rather less conscious of their leaders than the pronunciamentoes of those leaders would lead others to believe.

DuBois's significance will emerge more clearly if the extravagant claims made by him and for him are scuttled. His position depends not on his scholarly and literary work; it does not require a consistent thirty-year record of working for integration against rapacious "Uncle Tom" Negroes and stubborn whites; it does not need an omnivorous concept of leadership which makes Negro history hinge on one man.

➤ DuBois's importance to the Negro's history in American society lies in two achievements: First, for thirty years he made himself the loudest voice in demanding equal rights for the Negro and in turning Negro opinion away from the acceptance of anything less. Whatever private racist notions may have contradicted this line of thought, DuBois's principal public statements from the publication of *The Souls of Black Folk* until 1933 hammered away at America's conscience and at the Negro's pride, arguing, cajoling, threatening, retreating when necessary, advancing when possible. Many weapons came to his hands—history, fact, fiction, invective, even humor. They all served one central purpose. His conceit and arrogance gave him cushions against abuse: he could ignore it, or relish it. From his pen came the arguments for others. When he left the road which he had done so much to pave, many other Negroes were well enough trained in his tradition to continue the work. One cannot say that the Negro's progress since 1903 is a result of DuBois's agitation—DuBois's ideas belonged to others as well, and many forces other than agitation have contributed to the Negro's advance in fifty years. But it is fair to say that DuBois in these years pointed the way for the Negro, not by his futile searches for extranational allies, but by steady refusal to accept or to allow the Negro to accept less than his full rights as an American.

DuBois's second achievement lies in his service to the Negro's morale. When Washington was training Negro youth for manual work, DuBois held high the ideal of a liberal education. When Washington measured civilization in material terms, DuBois reminded his people of Socrates and Saint Francis. As a younger generation grew up, it matured in the atmosphere which DuBois helped to create: it could not ignore and it frequently had to support his insistence on the ideal of full citizenship. At home, and abroad as well, his writings gave colored men courage for their fight. His monthly editorials held up the strong, recharged the wavering, and flayed the compromisers. The *Crisis* became the record of Negro achievement; its columns gave recognition to success in every field, and young artists could find there a place for their creations. In this context, even DuBois's aloofness became an asset; it removed him in Negro eyes from everyday life and, by giving him a transcendent quality, it raised the goal of aspiration. The austere Dr. DuBois reminded Negro intellectuals that courage and talent could carry a man—and a race—far.

In performing these two functions, propagandizing for equality and inspiring younger Negroes, DuBois achieved enough significance for one lifetime. It is not necessary to gild the lily with myths.

BIBLIOGRAPHICAL NOTE

The two most important sources for the study of W. E. B. DuBois are his collected papers and his published work. His papers, which are in his own possession, are now closed to outside students and presumably will remain so until his wife, Shirley Graham DuBois, completes her authorized biography of him. His published work is extensive: 18 books, more than 20 long pamphlets, hundreds of editorials in *Horizon* and *Crisis,* hundreds of columns in Negro newspapers, and an even larger number of articles in learned journals, periodicals of general circulation, and magazines under his own control. A partial bibliography of his published work up to 1952 is available at the Widener Library, Harvard University, and at the Schomburg Collection of the New York Public Library.

The Schomburg Collection has a handful of DuBois letters, a folder of his speeches given from 1947 to 1949, several volumes of newspaper clippings on DuBois, and a substantial vertical file of miscellaneous references to him. It also has some letters to and from Francis J. Garrison in which there is relevant material on DuBois and on Booker T. Washington; the John Edward Bruce Papers and the Paul Laurence Dunbar Papers, which touch on DuBois in his post-Germany period; and a few Washington letters. At Harvard University, the sources listed on p. 238 give information about his student days. At Yale University, two DuBois manuscripts and a file of correspondence with Joel Spingarn are available in the James Weldon Johnson Collection. The Spingarn letters throw light on DuBois's relations with the National Association for the Advancement of Colored People. Further information on this topic appears in the well-organized Oswald Garrison Villard Papers at the Houghton Library, Harvard University; see, for example, his correspondence with Mary White Ovington. The annual reports of the NAACP, the minutes of its board of directors, and its correspondence files, all available at the national headquarters in New York, are surprisingly enlightening.

The conflict with Washington is best approached through the Booker T. Washington Papers at the Library of Congress, a vast collection now well catalogued and very rewarding. Samuel R. Spencer, Jr., *Booker T. Washington and the Negro's Place in American Life* (Boston, 1955), is the best biography of Washington, fair to both Washington and DuBois. August Meier, who has done intensive work in the Washington papers, has opened a new era of understanding Washington with his three articles: "Booker T. Washington and the Negro Press: With Special Reference to the *Colored American Magazine*," *Journal of Negro History*, XXXVIII, 67–90 (January 1953); "Booker T. Washington and the Rise of the NAACP," *Crisis*, LXI, 69–76, 117–23 (February 1954); and "Toward a Reinterpretation of Booker T. Washington," *Journal of Southern History*, XXIII, 220–27 (May 1957). The Ray Stannard Baker Papers at the Library of Congress have much to say on the Negro question in general, and on DuBois and Washington in particular.

Elliott M. Rudwick's thoughtful manuscript study of DuBois, "W. E. B. DuBois: A Study in Minority Group Leadership" (typescript Ph.D. dissertation, 1956, University of Pennsylvania), is based on research in manuscript materials and quotes extensively from them. L. M. Collins, "W. E. B. DuBois's Views on Education" (Master's essay, Fisk University, 1937), and Mary M. Drake, "W. E. Burghardt DuBois as a Man of Letters" (Master's essay, Fisk University, 1934), summarize their topics uncritically.

Among the general studies, none compares in range and in quantity of information with Gunnar Myrdal, *An American Dilemma: The Negro Problem and Modern Democracy* (2 vols.; New York, 1944). Ralph J. Bunche prepared two splendid study papers for the Myrdal study in 1940: "Extended Memorandum on the Programs, Ideologies, Tactics and Achievements of Negro Betterment and Interracial Organizations" and "A Brief and Tentative Analysis of Negro Leadership"; both are available in typescript at the Schomburg Collection. John Hope Franklin, *From Slavery to Freedom: A History of American Negroes* (New York,

1947); Benjamin Brawley, *The Negro in Literature and Art in the United States* (3d ed.; New York, 1929); Sterling D. Spero and Abram L. Harris, *The Black Worker: The Negro and the Labor Movement* (New York, 1931); Herbert R. Northrup, *Organized Labor and the Negro* (New York, 1944); E. Franklin Frazier, *The Negro in the United States* (New York, 1949); and, for the earlier period of DuBois's career, Rayford W. Logan, *The Negro in American Life and Thought: The Nadir, 1877–1901* (New York, 1954), are the standard works in their fields. Abram Kardiner and Lionel Ovesey, *The Mark of Oppression: A Psychosocial Study of the American Negro* (New York, 1951), and Frazier, *The Black Bourgeoisie* (Glencoe, Illinois, 1957), are incisive works with important implications for my study. Herbert Aptheker, *A Documentary History of the Negro People in the United States* (New York, 1951), is a well edited and valuable collection; DuBois's twenty-fifth birthday dedication and the "Declaration of Principles" of the Niagara Movement are both reprinted there in full. Several articles and books may be mentioned as giving views of DuBois not available elsewhere: Aptheker, "The Washington-DuBois Meeting of 1904," *Science and Society*, XIII, 344–51 (fall, 1949)—an article based on research in the DuBois papers; John Henry Adams, "Rough Sketches: William Edward Burghardt DuBois," *Voice of the Negro*, II, 176–81 (March 1905); Ray Stannard Baker, *Following the Color Line* (Garden City, 1908); V. F. Calverton, "The New Negro," *Current History*, XXIII, 694–98 (February 1926); Roger Didier, "The Ordeal of DuBois," Pittsburgh *Courier Magazine Section*, May 25, 1957, pp. 4–6; James Weldon Johnson, *Along This Way* (New York, 1933); J. Saunders Redding, "Portrait: W. E. Burghardt DuBois," *American Scholar*, XVIII, 93–96 (winter, 1948); T. G. Standing, "Nationalism in Negro Leadership," *American Journal of Sociology*, XL, 180–92 (September 1934); George Streator, "A Negro Scholar," *Commonweal*, XXXIV, 31–34 (May 2, 1941); Ridgely Torrence, *The Story of John Hope* (New York, 1948).

Finally the Negro press, which must be consulted regularly at all points. In the early period, for example, the Boston *Guardian* on one side and the New York *Age* and the *Southern Workman* on the other give insight into the Washington-DuBois controversy, and after 1910 the more popular national newspapers like the Pittsburgh *Courier,* the Chicago *Defender,* and the Cleveland *Gazette* supply a running chronicle of Negro life.

A substantial part of my own notes on DuBois, on file at the Schomburg Collection, are available to other scholars with no restrictions other than those imposed by my sources.

NOTES

Chapter I

1. This account of DuBois's early life is based on unpublished material in the W. E. B. DuBois papers in Dr. DuBois's possession, and on his published autobiographical accounts, especially *Dusk of Dawn: An Essay Toward an Autobiography of a Race Concept* (New York, 1940); *The Souls of Black Folk: Essays and Sketches* (Chicago, 1903), especially Chapter VI; *Darkwater: Voices From Within the Veil* (New York, 1921), pp. 5–23; "My Evolving Program for Negro Freedom," in Rayford W. Logan, ed., *What the Negro Wants* (Chapel Hill, 1944), pp. 31–70; *A Pageant in Seven Decades, 1868–1938,* pamphlet, n.p., n.d.; "From McKinley to Wallace: My Fifty Years as a Political Independent," *Masses and Mainstream,* I, vi, 3–13 (August 1948); and various newspaper columns written during the course of a long life.

2. DuBois, "My Evolving Program for Negro Freedom," p. 32.

3. DuBois, *Darkwater,* p. 10; "Harvard and Democracy," typescript of speech, n.d., DuBois papers.

4. DuBois, *A Pageant in Seven Decades, 1868–1938,* p. 2.

5. DuBois, *Darkwater,* p. 17.

6. *Crisis* (New York), XXIII (April 1922), 248.

7. New York *Globe,* April 12, 1884, October 20, 1883, May 17, 1884, May 3, 1883, June 2, 1883; New York *Freeman,* December 27, 1884, January 10, 1885; New York *Globe,* April 14, 1883, September 29, 1883.

8. DuBois, "My Evolving Program for Negro Freedom," p. 35.

9. New York *Globe,* September 8, 1883.

10. New York *Globe,* October 18, 1884.

11. DuBois, "My Evolving Program for Negro Freedom," p. 36.

12. *Ibid.,* p. 36; *Dusk of Dawn,* p. 24.

13. DuBois, ms. of untitled, undated oration at Fisk, DuBois paper.

14. DuBois, "My Evolving Program for Negro Freedom," p. 37.

15. *Catalogue of . . . Fisk University . . . 1884–1885,* Nashville, 1885, p. 5.

16. *Catalogue of . . . Fisk University . . . 1887–1888,* Nashville, 1888, p. 42.

17. DuBois, "Diuturni Silenti," ms. of speech, 1924, DuBois papers; reprinted in the *Fisk Herald,* XXXIII (1924), 1–12.

18. These letters are in the "W. E. B. DuBois, Class of 1810" folder in the Harvard University Archives.

19. DuBois, "What the Negro Will Do," ms. of unpublished article, February 4, 1889, DuBois papers; written in reply to George Washington Cable, "A Simpler Southern Question," *Forum,* VI, 392–403 (December 1888).

20. C. Vann Woodward, *The Strange Career of Jim Crow* (New York, 1955), p. 30.

21. DuBois, "Political Serfdom," ms. of speech at Fisk, *ca.* 1887, DuBois papers.

22. Quoted in Benjamin Quarles, *Frederick Douglass* (Washington, D.C., 1948), p. 335.

23. DuBois, "Harvard and Democracy."

24. "W. E. B. DuBois, Class of 1890," folder.

25. DuBois to Evarts Scudder, February 3, 1886, DuBois papers.

26. DuBois, *Dusk of Dawn*, p. 33.

27. DuBois, "What the Negro Will Do."

28. DuBois, "The Renaissance of Ethics: a critical comparison of scholastic and modern ethics," ms., 1899, James Weldon Johnson Collection, Yale University Library.

29. DuBois, account book and diary, 1888–90, and scrapbook fragment, *ca.* 1891, DuBois papers.

30. This discussion of DuBois's academic work at Harvard is derived from successive issues of the *Harvard University Catalogue*, Cambridge, 1888–92; Registrar's Records, "Record of the Class of 1890," p. 314; the "Record of the Graduate Department, 1888 [*sic*]," at the office of the Graduate School of Arts and Sciences; and the "W. E. B. DuBois, Class of 1890," folder.

31. DuBois, *Dusk of Dawn*, p. 39.

32. DuBois, "Jefferson Davis as a Representative of Civilization," ms., 1890, DuBois papers; *Nation*, LI (July 3, 1890), 15.

33. DuBois, "Harvard and the South," ms. of commencement "part," June 1891, DuBois papers.

34. Herbert B. Adams, "The American Historical Association in Washington," *Independent*, XLIV (January 7, 1892), 10.

35. DuBois, *A Pageant in Seven Decades, 1868–1938*, p. 8.

36. Cleveland *Gazette*, November 4, 1893.

37. Instructor's note on DuBois, "Hunted Mouse," December 11, 1890, DuBois papers.

38. Robert Morss Lovett, "DuBois," *Phylon*, II (third quarter, 1941), 214.

39. DuBois, "What the Negro Will Do."

40. DuBois, "A Vacation Unique," ms. dated June 1889, DuBois papers.

41. DuBois, account book and diary, 1888–1890.

42. DuBois, "A Vacation Unique."

43. DuBois, "Comments on My Life," typescript, *ca.* 1943, DuBois papers; *Dusk of Dawn*, p. 38; *A Pageant in Seven Decades, 1868–1938*, p. 7.

44. The comment is on the paper, "The Renaissance of Ethics."

45. DuBois, "Harvard and Democracy."

46. DuBois, "My Evolving Program for Negro Freedom," p. 33.

47. DuBois, "Comments on My Life."

48. DuBois, *A Pageant in Seven Decades, 1868–1938*, p. 10.

49. DuBois, "Harvard in Berlin," diary fragment, November–December, 1892, DuBois papers.

50. DuBois, diary, February 23, 1893, DuBois papers.

51. DuBois to the Slater Fund Trustees, undated, *ca.* April 1893, DuBois papers.

52. These comments are all written on the paper, "The Renaissance of Ethics."

53. See note 52, above.

54. DuBois, *Darkwater*, p. 20.

Chapter II

1. DuBois to John A. W. Dollar, *ca.* 1896, DuBois papers.

2. DuBois, *Darkwater: Voices From Within the Veil* (New York, 1921), p. 18.

3. *Catalogue of Wilberforce University, 1894–1895* (Jefferson, Ohio, 1895), p. 20; Frederick A. McGinnis, *A History and an Interpretation of Wilberforce University* (Wilberforce, Ohio, 1941), p. 162.

4. DuBois, diary, February 23, 1896, DuBois papers.

5. DuBois, ms. fragment of a short story about a young professor at "Burghardt University," *ca.* 1895, DuBois papers.

6. DuBois, "The Enforcement of the Slave-Trade Laws," *Annual Report of the American Historical Association for the Year 1891* (52d Congress, 1st Session, *Senate Miscellaneous Document,* no. 173), Washington, D.C., 1892, p. 174.

7. Herbert B. Adams, "The American Historical Association in Washington," *Independent,* XLIV (January 7, 1892), 10.

8. Gunnar Myrdal, *An American Dilemma: The Negro Problem and Modern Democracy* (New York, 1944), p. 1132.

9. DuBois, "Sociology Hesitant," ms. of speech, *ca.* 1904, DuBois papers.

10. Thorstein Veblen, "Gustav Schmoller," *Quarterly Journal of Economics,* XVI (November 1901), 70.

11. DuBois, "Schmoller u. Wagner Notebook," 1893–94, DuBois papers.

12. DuBois, "The Study of Negro Problems," *Annals of the American Academy of Political and Social Science,* XI (January 1898), 16.

13. DuBois, "Reconstruction and Its Benefits," *American Historical Review,* XV (July 1910), 799.

14. Anon., "DuBois's Slave-Trade," *Nation,* LXIII (December 31, 1896), 499–500.

15. Howard W. Odum, *American Sociology* (New York, 1951), pp. 339–40.

16. DuBois, "Fifty Years Among the Black Folk," New York *Times,* December 12, 1909, 6:4.

17. DuBois, "The Negro South and North," *Bibliotheca Sacra,* LXII (July 1905), 511.

18. DuBois to the school children of Indianapolis, April 7, 1908, DuBois papers.

19. DuBois, "The Meaning of Business," ms. of speech, Chicago, 1898, DuBois papers.

20. DuBois, "The Talented Tenth," in Booker T. Washington *et al., The Negro Problem* (New York, 1903), pp. 63, 33.

21. DuBois, "Carlyle," ms. of speech, undated, *ca.* 1895, DuBois papers.

22. *Catalogue of Atlanta University* . . . *1898–1899,* Atlanta, 1899, pp. 7, 13.

23. DuBois, "Careers Open to College-Bred Negroes," in *Two Addresses Delivered by Alumni of Fisk University* . . . , pamphlet, Nashville, 1898, pp. 7–12.

24. These prayers, undated, are in the DuBois papers.

25. DuBois, *The Conservation of Races* (American Negro Academy, *Occasional Papers,* II), pamphlet, Washington, 1897, *passim.*

Chapter III

1. DuBois, *Darkwater: Voices From Within the Veil* (New York, 1921), p. 23.

2. DuBois, "The Twelfth Census and the Negro Problems," *Southern Workman,* XXIX (May 1900), 307–9.

3. Horace Bumstead to DuBois, April 6, 1907, DuBois papers.

4. Edward T. Ware to DuBois, January 28, 1909, DuBois papers.

5. Frank W. Taussig to DuBois, May 10, 1907, DuBois papers.

6. William Fremont Blackman, review of DuBois, ed., *The Negro Artisan* (Atlanta, 1902), in *Yale Review,* XII (August 1903), 221–22; J. A. Tillinghast, in *Political Science Quarterly,* XIX (December 1904), 701.

7. Anon., review of DuBois, *The Souls of Black Folk* (Chicago, 1903), in *Nation,* LXXVI (June 11, 1903), 481.

8. Walter F. Willcox to DuBois, March 13, 1904; DuBois to Willcox, March 29, 1904, DuBois papers.

9. DuBois, "The Souls of White Folk," *Independent,* LXIX (August 18, 1910), 342.

10. Washington [D.C.] *Colored American,* February 21, 1903.

11. Washington to the African Methodist Episcopal Zion Conference, Charlotte, N.C., May 9, 1912; quoted in E. Davidson Washington, ed., *Selected Speeches of Booker T. Washington* (Garden City, N.Y., 1932), pp. 208–12.

12. J. Saunders Redding, *They Came in Chains* (*The Peoples of America Series*) (Philadelphia, 1950), p. 197.

13. Quoted in DuBois, ed., *The Negro Artisan,* p. 5.

14. DuBois, *Dusk of Dawn: An Essay Toward an Autobiography of a Race Concept* (New York, 1940), p. 55.

15. Washington speech is reprinted in E. D. Washington, ed., *Selected Speeches of Booker T. Washington,* pp. 60–77; DuBois, "Carlyle," ms. of speech, undated, *ca.* 1895, DuBois papers.

16. See p. 51, above.

17. DuBois to Washington, July 12, 1899, Booker T. Washington Papers, Library of Congress; DuBois, ed., *The Negro in Business* (Atlanta, 1899), p. 11.

18. DuBois, ed., *The Negro Artisan*, p. 8.

19. DuBois, "The Religion of the American Negro," *New World*, IX (December 1900), 622–23.

20. DuBois, "The Evolution of Negro Leadership," *Dial*, XXXI (July 1, 1901), 54–55.

21. James Weldon Johnson, *Along This Way* (New York, 1935), p. 203.

22. *Colored American*, February 21, 1903.

23. *Southern Workman*, XXXI (June 1903), 262–63.

24. Cleveland *Gazette*, May 16, 1903.

25. DuBois to Clement Morgan, October 19, 1903, DuBois papers.

26. DuBois, "Possibilities of the Negro: The Advance Guard of the Race," *Booklover's Magazine*, II (July 1903), 7.

27. DuBois, "The Negro Problem From the Negro Point of View: V. The Parting of the Ways," *World Today*, VI (April 1904), 522.

28. DuBois, "The Joy of Living," ms. of speech in Washington, June 1904, DuBois papers.

29. DuBois, "The Hampton Idea," *Voice of the Negro*, III (September 1906), 632–35 and *passim*.

30. DuBois to Miller, November 2, 1903, DuBois papers.

31. DuBois to Miller, February 25, 1903, DuBois papers.

32. The circular is in the DuBois papers.

33. For a view of this conference favorable to DuBois, see Aptheker, "The Washington-DuBois Conference of 1904," *Science and Society*, XIII (fall, 1949), 344–51.

34. DuBois, "Debit and Credit," *Voice of the Negro*, II (January 1905), 677.

35. DuBois, "The Talented Tenth," in Booker T. Washington *et al.*, *The Negro Problem* (New York, 1903), pp. 58–59, 61, 73–74.

36. DuBois, "The Case for the Negro," ms. of unpublished article, 1901, DuBois papers.

37. DuBois, "The Value of Agitation," *Voice of the Negro*, IV (March 1907), 110.

38. Elliott M. Rudwick, "The Niagara Movement," *Journal of Negro History*, XLIII (July 1957), 177–200, is steeped in manuscript and newspaper material.

39. *The Niagara Movement, Declaration of Principles, 1905*, pamphlet, n.p., n.d., Schomburg Collection, New York Public Library. The text of the declaration is reprinted in Herbert Aptheker, *A Documentary History of the Negro People in the United States* (New York, 1951), pp. 901–4.

40. Joseph Summers to DuBois, August 4, 1909, DuBois papers.

41. Mary White Ovington to DuBois, April 24, 1908, DuBois papers.

42. Washington to Charles W. Anderson, December 30, 1905, Washington papers.

43. J. B. Watson, "Recalling 1906," *Crisis*, XLI (April 1934), 100.
44. DuBois, "A Litany at Atlanta," *Independent*, LXI (October 11, 1906), 856–58.
45. DuBois, "Negro Ideals," ms. of speech, 1907, DuBois papers.
46. DuBois, "Marrying of Black Folk," *Independent*, LXIX (October 13, 1910), 812–13.
47. DuBois, "The Negro and the YMCA," *Horizon*, V (March 1910), v, 3.
48. DuBois, "The Economic Aspects of Race Prejudice," *Editorial Review*, II (May 1910), 488–93.
49. This account summarizes DuBois's articles in *Horizon*, IV (July–October 1908), i–iv.
50. DuBois, "The Free Coinage Controversy Today," ms. of speech, *ca.* 1896, DuBois papers.
51. *Horizon*, I (February 1907), ii, 7–8.
52. Emmett J. Scott to Washington, November 30, 1909, Washington papers.
53. Ridgely Torrence, *The Story of John Hope* (New York, 1948), p. 162.

Chapter IV

1. The call is reprinted in its entirety in Ovington, *How the National Association for the Advancement of Colored People Began*, pamphlet, New York, 1914, pp. 3–4.
2. DuBois, "National Committee on the Negro," *Survey*, XXII (June 12, 1909), 409.
3. *Ibid.*
4. New York *Evening Post*, April 1, 1910.
5. DuBois, *Dusk of Dawn: An Essay Toward an Autobiography of a Race Concept* (New York, 1940), p. 225; ms. of *A Pageant in Seven Decades, 1868–1938*, pamphlet, n.p., n.d.; *Crisis*, I (November 1910), i, 10.
6. Ray Stannard Baker and William E. Dodd, eds., *The Public Papers of Woodrow Wilson* (3 vols., New York, 1926), II, 5.
7. DuBois, "The Forward Movement," ms. of speech, October 1910, DuBois papers.
8. DuBois to John E. Bruce, September 27, 1911, John Edward Bruce Papers, Schomburg Collection.
9. *Crisis*, VIII (May 1914), 26.
10. *Ibid.*, I (November 1910), i, 10.
11. *Ibid.*, 10–11.
12. *Ibid.* (January 1911), iii, 21.
13. *Ibid.*, IV (August 1912), 181.
14. C. Vann Woodward, *Tom Watson: Agrarian Rebel* (New York, 1938), p. 426.
15. Quoted in Alexander Walters, *My Life and Work* (New York, 1917), p. 195.

16. *Crisis,* IX (February 1915), 181.
17. DuBois to Walter Hines Page, March 18, 1903, DuBois papers.
18. *Crisis,* IV (July 1912), 131.
19. *Ibid.* (September 1912), 234.
20. *Ibid.,* II (October 1911), 243–44.
21. *Ibid.,* VIII (July 1914), 124.
22. *Ibid.,* XI (November 1915), 28.
23. Mary White Ovington, *The Walls Came Tumbling Down* (New York, 1947), p. 108.
24. DuBois to Villard, March 18, 1913, Villard papers.
25. Villard to Joel Spingarn, March 20, 1913, Villard papers.
26. Spingarn to DuBois, October 24, 1914, Johnson Collection. This copy in the Spingarn papers is a first draft corrected from memory somewhat later.
27. DuBois to Spingarn, October 28, 1914, Johnson Collection.
28. Minutes of the Board of Directors of the National Association for the Advancement of Colored People, January 3, 1916. The minutes are at the NAACP office in New York. Hereafter cited "NAACP Board minutes."
29. Quoted in *Crisis,* III (March 1912), 202.
30. DuBois, "The Great Northwest," *ibid.,* VI (September 1913), 238.
31. DuBois, "The Immediate Program of the American Negro," *ibid.,* IX (April 1915), 310–12.
32. DuBois, "The Economic Future of the Negro," *Publications of the American Economic Association,* 3d series, VII (February 1906), 230, 239.
33. E. H. Clement to DuBois, December 18, 1907; DuBois to Clement, December 30, 1907, DuBois papers.
34. DuBois, "The Social Evolution of the Black South," *American Negro Monograph,* I (March 1911), iv, especially 7–10.
35. *Crisis,* I (February 1911), iv, 20.
36. *Ibid.,* V (February 1913), 184–86.
37. *Ibid.,* XIV (August 1917), 166.
38. *Ibid.,* XVII (January 1919), 112–13.
39. DuBois *et al.,* "Race Relations in the United States," press release, October 26, 1910, DuBois papers.
40. *Crisis,* V (April 1913), 291.
41. *Ibid.,* I (February 1911), iv, 20; II (September 1911), 196–97; II (May 1911), 19.
42. *Ibid.,* II (September 1911), 195.
43. *Ibid.,* XII (October 1916), 270–71.
44. *Ibid.,* XIII (December 1916), 63.
45. *Ibid.,* IX (November 1914), 28–30.
46. DuBois, "The African Roots of War," *Atlantic Monthly,* CXV (May 1915), 707–14.
47. *Crisis,* XIV (June 1917), 61–62.
48. *Ibid.,* XV (December 1917), 77.
49. *Ibid.,* XVI (August 1918), 164.

50. *Crisis,* XVII (April 1919), 267.
51. *Ibid.,* XIV (September 1917), 216.
52. *Ibid.,* XV (March 1918), 216–17.
53. John Hope Franklin, *From Slavery to Freedom* (New York, 1947), pp. 472–74.
54. *Crisis,* XVIII (May 1919), 13–14.
55. *Ibid.* (September 1919), 231.
56. *Ibid.* (October 1919), 285, and XIX (November 1919), 335.
57. DuBois, "The Judge," *Brownies' Book,* II (February 1921), 41.
58. *Crisis,* XX (February 1920), 213.
59. E. Franklin Frazier, *The Negro in the United States* (New York, 1949), pp. 191–93.
60. Kelly Miller ("Fair Play," pseud.), "Washington's Policy," Boston *Evening Transcript,* September 19, 1903.
61. Washington to Charles D. Hilles, March 29, 1912, Washington papers.
62. Washington, "My View of Segregation Laws," *New Republic,* V (December 4, 1915), 113–14.
63. Washington to Villard, April 19, 1911, Washington papers.
64. DuBois, "The Great Northwest," 239.
65. Cleveland *Gazette,* October 8, 1910.
66. *Crisis,* VI (July 1913), 130–31.
67. *Ibid.,* IV (June 1912), 75.
68. *Ibid.,* III (November 1911), 21.
69. *Ibid.,* VIII (May 1914), 17.
70. *Ibid.,* I (November 1910), i, 10.
71. *Ibid.* (December 1910), ii, 16.
72. *Ibid.,* XVII (January 1919), 112.
73. Edwin R. Embree, *13 Against the Odds* (New York, 1944), p. 153.
74. *Crisis,* IV (May 1915), 25.
75. *Ibid.,* XI (December 1915), 82.
76. Though Moton had assured Washington that he was "absolutely" on Washington's side (Moton to Washington, April 8, 1914, Washington papers), he had refused to join in the abusive attacks on DuBois. H. B. Frisell, the principal of Hampton Institute, told Ray Stannard Baker that Moton thought it was a good thing to have men like DuBois stand up for Negro rights. (Frisell to Baker, May 1, 1908, Ray Stannard Baker Papers, Library of Congress.) August Meier records Moton's attempt to make peace between the two wings of the race, and he regards Moton's selection as Washington's successor at Tuskegee as a victory for moderation. "Booker T. Washington and the Rise of the NAACP," *Crisis,* LXI (February 1954), 118–22.
77. DuBois, "The Amenia Conference: An Historic Negro Gathering" (*Troutbeck Leaflets,* VIII) (Amenia, N.Y., 1925), pp. 14–15.
78. New York *Sun* (October 12, 1919), 7:5.
79. Anon., "Are We Menaced by a New Race War?" *Current Opinion,* LXIX (July 1920), 82.

80. C. Alphonso Smith, "Dialect Writers," in W. P. Trent *et al.*, *Cambridge History of American Literature* (3 vols., New York, 1918), II, 351.

81. Washington *Eagle*, July 27, 1918.

82. Gunnar Myrdal, *An American Dilemma: The Negro Problem and Modern Democracy* (New York, 1944), ch. 37.

Chapter V

1. *Crisis*, XVIII (September 1919), 234–35.

2. *Ibid.*, XXXIV (November 1927), 311.

3. DuBois, "Hopkinsville, Chicago, and Idlewild," *Crisis*, XXII (August 1921), 160.

4. *Ibid.*, XXVI (October 1923), 249.

5. *Ibid.*, XXXIV (September 1927), 227.

6. DuBois, "Woofterism," *ibid.*, XXXIX (March 1931), 81–83. The reference is to Thomas J. Woofter, *A Study of the Economic Status of the Negro*, manifold script issued by the Rosenwald Foundation, 1930.

7. *Crisis*, XXV (March 1923), 202–3.

8. *Ibid.*

9. DuBois, "The African Roots of the War," *Atlantic Monthly*, CXV (May 1915), 714.

10. *Crisis*, XIX (January 1920), 108.

11. *Ibid.*, XX (September 1920), 214–15.

12. *Ibid.*, XIX (April 1920), 298.

13. *Ibid.*, XX (October 1920), 261.

14. *Ibid.*, XXIV (June 1922), 55.

15. DuBois, "Liberia and Rubber," *New Republic*, XLIV (November 18, 1925), 329.

16. New York *Times*, January 6, 1930, 29:3.

17. DuBois, "What Is Civilization? II. Africa's Answer," *Forum*, LXXIII (February 1925), 178–88.

18. DuBois, *Africa, Its Geography, People and Products* (*Little Blue Books*, No. 1505) (Girard, Kansas, 1930), p. 3.

19. DuBois, "The Primitive Black Man," *Nation*, CXIX (December 17, 1924), 675–76.

20. DuBois, "Little Portraits of Africa," *Crisis*, XXVII (April 1924), 274.

21. DuBois, "Pan-Africa and New Racial Philosophy," *ibid.*, XL (November 1933), 247.

22. *Ibid.*, XVII (January 1919), 119–21.

23. *Ibid.*, p. 112.

24. DuBois, "Back to Africa," *Century*, CV (February 1923), 542.

25. *Crisis*, XVII (February 1919), 166.

26. For Pan-Africanism, see DuBois, "Pan-Africanism: A Mission in My Life," in *Africa in the Modern World* (a *United Asia* pamphlet, n.d.), pp. 23–28; and George Podmore, *Pan-Africanism: The Coming Struggle for Africa* (London, 1956).

27. *Crisis*, XVIII (May 1919), 7–9.

28. DuBois, "France's Black Citizens in West Africa," *Current History,* XXII (July 1925), 563.

29. DuBois, "A Second Journey to Pan-Africa," *New Republic,* XXIX (December 7, 1921), 42.

30. DuBois, "The Negro Takes Stock," *New Republic,* XXXVII (January 2, 1924), 144.

31. *Crisis,* XXXII (October 1926), 284; XXXIV (October 1927), 264.

32. *Ibid.,* XXIII (April 1922), 247.

33. *Ibid.,* XXXIV (June 1927), 111.

34. *Ibid.,* XXXVI (October 1929), 350.

35. *Ibid.,* XLI (January 1932), 448. The pagination and volume numbering of the *Crisis* are somewhat confused about this time. The date is the most useful referrent.

36. *Ibid.* (March, April 1932), 93, 116.

37. DuBois, "A Forum of Fact and Opinion," Pittsburgh *Courier,* October 2, 1937.

38. *Crisis,* XL (December 1933), 293.

39. DuBois, "Ethiopia," ms. of article, *ca.* 1930, Johnson Collection.

40. *Crisis,* XXVIII (May 1924), 11.

41. Quoted in DuBois, *Dusk of Dawn: An Essay Toward an Autobiography of a Race Concept* (New York, 1940), pp. 124–25.

42. Schuyler's comment is in *Crisis,* XLI (March 1932), 92.

43. Margaret Halsey, *Some of My Best Friends Are Soldiers* (New York, 1944), p. 49.

44. New York *Times,* January 11, 1930, 10:6.

45. *Crisis,* XXXVI (December 1929), 424.

46. DuBois, "Worlds of Color," *Foreign Affairs,* III (April 1925), 423–44.

47. *Crisis,* XXII (September 1921), 200.

48. *Ibid.,* XXXII (June 1926), 64.

49. *Ibid.,* XXII (September 1921), 199–200.

50. *Ibid.* (May 1921), 8.

51. *Ibid.* (July 1921), 102–4.

52. *Ibid.,* XXIII (April 1922), 247.

53. *Ibid,* XXXIV (December 1927), 348.

54. *Ibid.,* XXXIII (November 1926), 8.

55. DuBois, "Judging Russia," *ibid.,* XXXIII (February 1927), 189–90.

56. *Ibid.,* XXII (September 1921), 200.

57. DuBois, "The Hosts of Black Labor," *Nation,* CXVI (May 9, 1923), 541.

58. DuBois, "These United States. XLIX. Georgia: Invisible Empire State," *Nation,* CXX (January 21, 1925), 67.

59. *Crisis,* XXXVII (May 1930), 160.

60. *Ibid.,* XXIV (May 1922), 11.

61. *Ibid.,* XXXV (December 1928), 418.

62. *Ibid.,* XXII (August, October 1921), 151–52, 245–47.

63. Robert Minor, "The First Negro Workers Congress," *Workers Monthly*, V (December 1925), ii, 68; quoted in Wilson Record, *The Negro and the Communist Party* (Chapel Hill, 1951), p. 32.

64. Quoted in Record, *The Negro and the Communist Party*, pp. 44, 80–81.

65. *New Masses*, VII (February 1932), ix, 10.

66. Reprinted, undated, in *Crisis*, XXXIX (July 1932), 232.

67. *Ibid.*, XL (September 1931), 314.

68. *Ibid.*, XXXVII (April 1930), 137.

69. *Ibid.*, XL (September 1931), 313–15, 318, 320.

70. *Ibid.*, XXXIX (July 1932), 234.

71. *Ibid.*, XL (April 1933), 93.

Chapter VI

1. See above, pp. 103–4.

2. *Crisis*, XXIII (January 1922), 105.

3. *Ibid.*, XXXV (March 1928), 96.

4. *Ibid.*, XX (October 1920), 263, 266.

5. *Ibid.*, XXII (June 1921), 55–56, and XXVIII (June 1924), 57.

6. *Ibid.*, XXII (June 1921), 55–56.

7. DuBois, "The Negro in Literature and Art," in "The Negro's Progress in Fifty Years," *Annals of the American Academy of Political and Social Science*, XLIX (September 1913), 233, 236–37.

8. *Crisis*, XXVIII (May 1924), 12; XXXIII (February 1927), 183; XXXIV (April 1927), 70.

9. Alain Locke, "The Negro Intellectual," New York *Herald Tribune Books*, May 20, 1928, 12: 12.

10. Dewey R. Jones in the Chicago *Defender*, June 9, 1928.

11. DuBois, *The Gift of Black Folk* (Boston, 1924), p. 341.

12. *Crisis*, XXX (May 1925), 8.

13. DuBois, "Criteria of Negro Art," *ibid*, XXXII (October 1926), 296.

14. *Ibid.*, XXXIII (December 1926), 81.

15. *Ibid.*, XXXIV (June 1927), 129.

16. DuBois, "The Browsing Reader," *ibid.*, XXXVI (April 1929), 125.

17. *Ibid.*, XXXV (June 1928), 202.

18. *Ibid.*, XXXVI (July 1929), 234.

19. DuBois, "The Browsing Reader," *ibid.*, XXXV (November 1928), 374; XXXVII (April 1930), 129.

20. *Ibid.*, XL (September 1931), 304.

21. J. Saunders Redding, *They Came in Chains* (*The Peoples of America Series*) (Philadelphia, 1950), p. 265.

22. DuBois, "Fall Books," *Crisis*, XXXIX (November 1924), 25.

23. DuBois and Locke, "The Younger Literary Movement," *ibid.*, XXVII (February 1924), 161–62.

24. *Ibid.*, 161.

25. DuBois, "Browsing Reader," *Crisis*, XXX (May 1925), 26.
26. DuBois, "Criteria of Negro Art," p. 296.
27. *Ibid.*, XL (July 1931), 230.
28. DuBois, "Our Book Shelf," *ibid.*, XXXI (January 1926), 141.
29. *Ibid.*, XXXV (May 1928), 168.
30. DuBois, "Frederick Q. Morton," *ibid.*, XXX (July 1925), 116.
31. *Ibid.*, XXIV (June 1922), 57.
32. *Ibid.*, XXXI (March 1926), 216.
33. *Ibid.*, XXIX (April 1925), 250.
34. Reprinted as DuBois, "Education and Work," *Journal of Negro Education*, I (April 1932), 60–74.
35. DuBois, "The Negro College," *Crisis*, XL (August 1933), 175–77.
36. DuBois, "Education and Work," *Journal of Negro Education*, I (April 1932), 64.
37. DuBois, "The Negro College," p. 177.
38. *Ibid.*, XXXVII (November 1930), 389.
39. DuBois, "On Being Ashamed of Oneself," *ibid.*, XL (September 1933), 200.
40. This account draws on the minutes of the Board of Directors, the correspondence files of the NAACP, and the pages of the *Crisis* from January through August 1934.
41. Ovington to Villard, July 22, 1934, Villard papers.
42. NAACP Board minutes, October 14, 1924.
43. George E. Cannon to Ovington, October 25, 1924; reprinted in part in *Crisis*, XXIX (January 1925), 126–27.
44. Walter White's introduction to DuBois, "Black America," in Fred J. Ringel, ed., *America as Americans See It* (New York, 1932), p. 139.
45. *Crisis*, XXXI (February 1926), 166.
46. *Ibid.*, XLI (February 1932), 59.
47. *Ibid.*, XXXV (July 1928), 239.
48. *Ibid.*, XXXVI (November 1929), 388.
49. Quoted in Vernon F. Calverton, ed., *Anthology of American Negro Literature* (New York, 1929), pp. 252–53.
50. The resolutions of the conference were reprinted in DuBois, "Youth and Age at Amenia," *Crisis*, XL (October 1933), 226–27. See also, Bunche, "Extended Memorandum," 208–10, and the mimeographed "Findings" of the conference, n.d., Johnson Collection.
51. DuBois to Spingarn, May 31, 1934, Johnson Collection.
52. Chicago *Defender*, March 24, 1934.

Chapter VII

1. DuBois, ed., "Report of the First Conference of Negro Land-Grant Colleges . . ." (Atlanta University *Publications*, XXII) (Atlanta, 1943), p. 9.

2. DuBois, "Phylon: Science or Propaganda," *Phylon*, V (first quarter, 1944), 6–8.

3. DuBois, "As the Crow Flies," New York *Amsterdam News*, February 27, 1943.

4. DuBois, "Does the Negro Need Separate Schools?" *Journal of Negro Education*, IV (July 1935), 332.

5. DuBois, "A Forum of Fact and Opinion," Pittsburgh *Courier*, June 5, 1937.

6. *Ibid.*, August 15 and 22, 1936.

7. *Ibid.*, August 14, 1937.

8. DuBois, *Dusk of Dawn: An Essay Toward an Autobiography of a Race Concept* (New York, 1940), p. viii.

9. Benjamin Stolberg, "Black Chauvinism," *Nation*, CXL (May 15, 1935), 570.

10. DuBois, "Inter-Racial Implications of the Ethiopian Crisis," *Foreign Affairs*, XIV (October 1935), 92.

11. DuBois, "A Forum of Fact and Opinion," Pittsburgh *Courier*, May 23, 1936.

12. *Ibid.*, June 13 ,1936.

13. *Ibid.*, March 7, 1936.

14. DuBois, "As the Crow Flies," New York *Amsterdam News*, April 12, 1941.

15. *Ibid.*, January 18, 1941.

16. *Ibid.*, August 9, 1941.

17. *Ibid.*, October 23, 1943.

18. *Ibid.*, February 14, 1942.

19. DuBois, "Prospects of a World Without Race Conflict," *American Journal of Sociology*, XLIX (March 1944), 450–56.

20. DuBois, "As the Crow Flies," New York *Amsterdam News*, August 19, 1944.

Chapter VIII

1. DuBois, *In Battle for Peace* (New York, 1952), p. 180.

2. DuBois, "The Negro and Imperialism," ms. of broadcast, November 15, 1944, NAACP files.

3. DuBois, "Winds of Times," Chicago *Defender*, March 23, 1946.

4. DuBois, "Jan Christian Smuts: Story of a Tyrant," *New Masses*, LXII (March 4, 1947), x, 7.

5. DuBois, *The World and Africa* (New York, 1947), p. 14.

6. DuBois, "Winds of Time," Chicago *Defender*, September 27, 1947.

7. *Ibid.*, June 23, 1945.

8. DuBois, "Roosevelt," ms. of speech in Baltimore, January 30, 1948, Schomburg Collection.

9. DuBois, *In Battle for Peace*, p. 46.

10. New York *Times*, September 9, 1948, 27:1.

11. DuBois, "None who saw Paris will ever forget," *National Guardian*, I (May 16, 1949), xxxi, 12; *In Battle for Peace*, p. 28.

12. DuBois, *In Battle for Peace*, p. 41.

13. New York *Times*, July 17, 1950, 5:1.

14. *Daily Worker* (New York), September 25, 1950.

15. E. Clay, "The Negro Writer and the Congress," *New Masses*, XIV (March 19, 1935), xi, 22.

16. Aptheker, "W. E. B. DuBois: Story of a half-century of distinguished service to humanity," *National Guardian*, II (February 8, 1950), xvii, 6–7.

17. *Daily Worker*, September 11 and 13, 1950.

18. DuBois, "Winds of Time," Chicago *Defender*, November 16, 1946.

19. New York *Times*, June 20, 1949, 7:6.

20. His talk was reprinted as DuBois, "Bound by the Color Line," *New Masses*, LVIII (February 12, 1946), vii, 8.

21. DuBois, "From McKinley to Wallace: My Fifty Years as a Political Independent," *Masses and Mainstream*, I, vi, 7.

22. This account of the trial is based on DuBois, *In Battle for Peace;* United States District Court for the District of Columbia, "United States v. Peace Information Center, *et al.*," Criminal file No. 178–51; and the New York *Times*, August 25, 1950; February 10, 17, April 28, May 10, June 21, July 1, November 8, 19, 1951.

23. DuBois, "The Freeing of India," *Crisis*, LIV (October 1947), 316.

24. DuBois, review of Ralph Linton, ed., *Most of the World: The Peoples of Africa, Latin America and the East Today* (New York, 1949), in *Science and Society*, XIII (fall, 1949), 367; New York *Times*, June 2, 1949, 10:6.

25. DuBois, *In Battle for Peace*, p. 154.

26. DuBois, "America's Responsibility to Israel," ms. of speech to the American Jewish Congress, New York, November 30, 1948, NAACP files.

27. Gordon B. Hancock, a sociologist, quoted in DuBois, *In Battle for Peace*, p. 191.

28. DuBois, *In Battle for Peace*, pp. 75–76, 77, 155.

29. DuBois to author, May 31, 1951.

30. Kwame Nkrumah to Bernard Reswick, April 25, 1957, Schomburg Collection.

Chapter IX

1. DuBois, *A Pageant in Seven Decades, 1868–1938*, p. 44.

2. DuBois, "Winds of Time," Chicago *Defender*, January 6, 1945.

3. Aptheker, "W. E. B. DuBois: The First Eighty Years," *Phylon*, IX, 59 (first quarter, 1948). This whole essay is a well informed statement of the myth.

4. The remark appears in one of Miss Graham's (*i.e.*, Mrs. DuBois's) "Comments," in DuBois, *In Battle for Peace* (New York, 1952), p. 12.

5. See p. 214, above.

6. Van Wyck Brooks, *The Confident Years, 1885–1915 (Makers and Finders: A History of the Writer in America, 1800–1915)* (New York, 1952), p. 547.

7. John Gunther, *Inside U.S.A.* (New York, 1947), p. 681.

8. Henry Steele Commager, "The Men Who Make Up Your Mind," *'48*, II, v, 33 (May 1948).

9. J. Saunders Redding, *To Make a Poet Black* (Chapel Hill, 1939), p. 80.

10. Youra Qualls, "Authors and Books," *Southwestern Journal*, I, 275 (Spring 1945).

11. William Stanley Braithwaite, "A Tribute to W. E. Burghardt DuBois, First Editor of Phylon," *Phylon*, X, 302 (fourth quarter, 1949).